ARCHAEOLOGY OF EARLY BUDDHISM

ARCHAEOLOGY OF EARLY BUDDHISM

LARS FOGELIN

DEV PUBLISHERS & DISTRIBUTORS

New Delhi

Published by:
DEV PUBLISHERS & DISTRIBUTORS
2nd Floor, Prakash Deep,
4735/22, Ansari Road,
Darya Ganj,
New Delhi-110002
Phone : 011-43572647, 9810236140
e-mail: devbooks@hotmail.com
website: www.devbooks.co.in

ISBN 978-81-920752-8-0
First Indian edition 2012

This edition is published by arrangement with AltaMira Press, A Division of Rowman & Littlefield Publishers Inc.

This edition is for sale in India, Pakistan, Myanmar, Sri Lanka, Nepal, Bhutan, and Bangladesh.

Printed in India.

For my parents,
Robert Fogelin and Florence Fogelin

Contents

Preface

THIS BOOK IS A REVISED VERSION of my Ph.D. dissertation, submitted in 2003 to the University of Michigan Department of Anthropology (Fogelin 2003c). Most of the revisions have consisted of removing extraneous information unrelated to the specific goals of this book, but I have also expanded some portions of the original, particularly those dealing with the method and theory of the archaeology of religion.

The original dissertation had several appendices containing the data that I had collected during fieldwork—summaries of my site forms, field maps, ceramic drawings, and ceramic measurements. I have chosen not to reproduce them here because of space limitations. The primary data and more extensive discussions of the specific material remains can be found in the original dissertation. I am also happy to provide all of this information in a digital format to any legitimate researcher.

All of the archaeological materials collected during survey were given to the Andhra Pradesh Department of Archaeology and Museums for long-term curation. The department has stored all of the archaeological materials collected during fieldwork in its warehouse in Visakhapatnam, Andhra Pradesh. No archaeological remains were removed from India or Andhra Pradesh at any time.

Small portions of this book were adapted from recent and forthcoming publications (Fogelin 2003a, 2003b, 2004, and in press a) to suit the particular needs of this book. Most excerpts are only a few paragraphs long. In some cases, I have incorporated a few pages.

Acknowledgments

My thanks go first to Carla Sinopoli, the chair of my dissertation committee, for the guidance she has provided me over the years. I cannot overstate the value I place on the advice she has given me on this book specifically and on archaeology as a whole. I also thank the other members of my dissertation committee, Jeffrey Parsons, Norman Yoffee, Henry Wright, and Donald Lopez Jr. Each has provided critical insights toward my research, and this book is far better for their comments. A final, unofficial, member of my dissertation committee was Himanshu Ray. Initially through her writings, and later through long conversations over coffee, she has greatly helped my thinking on all things relating to the Early Historic Period in South Asia.

I thank David Whitley and Mitch Allen, as well as the two anonymous reviewers they contacted, for providing extremely constructive comments on the prospectus of this book. I also thank Alden Perkins of Rowman & Littlefield for shepherding this book through the publication process, and Jeanne Pinault for attending to the details.

While I was in India, the Andhra Pradesh Department of Archaeology and Museums and Commissioner Dr. Lal Rosem extensively assisted me in my research. From the beginning, they have graciously allowed access to their collections and permission to research sites under their control. I particularly thank Dr. B. Subrahmanyam and Dr. E. Sivanagi Reddy for the time they spent with me in Visakhapatnam, discussing my material and guiding me through other sites in the area. The high quality of the excavations and site reports by the Andhra Pradesh Department of Archaeology and Museums allowed my subsequent analyses of Thotlakonda Monastery to proceed. I also thank Vice Chancellor Dr. N. Gopi, Dr. D. R. Raju, Dr. T. Gowrishankar, and the staff of Telugu University in Hyderabad for providing logistical support and academic affiliation in Andhra Pradesh. My research was also greatly assisted by the advice of Dr. Aloka Parasher-Sen of the University of Hyderabad.

Funding for this project was provided by the Wenner-Gren Foundation for Anthropological Research (Gr. 6597), the University of Michigan Rackham School of Graduate Studies, and the University of Michigan Museum of Anthropology. Additional logistical support was provided by the American Institute of Indian Studies. I particularly thank Dr. Pradeep Mehendiratta and Mrs. Purnima Mehta for their assistance in obtaining the necessary permits and providing contacts in Andhra Pradesh. The Archaeological Survey of India has provided critical support for this project.

I also thank the students from Jawaharlal Nehru University and Deccan College (Smita Sahay, Chhaya Bhardwaj, Hemanth Kadambi, Garima Misra, Dilip Sebak, Abhishek Singh, N. Sivakumar, and R. Chumbeno Ngullie) who worked with me in Visakhapatnam. Their efforts and insights made this book possible. Throughout the project I was assisted by Praveena Kumar. Without any training in archaeology, she quickly became invaluable. Finally, I thank Dr. S. V. R. Rao for the steady supply of buffalo-milk cappuccinos and chitchat.

I thank Laura Villamil, Jason Sherman, Severin Fowles, Ellen Morris, Amy Lawson, Dan Pugh, Jim Noone, Bill Parkinson, Geoff Curley, and Robert Brubaker for their advice (archaeological and otherwise), friendship, and support. I have learned as much from them as I have from anyone. I thank Alice Ritscherle for far more than I can state here, really. Finally, I thank my parents. I am the child of a poet and a philosopher. From them I have learned the beauty of silly ideas, well explored.

A Note on Transliteration

Throughout this book I phonetically transliterate Sanskrit terms rather than using the more modern system of diacritical marks that is commonly employed in Buddhist studies. This was a difficult decision. Diacritical marks undoubtedly allow for the most accurate pronunciation of Sanskrit. I chose to use phonetic transliteration for two reasons. First, archaeological sites are by convention named by their excavators. In almost all cases the names of archaeological sites are phonetically transliterated. For reasons of consistency, other Sanskrit words should be similarly transliterated. Second, I expect that many of the people reading this book will be archaeologists who work outside South Asia. While phonetic transliteration is less accurate than the use of diacriticals, it is the quickest and easiest way to approximate proper pronunciation for the nonspecialist.

Using phonetic transliteration, Sanskrit and other terms are pronounced pretty much as an English speaker would expect. The one difference is the use of the letter *h* to mark certain consonants as aspirated (e.g., *th, bh,* and *dh*). With the exception of *th,* this does not cause any significant confusion. As for *th,* it is never pronounced as a fricative as in *them,* but rather as an aspirated *t* as in *stop. Ch* and *sh* are pronounced as they are in English.

Introduction: Archaeology and Early Buddhism — 1

Archaeologists have a long, problematic relationship with religion. From the beginning of the discipline, many of the largest and most impressive archaeological remains have had obvious religious function and significance to people in the past. It is also clear that ancient religions often bore little resemblance to religions practiced today. At times, archaeological interpretations have been little more than fanciful reconstructions, with religious monuments serving as elaborate Rorschach tests for archaeologists carrying their own religious baggage. Thus, early researchers of the Maya saw a peaceful kingdom ruled by astronomer-priests in the jungles of southern Mexico (Morley 1946; Thompson 1950) and ignored evidence for bloodletting, warfare, and human sacrifice. Stonehenge has served as the foil for almost every interpretation of religion imaginable, ranging from human sacrifice to alien encounters. When dealing with the origins of world religions, particularly Christianity, archaeologists have often worked to confirm that events in written scripture actually occurred (see Insoll 2001). This process was made all the easier by the assumption that these events had actually happened, so the only real purpose for archaeology was in finding where they had taken place.

As the discipline of archaeology developed, with a corresponding increase in the demands for rigorous archaeological interpretations and scientific reasoning, a new approach to the archaeology of religion emerged—avoidance. This approach was most articulately advocated by Christopher Hawkes in his "ladder of inference" (Hawkes 1954, 162):

> If material techniques are easy to infer to, subsistence-economics fairly easy, communal organization harder, and spiritual life hardest of all, you have there a climax of four degrees in reasoning.

In essence, Hawkes's position was that religion is a particularly unbounded, immaterial aspect of human life. Reconstructions of past religions could not be anything but fanciful reconstructions and should therefore not be attempted in the first place. Archaeologists, he argued, should focus on what they were good at—the environment, economy, and other more materially grounded phenomena. This position was later taken up by Lewis Binford and other processual archaeologists (but see Fritz 1978; Renfrew 1985; and Marcus 1998 as some notable exceptions). While the rhetoric of Binford (1962) suggested that everything in the past was fair game for archaeological inquiry, in practice processual archaeologists focused on the interaction of people with their environment. Where religion was addressed, it was typically understood in simplistic terms, as regulating peoples' interactions with the environment or serving to legitimize elite power.

All of this began to change in the 1980s with the development of postmodern archaeology (referred to within the discipline as post-processual archaeology). Among the central tenets of this movement was that previous research had overemphasized issues regarding subsistence, economy, and the environment. In contrast, post-processual archaeology was interested in more ideological issues, with religion among them. Despite this newfound interest, even some proponents of post-processual archaeology have recognized that specific methods for investigating religion were slow in developing (see Insoll 2004, 76–84). Post-processual archaeology expressed an interest in studying religion but, with some exceptions (see chapter 4), lacked the tools to fulfill it.

Over the last twenty years a number of new approaches to the archaeology of religion have developed. These can be roughly grouped into two categories. The first is an outgrowth of processual archaeology, taking seriously the idea that past religions could be investigated through the construction of interpretive methodologies for the identification of the material remains of religious practice. This approach has been most clearly articulated by Colin Renfrew (1985, 1994), particularly in his studies of the sanctuary of Phylakopi on the Greek island of Melos. In this study Renfrew developed a list of specific material criteria to determine if a specific set of rooms were, or were not, a center of religious activity. He then compared the material remains found in the rooms with his criteria and determined that a religious or ritual explanation was most likely. Since this original study, Renfrew and others have continued to develop and refine their methods within an overall approach they refer to as cognitive archaeology (see Renfrew and Zubrow 1994).

A second approach toward the archaeology of religion focuses on more theoretical issues regarding religion, arguing that a fundamental misunderstanding of what religion actually is has hobbled archaeological inquiry (see Insoll 2004). Research in this vein has focused on mining other disciplines (e.g., cultural anthropology, sociology, and religious studies) for more sophisticated understandings of religion, and examining their implications for archaeology. These new theoretical perspectives have often been applied to examinations of iconography, ethnohistory, and historical sources. I address the value of these perspectives in greater detail in chapter 4.

From my point of view, both recent approaches to the archaeology of religion have tremendous value and potential. The development of the archaeology of religion requires both a greater theoretical sophistication and more developed material sensibilities. I do not see this as a radical position. I have no doubt that almost all archaeologists interested in religion would agree. The two categories of research presented above do not translate into categories of archaeologists. Renfrew is interested in broader theoretical issues, just as Insoll attempts to develop archaeological methodologies. The difficulty for all concerned is bringing these two approaches together. In my own research I have found ritual to be an effective bridge between the materials I typically come across as an archaeologist and the broader theoretical concerns that orient my interest in religion.

Ritual

> Ritual is religion in action; it is the cutting edge of the tool. ... It is ritual which accomplishes what religion sets out to do.
>
> —WALLACE 1966, 102

The principal difficulty in the study of ancient religion is the identification of something as immaterial as belief or faith. When religion is viewed as a collection of myths, origin stories, and ethical principles, there is little in the material world that can be used to investigate it. Admittedly, archaeologists regularly come across iconographic elements depicting gods or similarly religious themes. But what are we to do with them? We might find depictions of what appear to be divine turtles, for instance. As for the significance of the turtles—it is almost impossible to say without some other, nonarchaeological, source to rely on. The solution to this problem is the recognition that religion is not simply something that people think, but is also something that people do (see Fogelin in press b for an expanded discussion of this point). Ritual is religiously motivated action, and these actions can and do leave material traces of their practice. If people sacrifice for their gods, archaeologists can identify the sacrificed materials. If people congregate to engage in worship, archaeologists can identify the spaces used to congregate in. As will be discussed in greater length in chapter 4, rituals are typically regularized and repeated affairs. Thus, the material traces will often be added to, and made more distinct, with each performance.

Not all rituals are religious. Nor are all religious ideas or principles enacted through rituals (see Bell 1997 for an excellent review of ritual). That said, the archaeological investigation of ritual can serve as a foundation upon which understandings of past religions can be constructed. These understandings can, in turn, be analyzed in terms of existing theories concerning the nature, function, and form of religion.

These interests brought me to Thotlakonda, an Early Historic Period (c. 300 B.C.–A.D. 300) Buddhist monastery in north coastal Andhra Pradesh, India. My research at Thotlakonda Monastery is situated within broader anthropological approaches to ritual. In my investigations I examine religion, as it was practiced, within a dynamic social structure of competing concerns in daily life. The challenge of my work is the identification of the material consequences of religious practice. To this end, I focus on architecture and landscape. While I am interested in religious symbolism, I also consider the implications of the physical layout of architecture on social interactions among ritual participants. These interactions are shown in patterns of visibility and through principles derived from Western and non-Western theatrical design. My approach links religious and other architectural spaces within a regional landscape of meaning and interaction. I employ architecture to derive the social implications of spaces, and landscape to link them within a larger social context. Though the focus of this book is on Early Buddhism in South India, it is my hope that the methods and approaches I present here will have value for archaeologists working in a wide variety of geographic and religious contexts.

Early Historic Period Buddhist Monasteries

Since its beginnings in the nineteenth century, the study of Early Buddhism has combined investigations of early Buddhist texts and archaeological remains. The twentieth century brought new approaches and insights to the study of Early Buddhism. To simplify the range of earlier interpretations of Buddhist monasticism, two different approaches to their broader social role can be identified. The first sees monasteries as retreats where monks could, as Brown (1965, 13) stated, "conduct their observances undisturbed by the distractions of any human environment." This position, or some variation on it, was also suggested by Fergusson and Burgess ([1880] 1988), Cunningham ([1854] 1997, [1876] 1962, [1892] 1998), Basham (1967), Lamotte (1988), and others. Using Buddhist monastic texts as a guide, these scholars believed that monasteries were centers for extended meditation and religious learning.

By the 1960s, with an emphasis on materialism, a new interpretation of Buddhist monasticism began to emerge. Again to simplify, this approach saw monasteries as economically oriented and actively engaged in broader social relations. In the work of Romila Thapar (1966, 2002), Buddhism was viewed as fostering trade by breaking down caste barriers that had formerly limited the ability of merchants and traders to interact. This economic approach was extended by subsequent scholars such as Ray (1986, 1989), Lahiri (1992), and Heitzman (1984, 1997). In Ray's early work, she argued that Buddhist monasteries played an active role in organizing and promoting trade, both as consumers and direct facilitators. Heitzman, and to a lesser degree Ray, suggested that Buddhist monasteries were also actively engaged in promoting agricultural production, serving as the nuclei of agrarian communities on the peripheries of developing states.

When comparing the newer and older interpretations of Buddhist monasticism, an interesting contrast is formed—religious disengagement versus economic engagement. What follows is an argument for a third permutation—religious engagement. In this I do not mean engagement in terms of Buddhist doctrine, but in the practice and conduct of daily ritual. I argue that this ritual role in society has been underappreciated in the existing scholarship on Early Historic Period Buddhist monasticism. An element common to all of the previous discussions of Buddhist monasticism is that they are based upon a combination of Buddhist texts and archaeological excavations of the monasteries in isolation (for an exception, see Shaw 2000, 2002). Yet most previous interpretations of the social role of monasteries make claims to the broader social context in which monasteries were found. My research over the last two years in Andhra Pradesh has been oriented toward investigating and evaluating all of these potential roles for Buddhist monasticism by directly examining the local context of a single monastery.

Thotlakonda Monastery

The Buddhist monastery of Thotlakonda is located sixteen kilometers north of the modern city of Visakhapatnam in north coastal Andhra Pradesh (see figure I.1). Sitting on a low hill overlooking the Bay of Bengal, it is one of three monasteries in the immediate area. The closest monastery, Bavikonda, lies on an adjacent hill less than two kilometers from Thotlakonda (Prasad 1993, 1994). Thotlakonda was excavated between 1987 and 1991 by the Andhra Pradesh Department of Archaeology and Museums (hereafter APDAM) (Sastry, Subrahmanyam, and Rao 1992). The excavators dated occupation of the site between the second and third centuries B.C. through the second or third centuries A.D.

Between November 2000 and March 2001, and again in January through March 2002, I directed a program of systematic archaeological surface survey in the area immediately surrounding Thotlakonda with a team of Indian graduate students (Fogelin 2003b, 2003c, 2004, in press a). After six months of fieldwork over two years, we surveyed 7.3 square kilometers and identified 328 archaeological features, including walls, terraces, reservoirs, and a *stupa* (a Buddhist ritual structure). In the floodplain below the hill we found a large non-monastic settlement. The

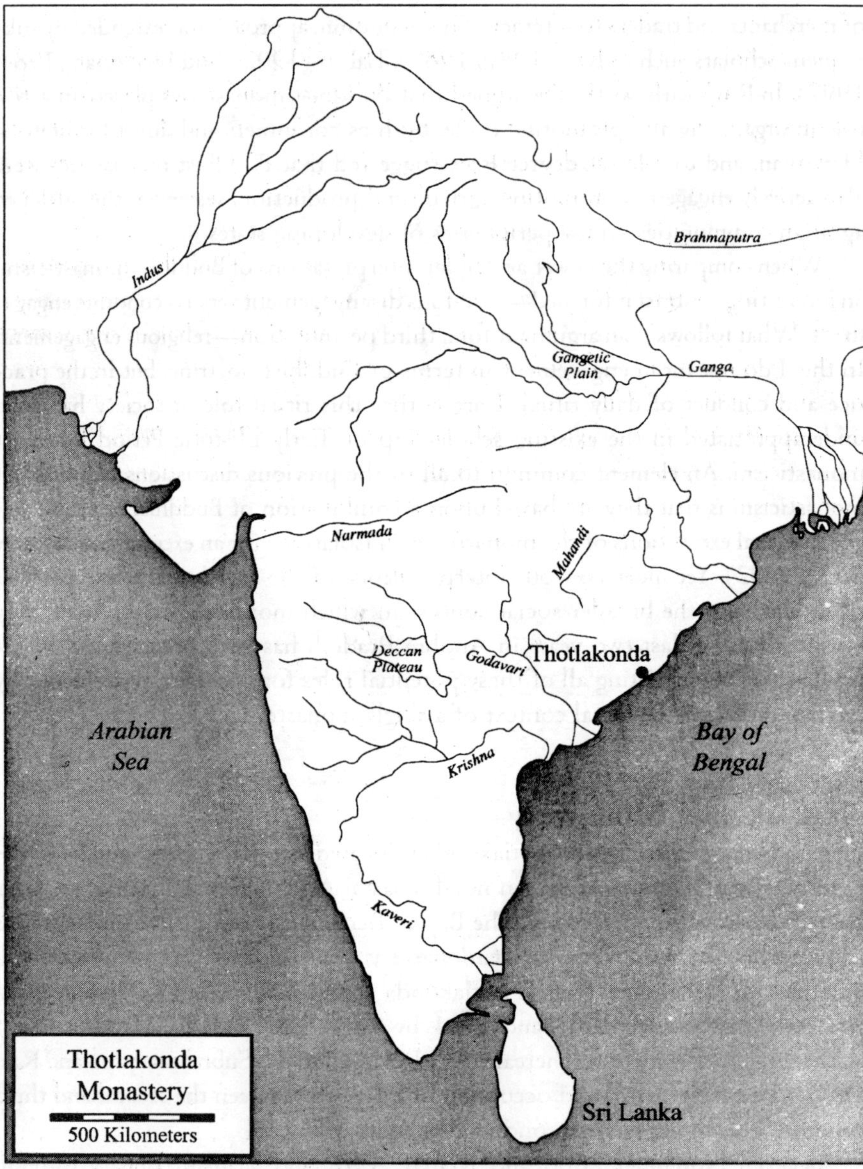

Figure 1.1. The location of Thotlakonda in South Asia.

most numerous sites identified were small cairns constructed of natural boulders. These cairns constituted a large mortuary landscape covering the hill on which Thotlakonda was found and several neighboring hills. Throughout the survey, a large number of ceramics were collected and analyzed, with similarities between the assemblages at different sites used to establish the ties between the different sites.

The goal of my research was to examine the relationship between Buddhist monks and laypeople during the Early Historic Period by directly examining the local context of these monasteries—to investigate the smaller, non-monastic archaeological remains that surround a single Buddhist monastery in conjunction with an examination of the monastery itself. My studies of Thotlakonda's architecture and landscape suggest that the monastery and local populations were actively engaged, both economically and ritually, with each other. Ritual ties are shown in the creation of a public worship space at the monastery and of paths leading to it. The ritual ties are further shown in a complex mortuary landscape combining the memorials of both monks and nuns scattered across the nearby hills.

In contrast to the emphasis on ritual interaction with the laity, there is also ample evidence for monastic isolation. This is shown in an architecturally isolated cloister at the heart of Thotlakonda, and its location on top of a hill, distant from any non-monastic settlements. The divergent roles of the monastery (ritual engagement versus religious isolation) created a tension in its broader social role. This tension was most clearly shown in the monastery's economic relationships with local populations.

Day-to-day support of the monks at Thotlakonda required the substantial movement of food and other resources to the monastery. A variety of mundane tasks were performed for the monks by laborers, most likely from the local villages. The relationships between the monks and the labor force that supported their lifestyle were strongly ambivalent. Through patterns of architectural separation, interaction with the laborers was kept to an absolute minimum. For the most part, the laborers worked outside the monastery walls, out of sight of the monks in the monastery. Further, the primary point of contact between the two groups, the refectory, was architecturally isolated from the rest of the monastery.

An Outline of This Book

This book is intended to serve several audiences—each with its own interests and background knowledge. I expect that archaeologists who study South Asia will be particularly interested in the results of my fieldwork and the specific conclusions concerning Thotlakonda Monastery. Further, I want my discussions of Thotlakonda and the methods I employ to serve as a case study for the archaeological investigation of religion and ritual for archaeologists who work outside of South Asia. Finally, I hope this book will demonstrate the value of recent archaeological approaches for historians of South Asia and Buddhism. For this final group, this book is intended to illustrate how archaeology can be more effectively employed in a collaborative investigation of ancient Buddhism.

I have written this book with these different audiences in mind. The chapters on South Asian history and Buddhism are written for those with little or no background in either. I provide more background on archaeological methods than most archaeologists would ever want to read. Discipline-specific jargon is avoided whenever possible, or clearly defined when unavoidable. Specialists in archaeology, South Asian history, and Buddhism are likely to find portions of some chapters overly simplistic. I ask that readers have patience in these sections. Many of the archaeologists have never heard the name Ashoka, just as some historians cannot tell the difference between an excavation unit and a hole in the ground. I am a committed convert to the cause of cross-disciplinary studies. I have gained tremendously from Buddhologists who patiently explained (and re-explained) the simplest concepts of Buddhist doctrine. For my part, I have tried to remain enthusiastic when asked to show how a small fragment of pottery can inform the study of past societies. Cross-disciplinary studies require a bit more background than discipline-specific studies, but the conclusions are strengthened by the collaboration.

Given the disparate sources employed, the arguments presented in this book often combine information from widely separated chapters. Ideas and arguments from earlier chapters are only completed in later chapters when other lines of evidence are considered. Throughout the text I indicate in what chapter, and in what way, particular points will reappear. Chapters 2 and 3 review the existing scholarship on South Asian history and Buddhism, respectively. In chapter 4, I examine the theoretical and methodological approaches employed in my archaeological analyses of religion and ritual. Chapters 5 and 6 present the archaeological background to north coastal Andhra Pradesh in general and Thotlakonda Monastery specifically. Chapters 7 and 8 synthesize the information from the preceding chapters to address the specific social context and underlying social tensions of Thotlakonda Monastery. I conclude the book with a discussion of the implications of this research on current understandings of Early Buddhism and the archaeological investigation of religion.

In the end, the picture of broader social relations developed for Thotlakonda Monastery is messier than typical depictions of early Buddhist monasticism. My interpretation more closely resembles the practice of modern Buddhist monasteries, with all of their conflicting roles and idiosyncrasies. By moving investigations beyond the monastery walls, my analyses emphasize the tensions, conflicts, and complex ritual relationships between the monks at Thotlakonda and the lay Buddhists who engaged, both economically and spiritually, with them. Rather than the idealized monastery of Buddhist literature, my analyses focus instead on the practice of Buddhist monasticism, with all of its inconsistencies and tensions intact.

Some Terms and Definitions

Several terms require clear definitions at the outset. The first of these is "Early Buddhism," a phrase that is even found in the title of this book. As used here it is intended to be a substitute for the term "*Hinayana* Buddhism." Literally, *Hinayana* translates as "lesser vehicle" and refers to the earliest forms of Buddhism that existed in South Asia. This was not the term used by early Buddhists themselves; it was applied by later *Mahayana* (greater vehicle) Buddhists as a somewhat derisive label for those who preceded them. In the academic literature of Buddhist studies, *Hinayana* also became a term used to describe the later forms of Buddhism found in Sri Lanka and parts of Southeast Asia. The use of *Hinayana* for these later forms of Buddhism was predicated on the idea that these forms of Buddhism, particularly those found in Sri Lanka, had undergone less change (or corruption) than the *Mahayana* Buddhism of Central and East Asia.

As will be discussed at greater length in chapters 2 and 3, I am skeptical about whether Sri Lankan Buddhism is a better model for Early Buddhism than any other form of Buddhism. There is ample reason to suspect that it has gone through as many profound changes as any other Buddhist tradition. Almost all Buddhist sects claim that their teachings represent the original words of the Buddha. From my perspective, I see no reason to privilege one *a priori*. For this reason—in addition to negative connotations of *Hinayana*—I prefer to use the term Early Buddhism. Further, the focus of this work is on Early Buddhism in South India. Thus, my conclusions do not necessarily have direct relevance to Early Buddhism in Sri Lanka. It is my hope that these analyses have value there, but I will leave it to those who have a greater knowledge of that material to make this determination.

Early Buddhism, in the sense used here, would date from the time of the Buddha (as early as the sixth century B.C.) through the second or third centuries A.D. It should be noted, however, that the terminal date is extremely fluid. The process in which *Mahayana* Buddhism developed is exceedingly complex and existing academic understandings of it contested (see Schopen 2000). It is likely that some Buddhist sects adopted *Mahayana* practices more quickly than others. Even within individual sects, some practices changed quickly while other practices continued to follow earlier forms. Thus the boundary between Early Buddhism and *Mahayana* Buddhism is permeable and likely indefinable.

There are also numerous difficulties in establishing the dates of origin of Early Buddhism. This is partly due to problems dating the life of the Buddha (see chapter 3), but also from the lack of any significant archaeological evidence for Buddhism prior to the third century B.C. (see Coningham 2001). Buddhism almost certainly existed prior to this, but in terms of this archaeological study, little or nothing can be said about it. Rather than trying to reconstruct an "original" Buddhism, here I focus on the earliest forms of Buddhism for which archaeological evidence can be obtained—a period beginning in roughly the third century B.C. and ending sometime in the second or third century A.D.

South Asian historians and archaeologists may have already noted another term that needs further explanation—the *Early Historic Period*. Traditionally the Early Historic Period refers to a time in the Gangetic Plain in northern South Asia to which many of the earliest written sources refer, a period beginning in about the sixth century B.C. and ending in the third or fourth century A.D. (but see chapter 2 for a more complete discussion of these historical sources). This term has been applied to South India, but here the earliest historical sources can only be said to date to the third century B.C. (see chapter 2). Given the South Indian focus of this work, I use the later date to mark the advent of the Early Historic Period. I only use the earlier date when specifically addressing the Early Historic Period in northern South Asia.

Throughout this book I make use of numerous Sanskrit terms. I define each of them as they come up. Most refer to either specific elements of Buddhist architecture or Buddhist religious concepts. I also employ various technical terms in the archaeological analyses. These terms, too, are explained in language that a nonspecialist can understand. For convenience, I also provide a glossary at the end of this volume.

A Brief History of the Early Historic Period in South Asia

2

Despite a long tradition of historical inquiry in South Asia, little is known of the early history of north coastal Andhra Pradesh. Most discussions of the region postulate shifting political control depending upon the relative power of neighboring, better documented states to the north and south. Exploring a more generalized historical framework for South Asia, this chapter outlines the broad historical context of north coastal Andhra Pradesh.

Lying at the edge of the traditional linguistic division between North India and South India, north coastal Andhra Pradesh was affected by both. Yet it was always somewhat peripheral to the Kalinga state to the north and the Satavahana state to the south. Its position is particularly interesting in that the Satavahanas are often considered the prototypical South Indian state, while the Kalinga were linguistically and geographically North Indian.

Here I will review the broader theoretical and historical topics that inform upon the geographic and cultural position of north coastal Andhra Pradesh. While part of South India, it was among the first areas in the peninsula to feel the effects of the spread of North Indian religions, political practices, and economic institutions. This "Sanskritization" of peninsular India is believed to have occurred in the first few centuries B.C. as a continuation of the alleged invasion of Indo-European people (Aryans) into northern South Asia that began in the second millennium B.C. The division between North India and South India is among the central concepts in South Asian history and is heavily entwined within colonial and postcolonial historical traditions. Given the importance of the North/South narrative in the formation of our historical understandings, I will investigate its creation before outlining the historical sequences that bear on a study of north coastal Andhra Pradesh. First, however, I will quickly review the primary sources for the study of South Asian history.

Sources for the Study of South Asian History

Primary source materials for the study of South Asian history fall into four categories. The first consists of literary sources written in South Asia. The second is foreign accounts of South Asia in Greek, Roman, Persian, and Chinese sources. Third, a large number of inscriptions are found throughout South Asia. Finally, archaeological remains provide a nontextual record of South Asian history. Each of these sources provides different types of information, as well as unique problems of interpretation.

It should be noted at the outset that most of the literary sources are versions of older oral and written histories. For this reason, such sources have two important dates. The first is the date that scholars believe the existing texts were written. The second is the period these texts refer to and from which they are presumed to have originated as oral histories. For example, many scholars argue that the *Rig Veda*, the earliest readable text in South Asia, records oral histories referring to the mid second millennium B.C. However, the *Rig Veda* was not written down until sometime in the early- to mid-first millennium B.C., at the earliest (Basham 1967; Thapar 2002). It can be expected that, just as modern texts are constructed within a particular social context, the versions of the primary texts available today were also written in specific social contexts. The result is a mediation between what was written and the source material they were based upon, either written or oral (see Thapar 2000 for an excellent discussion of this point). These texts can be used for investigating periods to which they refer, but not uncritically.

South Asian Literary Sources

Of the primary literary sources originating in India, the earliest, by far, are the *Vedas*, with the *Rig Veda* being the earliest. The four *Vedas* contain descriptions of early religious beliefs, rituals, medical practices, and heroic stories of kings. Together the *Vedas* are often seen as the foundation for the rest of Indian history, referred to in the subsequent religious literature of Brahmanism, Hinduism, Jainism, and Buddhism. Scholars have cited varying passages to identify the origin of caste, cosmology, and, most problematically, the Aryan invasion. Particularly in the case of the Aryan invasion, these references are overplayed. As Trautmann (1997) has argued, evidence of Dravidians (*Dasas*) in the *Rig Veda* consists of two vague references to dark-skinned people, plus one even vaguer reference to flat noses. References to warfare and conquest are far more often presented among various Aryan groups than between Aryans and *Dasas*. The *Vedas* may provide a window into the religious and cultural patterns of early Indian pastoralists who lived in northwestern South Asia in the second millennium B.C., but they are less useful for investigating sedentary state societies of the Early Historic Period.

The rest of the primary source material from South Asia was written in the first millennium A.D. These sources include the Hindu epics, the *Mahabharata* and *Ramayana*, a more scholastic text on statecraft (the *Arthashastra*), and a collection of histories and religious stories called the *Puranas*. In the peninsula, Tamil *Sangam* literature consists of collections of poems. Another important source is the Pali Canon of Sri Lanka. All of these literary sources are believed to refer to the Early Historic Period. However, the forms available to modern scholars all postdate the Early Historic period by several centuries. The earliest available versions of the *Ramayana* and *Mahabharata* date to the second or third centuries A.D. (Thapar 2002). Trautmann (1971) and Thapar (2002) argue that the *Arthashastra*, though typically ascribed to Kautilya, a third century B.C. royal advisor, was likely collated only in the second or third century A.D. The *Sangam* literature of Tamil Nadu is more difficult to date but most likely was composed in the first half of the first millennium A.D. (Basham 1967; Thapar 2002). As for the Pali Canon of Sri Lanka, it was extensively redacted in the fifth or sixth centuries A.D. (Bechert 1978; Collins 1990; Trainor 1997).

The *Puranas*, a collection of histories, myths, stories, and poems, are particularly difficult to date and interpret. They appear to have been collated in the mid first millennium A.D. (Basham 1967; Rocher 1986; Thapar 2000, 2002). As historical documents, the *Puranas* are notoriously difficult to use (Kosambi 1965; Ray 1986; Thapar 2000; Trautmann and Sinopoli 2002). The historical and mythical components are mixed to such a degree that determining strict chronological and historical data is often impossible. In several key areas (for example, dynastic lists of the Satavahana state) the *Puranas* present multiple versions of the same event. While problematic for developing chronologies, the *Puranas* do provide a window into the social patterns of the Early Historic Period, as long as it is remembered that this view is filtered through the third century A.D. context in which the *Puranas* were written. (See Thapar 2000 for a more detailed investigation of the historical value of the *Puranas*). In this way, the *Puranas* are no better, or worse, than the other early literary sources from South Asia.

Foreign Literary Sources

Foreign literary sources provide a different perspective on the Early Historic Period in South Asia. While they often contain obvious confusions on South Asian practices, in many cases they both date and refer to the Early Historic Period itself. The earliest of these sources record the campaign of Alexander the Great into northwestern South Asia in 326 B.C. (Thapar 2002; Briant 2002; McCrindle [1926] 2000). Upon his departure from South Asia, Alexander left governors to rule over the territories he had conquered. Many of the most useful Western accounts of early South Asia are derived from court officials posted in these territories. The best of these sources is the *Indika* of Megasthenes, a Greek ambassador who traveled in India during the fourth century B.C. (McCrindle [1926] 2000). Unfortunately, Megasthenes's writings are preserved only as long quotations in later, secondary works. Other accounts of India are found in the writings of numerous Greek and Roman authors (e.g., Ptolemy, Arrian, Strabo, Pliny, and Herodotus), but are generally based upon secondhand accounts and are of lesser value (see McCrindle [1901] 1979, [1927] 2000).

Among the most important later Greek sources for the study of South Asia is the *Periplus of the Erythraean Sea* (Casson 1989; Schoff 1974; Parker 2001). The *Periplus* was a guide for Greek sea captains trading on the west coast of India in the first century A.D. It provides valuable information on the geography of the west coast as well as political, economic, and social issues. The *Periplus* is less useful for studies of the east coast of the peninsula. While there is some discussion of the main ports and geography of the east coast, it appears that most of this is reported secondhand. This suggests that transport, either overland or coastal, from the west coast to the east coast of India was conducted by the Indians themselves (see Ray 1999).

In addition to the Greek and Persian accounts are two important Chinese sources. These record pilgrimages to South Asia by Chinese Buddhist monks in the third and seventh centuries A.D. The first pilgrim was Faxian (Giles 1923; Liu 1988). For the most part, his travels were limited to the Gangetic plains in the north. To a great extent, the *Chronicle of Faxian* guided much of the archaeological research conducted in India in the nineteenth century (Trautmann and Sinopoli 2002). In the seventh century another pilgrim, Xuanzang, traveled throughout south Asia, providing careful descriptions of numerous Buddhist establishments (Beal 1908). Although he did travel the east coast of the peninsula, the later date of the *Chronicle of Xuanzang* lessens its relevance to my own study of the Early Historic Period.

Inscriptions

A large number of inscriptions dating from the Early Historic Period have been found carved onto architectural elements at *stupa* complexes and monasteries throughout South Asia. For the most part, they record the donations to the complexes by monks, nuns, kings, guilds, and other members of the Buddhist laity. Schopen (1997, 31) has argued that these inscriptions provide the only South Asian textual sources that unquestionably date to the Early Historic Period itself. For this reason inscriptions can serve, along with archaeological material, as a check on the interpretations based upon contemporary foreign accounts or South Asian literary sources that postdate the Early Historic Period by several centuries. The earliest dated inscriptions in South Asia were produced by the Mauryan emperor

Ashoka in the third century B.C. As will be discussed in chapter 3, these inscriptions were erected throughout the subcontinent and glorify the rule of Ashoka. They provide useful political, social, and religious information. Other inscriptions record gifts to monasteries and religious establishments by kings, guilds, and others.

Archaeology

Traditionally, most archaeological studies of historical periods in South Asia have relied heavily upon literary sources. For example, a great deal of archaeological research has attempted to identify cities or monuments mentioned in the Hindu Epics, the Pali Canon, or the *Chronicle of Faxian*. Recently, some archaeologists have argued that an overreliance on historical sources has limited the practice of archaeology in South Asia (see Coningham 1998, 2001). Coningham suggests that archaeology can complement historical sources, providing information on aspects of life in the Early Historic Period that historical sources do not supply. Further, given that most of the historical sources were codified many centuries after the Early Historic Period, archaeology and epigraphy provide the only direct means of studying the time period. Although I agree with these archaeologists for the most part, I feel it is also important to use the historical sources wherever possible. Rather than simply interpret archaeological remains based upon these sources, archaeology and history should complement each other, with each supplementing its weaknesses with the other's strengths. (The relations between history and archaeology in South Asia are explored in Trautmann and Sinopoli 2002.) In the latter half of this chapter I present an outline of the historical and archaeological sequences in the Gangetic Plain and peninsular South Asia. As I intend to do throughout this book, I will combine archaeological and historical information. However, first I will briefly discuss a few of the major themes that run through South Asian archaeology—most importantly, the identification of chronological periods by the use of ceramics.

Archaeological research in South Asia has been conducted for more than two centuries (see Allchin 1995 for a good introduction to the archaeology of the Early Historic Period). In the nineteenth and early twentieth centuries, much of this research focused on early Buddhist monasteries and pilgrimage sites throughout the subcontinent. Among the more important of the early researchers was Alexander Cunningham ([1854] 1997, [1876] 1962, [1892] 1998). As the first Director General of the Archaeological Survey of India, he helped establish the systematic study of archaeology in South Asia. Excavations under his direction at Sanchi, Bharhut, Bodh-Gaya, and numerous other locations established archaeological investigation of Early Buddhism. Other researchers (e.g., Fergusson and Burgess [1880] 1988) continued these studies, revealing large numbers of early Buddhist monuments and monasteries.

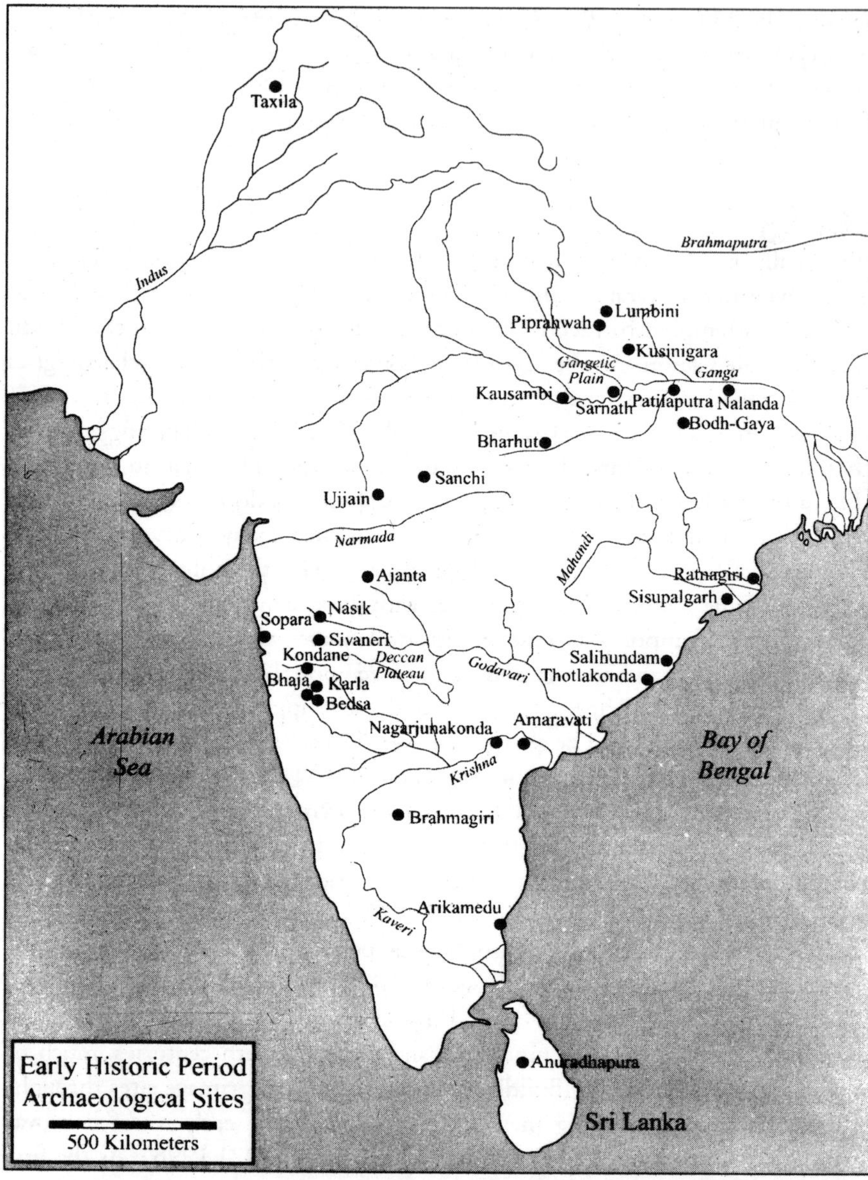

Figure 2.1. Major Early Historic Period archaeological sites in South Asia.

In the first half of the twentieth century, research continued on early Buddhist sites, but a new emphasis on Early Historic Period cities and large settlements began to develop. Major excavations were carried out at Arikamedu (Wheeler et al. 1946), Taxila (Marshall [1951] 1975), and several other Early Historic Period cities.[1] Together, these excavations allowed for a more nuanced understanding of the Early

Historic Period to emerge. In this research Buddhism was understood as part of a process of increasing urbanism, the development of regional exchange systems, and the establishment of craft guilds throughout the subcontinent. At this time, a strong interest in the importance of trade between India and Rome developed, particularly after Wheeler's excavations at Arikamedu revealed numerous artifacts of Mediterranean origin (Wheeler 1954). Wheeler's interpretation of these remains as indicating a Roman trading colony on the east coast of India became central to understandings of the development of South Asian history. While Wheeler's claim that Arikamedu housed a Roman colony has now been cast into doubt (Begley 1983), a focus on the role of India in long-distance trade has continued to be among the central concerns of Early Historic Period archaeological inquiry (see Ray 1994b, 1999; Begley and De Puma 1992; Chakravarti 2001).

In the last thirty years, archaeological study of the Early Historic Period has continued with the investigation of numerous sites.[2] With some exceptions (see Smith 1997, 2002; Shaw 2000, 2002), much of this work has followed closely the work of Wheeler. Both Wheeler's field methodologies and historical interpretations have, until recently, gone relatively unchallenged. In particular, his excavations at Brahmagiri (Wheeler 1948) have served as the baseline for interpreting the ceramic sequence of most sites in peninsular South Asia. Despite the advent of carbon-14 dating in the 1960s, most sites are still dated using Wheeler's ceramic chronology. A recent reanalysis of the ceramics from Brahmagiri by Kathleen Morrison (in press) suggests that the periods assigned by Wheeler are too short. Morrison argues that, in most cases, wares persisted for several centuries longer than previously believed. If correct, and her use of carbon-14 dating makes this likely, many of the sites once thought to be firmly dated in South Asia must be reevaluated. Chronology, once thought to be more or less resolved in South Asia, has reemerged as a central concern among archaeologists.

Wheeler and others identified several widespread ceramic wares found at numerous Early Historic Period sites throughout South Asia. These widespread wares exist side by side with numerous, often poorly defined, local wares that dominate most ceramic assemblages. For the most part, the widespread wares are defined on the basis of color and surface treatment. The most distinctive of these are Northern Black Polished Ware (Erdosy 1995, 1993), Russet Coated Painted Ware (Begley et al. 1996; Wheeler, Ghosh, and Deva 1946), Rouletted Ware (Begley 1986, 1988, 1996; Wheeler, Ghosh, and Deva 1946), and Southern Black-and-Red Ware (Gurumurthy 1981). The primary value of these wares has been in establishing the chronological framework in South India and, to some degree, patterns of interaction between sites. That said, all of these wares have broad temporal ranges (see table 2.1) that limit their usefulness.

With the exception of Northern Black Polished Ware, primarily found in North India, the dates for these wares were established by Wheeler through excavations

Table 2.1. Four widespread ceramic wares from the Early Historic Period in South Asia

Northern Black Polished Ware	c. 500 B.C.–100 B.C.
Russet Coated Painted Ware	c. 300 B.C.–A.D. 200
Rouletted Ware	c. 150 B.C.– ?
Southern Black-and-Red Ware	c. 1000 B.C.–A.D. 400

at the site of Brahmagiri in Karnataka (Wheeler, Ghosh, and Deva 1946). While subsequent research has amended the chronology to some extent, for the most part the dates reported in table 2.1 follow Wheeler's original formulation. With Morrison's recent reanalysis (in press) of excavated materials from Brahmagiri, it is now clear that most of Wheeler's ceramic sequence is not reliable. However, even if Wheeler's ceramic chronology is correct, the periods are too broad to identify sub-periods within individual Early Historic Period sites, or even precisely date in which centuries a site was occupied.

The existing ceramic chronology for South India has several other limitations as well. First, all of these wares were presumably of high value due to superior craftsmanship and superior materials. Thus, these types typically comprise only a small fraction of the total ceramic assemblage at any site. Within the ceramic assemblage at Thotlakonda, no sherds of Russet Coated Painted Ware were found (Sastry, Subrahmanyam, and Rao 1992, 60–77). A few fragmentary sherds were found that may have been Northern Black Polished Ware, but they are too small to identify reliably. Only two sherds of Rouletted Ware were found. While a large number of sherds were found that could be labeled southern Black-and-Red Ware, their identification is problematic for several reasons.

Black-and-Red Wares occur in many different contexts in South Asia. One type is found in the Gangetic Plain and dates as early as the late Harappan Period (Gurumurthy 1981). A different Black-and-Red Ware is found in peninsular India, associated with megalithic graves. This ware continues into the Early Historic Period in the peninsula, overlapping with the construction of megalithic graves. Though found throughout the peninsula, the wide variety of different pastes, forms, and other features suggests that Black-and-Red Ware was produced in many different areas (Gurumurthy 1981). The similarities between these different regions are the product of similar production techniques, not trade in the ceramics from one central place. Thus, while the presence of Black-and-Red Ware testifies to cultural contacts within the areas where it is found, it does not necessarily suggest that these ties were frequent or pronounced.

In north coastal Andhra Pradesh, numerous Early Historic Period sites yielded Black-and-Red Ware sherds (Bavikonda, Pavuralakonda, Sankaram, Salihundam, etc.; see Sastry 1983). Given its widespread geographic and temporal use,

Black-and-Red Ware is a poor chronological marker. This does not cast the dating of Thotlakonda Monastery into doubt, as numerous other archaeological remains and inscriptions serve to date the monastery (see chapter 5). The difficulty I encountered was in dating sites found during survey around the monastery. Given that the existing ware categories are insufficient for the precise dating of any site, I needed to find new criteria to characterize ceramics from the four centuries in which Thotlakonda was occupied. For this reason, a major part of my research was an attempt to create a local ceramic chronology based on local pottery traditions rather than the widespread wares that have dominated much of the archaeological literature in South Asia. I present the results of these analyses of local ceramics in chapter 6.

Historiography: Aryans and Dravidians

A massive body of literature focuses on colonialism and postcolonialism in South Asia.[3] With each year, these investigations become more nuanced and subtle, tracking the effects of colonialism and postcolonialism with increasing detail. Although my focus is not on the history of colonialism itself, it is important to examine the effects that colonialism has had on the study of precolonial South Asia (Chakrabarti 1997, 2001b). These effects color both the colonial and postcolonial historical texts that I rely upon. For this reason it is necessary to approach historical sources with an understanding of the context in which they were created. Many of the historical themes I explore here are based upon one simple "fact"—that Sanskrit is an Indo-European language related to Persian, Greek, Latin, and most other European languages. Further, the *Rig Veda,* the earliest readable text from South Asia, is written in Sanskrit. For the British and other Europeans, this established that some ancient link existed between the European and South Asian "civilizations." Explanations of this connection produced the first major theme of South Asian history, the Aryans.

With the recognition of the common origin of Sanskrit and European languages by Sir William Jones near the end of the eighteenth century (Jones 1824), modern European narratives of Indian history began to emerge. Thomas Trautmann (1997) provides a nuanced investigation of these narratives, arguing that the development of the European concept of the Aryans emerged as a synthesis of the work of European Sanskritists and the racial science of nineteenth-century anthropology. In this synthesis, the introduction of Indo-European languages was assumed to coincide with the migration of Indo-European people from Central Asia—the Aryans—into South Asia during the second millennium B.C. The Aryans were credited with introducing "civilization" to South Asia.[4] They were considered a race superior to the indigenous South Asians, who were forced southward as the

Aryans assumed control over northern India. This served to explain the modern distribution of languages and races found in South Asia today.

By the mid-nineteenth century, the Dravidian and Munda language families of peninsular India were shown to be different from the Indo-European languages of North India (Ellis 1816; Campbell 1816; Caldwell 1856; see Trautmann 1997 for a review of the identification of the Dravidian language family). European historians postulated that the people who spoke these languages were the descendants of the people displaced by the Aryans. Thus, a linguistic divide between the north and south was explained as the product of the historical replacement and migration of different races. This racial explanation was buttressed by the observation that people in the south were dark skinned in comparison to the lighter skin of the descendants of the Aryans in the north.[5] The one "fact" left to account for was the apparent sophistication of the Dravidian speakers of the south. This was explained by a process of "Aryanization" or "Sanskritization," in which northern Aryans were postulated to have moved south to become the political and religious elite over the Dravidian speakers of the south (see Srinivas 1966). Just as the British employed local languages in their own colonial endeavor, the Aryans who moved south adopted the local languages of their new homes, slowly losing their original Aryan tongue. The presence of numerous Sanskrit loan words in Dravidian languages, and common religious elements between the north and south, were seen as survivals of the process of Aryanization.

Over the course of two centuries of European investigation, a simple story of Indian history was constructed. The origins of Indian civilization were viewed as the product of an earlier influx of colonizers, who were themselves the progenitors of the Europeans who were then in the process of recolonizing South Asia. Today it is almost impossible not to recognize that this historical narrative was a product of the colonial process itself and that it served to legitimize the colonial practices of the British in South Asia (see Trautmann 1997; Chakrabarti 1997, 2001b). Nevertheless, it should also be remembered that much of the colonial scholarship remains valuable to this day. That this scholarship existed within the context of British colonialism does not necessarily limit its usefulness in studying precolonial South Asian history and archaeology.

Antecedents: North India

With this background, it is possible to briefly outline South Asian history through the Early Historic Period. This outline will combine archaeological and historical information, though the archaeology of north coastal Andhra Pradesh will be discussed in chapter 5. Since there are other histories (See Basham 1967; Thapar 2002, [1961] 1997; Allchin 1995; Ray 1986), this outline can be brief. In later chapters I will present progressively more specific historical data and interpretations. Where possible, these will be backed by relevant archaeological data. The following outline is intended only to situate my archaeological research in north coastal Andhra Pradesh within the broader historical context of South Asia.

The Early Historic Period

There is no clear break between the Early Historic Period and the preceding Vedic Period in North India. The selection of 600 B.C. as the start of the Early Historic Period in the Gangetic Plain has more to do with an increase in the available historical sources than with any clear historical boundary. This is not to suggest that the written sources actually date to this period. As stated earlier, sources such as the *Mahabharata* and *Ramayana* were collated as much as a thousand years later. Since the extant versions were written in periods with much greater political centralization and stratification, it is likely that they project later political and religious attitudes into earlier time periods (see Thapar 2000).

Thapar (1966, 1984, 2002) has argued that at the start of the Early Historic Period polities of the Gangetic Plain included both kingdoms and republics. In the heart of the Gangetic Plain, new polities emerged with more autocratic and prominent kings at their centers. In contrast, on the peripheries of these kingdoms, polities retained more aspects of the communal leadership that characterized the Vedic Period. These larger tribes or tribal confederacies organized themselves as republics. Here assemblies were created of village and tribal leaders who made communal decisions for the republics. More recently, several scholars have argued that these early republics and kingdoms can be subsumed within a broader rubric of city-states (see Kenoyer 1997; Erdosy 1995; Chakrabarti 2001, 1995). In this view, small states, centered around single cities, were in constant interaction with one another. Periodically a city-state might gain advantage over others, but territorial expansion was just as often followed by withdrawal.

Along with these political developments came increases in trade, communication, and warfare. Particularly in the plains, cities developed, often with elaborate defensive walls. Merchants, traders, craftspeople, and religious specialists augmented the bulk of the population, who remained agriculturalists. In short, the first few centuries of the Early Historic Period in northern South Asia was a time of multiple small competing polities centered around developing urban centers. At times one or another would make gains, consolidating power over larger areas, but just as often these polities collapsed. The Vedic rituals from the earlier periods continued to be practiced but were soon challenged by the development of several new religious sects.

During the Early Historic Period a wide variety of religious traditions emerged to challenge the orthodoxy of Brahmanism, which continued the practice of Vedic sacrifices. The textual sources mention numerous wandering ascetics propounding a bewildering variety of religious views. Over time, some of these wandering ascetics began to attract followers and settle in small monasteries throughout the subcontinent. Of these sects, two became major religions that persist to this day, Jainism and Buddhism. Originating in the sixth century B.C., they share many common elements. Jainism was founded by Mahavira around 500 B.C. (see Dundas 1992 for a good introduction to Jainism). Mahavira argued that everything (people, animals, plants, rocks, and even air) had a soul. Jains attempted to purify their own souls in order to attain a state of bliss. Purification of the soul was accomplished by leading a balanced life, principally by refraining from causing injury to any creature.

Given that everything had a soul, a Jain monk was forced to employ drastic measures to avoid injuring them. They wore mesh masks to avoid injury to air spirits; they swept the path before them to avoid stepping on insects. Unavoidable injuries such as eating and drinking were atoned by fasting and prayer. Given these prohibitions, people who practiced agriculture or craft activities that required the killing of animals could not hope to follow Jain practice. Rather, Jains tended to occupy themselves in trade and other commercial activities centered in the developing urban centers of the period (Thapar 2002; Dundas 1992). Even with these occupations, only Jain monks could hope to perform the austerities and purification rituals necessary to attain bliss. For others, the goal was to lead as balanced a life as possible to ensure that they were themselves reborn as monks. In this sense Jainism was similar to its contemporary new religion, Buddhism.

Buddhism and the development of the Buddhist order of monks will be discussed in the next chapter. Here I only present the barest outlines of Buddhism. The Buddha is believed to have been a contemporary of Mahavira, living from 563 through 483 B.C., though recently several scholars have argued that he may have lived as much as one century later (see Bechert 1995). The Buddha was born to the chief of a republic (the Shakyas) in what is now southern Nepal. At age twenty-nine he left the palace for a life as an ascetic. After six years he achieved enlightenment, understanding the causes of suffering and the means to overcome it. Over time, the Buddha attracted a large number of followers and established an order of monks and nuns. Like the Jains, Buddhists downplayed the importance of caste in their teachings. As Thapar (2002) has suggested, this allowed Jains and Buddhists to engage in trade more easily than Brahmans, who were forced to follow strict caste prohibitions. The result was that both Buddhism and Jainism thrived in the developing cities of the Gangetic Plain and spread rapidly from city to city from the fourth through first centuries B.C.

In sum, the picture that emerges of religious practice in the Early Historic Period is of multiple rival sects vying with each other (Ray 2004). Forms of

Brahmanism, Jainism, and Buddhism have survived to this day, but other sects (e.g., Ajivikas and Charvakas) have disappeared (Basham 1967; Thapar 2002). While this book focuses on Buddhism and Buddhist monasteries, Buddhism was only one of many religious traditions in simultaneous practice throughout the subcontinent. Moreover, kings often supported multiple religious institutions. While the monastic literature emphasizes the differences between these sects, it is very likely that the laity did not. The fluidity of these traditions can be clearly illustrated by the Mauryan kings Chandragupta and his grandson Ashoka. Jain literary sources record that the grandfather became a Jain monk in his old age, while Ashoka is credited in the Pali Canon as the greatest royal sponsor that Buddhism ever had.

The Mauryas

In 326 B.C. Alexander the Great led his armies into northwestern South Asia. Alexander was not pushing into unknown territory. He was consolidating his victory over the Persians, who had claimed Gandhara as one of their territories. For at least two centuries prior to the arrival of Alexander, the Persians had received sporadic tribute and support from the Northwest (McCrindle [1926] 2000; Thapar 2002; Briant 2002). Alexander's campaign in South Asia lasted only a few years. With his death soon after his departure from South Asia, the provinces he had established slowly collapsed. Although a Greek presence remained in the Northwest for a few more centuries, the Greeks were rapidly absorbed into the local populations. Alexander himself had little impact on South Asia. He is not mentioned in any South Asian literature or inscriptions.

Alexander's Gandharan campaign did have one important consequence—it cleared away rivals, allowing Chandragupta Maurya to establish the Mauryan Empire in the area recently held by the Persians and Greeks (Thapar 2002; see figure 2.3). Over the next two centuries the Mauryan Empire expanded under several subsequent kings, consolidating power in the Gangetic Plain, with areas of significant influence in the peninsula. The southward expansion of the Mauryas is critical to the spread of northern religions and cultural practices into the peninsula beginning in the third century B.C. The following historical abstract is derived, for the most part, from the writings of Basham (1967) and Thapar (1966, 2002).

By 321 B.C. Chandragupta Maurya had defeated his main rivals, the Nandas. He continued his conquest of the Gangetic Plain until 297 B.C. when he abdicated the throne in favor of his son, Bindusara, and became a Jain monk. Bindusara continued his father's conquests, principally toward South India. Between them, Chandragupta and Bindusara successfully established the first large empire in South Asia. However, the specific borders and forms of imperial control established by Chandragupta and Bindusara are not clear. What is known of the Mauryan Empire must be inferred from the legacy of their successor, Ashoka.

Ashoka has become a central figure of Indian history. His importance is, in part, derived from the large number of inscriptions he had incised on rock faces and pillars throughout South Asia. (The content of the inscriptions will be discussed in greater detail in chapter 3). These inscriptions are among the best records of the Mauryan political and social systems, since, unlike the *Arthashastra,* they were not written centuries after the Mauryan Empire collapsed. The inscriptions were written in the local languages of the area in which they are located. For this reason it is likely that Ashoka intended them to communicate his proclamations to local audiences rather than simply to Mauryan officials. They include specifics of Ashoka's life and elaborate statements on what Ashoka saw as the appropriate behavior of his subjects.

Ashoka became king in 272 B.C. and ruled for roughly forty years. In 260 B.C. he conquered the Kalinga, a kingdom in what is now coastal Orissa. Both Ashoka's rock inscriptions and Buddhist sources document that the carnage, death, and enslavement of the Kalinga caused Ashoka to enter a period of religious contemplation. According to the Pali Canon, Ashoka actively proselytized for Buddhism, sending missionaries to Sri Lanka, redistributing relics of the Buddha, and supporting Buddhist monks. For these actions he is remembered in the Buddhist chronicle of Sri Lanka as a great hero-king (*chakravartin*) of Buddhism. Clearly his actions enabled Buddhism to expand within the subcontinent and start to spread throughout Asia. That said, Ashoka was not simply a promoter of Buddhism. While a small body of his inscriptions may have been intended to promote Buddhism, the greater number were directed toward the creation of an imperial ideology that fostered a more inclusive empire (Thapar 1997; Strong 1983, 1994).

Ashoka's inscriptions make clear his view that a ruler should support all of the religions within his domain. While a preference for Buddhism may be present, Ashoka advanced a more generalized religious point of view in the majority of his edicts. Specifically, he advocated pacifism, vegetarianism, and respect for family and authority. These proscriptions, while greatly influenced by Buddhist thought, had resonance throughout most of the religions of South Asia (Thapar 1997, 2002; Strong 1983, 1994). In this sense, Ashokan inscriptions are nonsectarian. This said, it should also be noted that these broad concepts would have served imperial interests well. In essence, they promoted activities, such as pacifism and respect for authority, that eased the process of governance. The Ashokan inscriptions also provide some information upon the political structure and history of the Mauryan Empire. Several inscriptions record embassies and trade missions to Greece, Syria, and Egypt. The inscriptions also record the names of territories not under Mauryan control, principally several in the extreme south. They record the existence of Mauryan provinces, tax collectors, and courts. Together all of these references suggest that the Mauryan Empire had a strong degree of centralized control, or at least had aspirations to it.

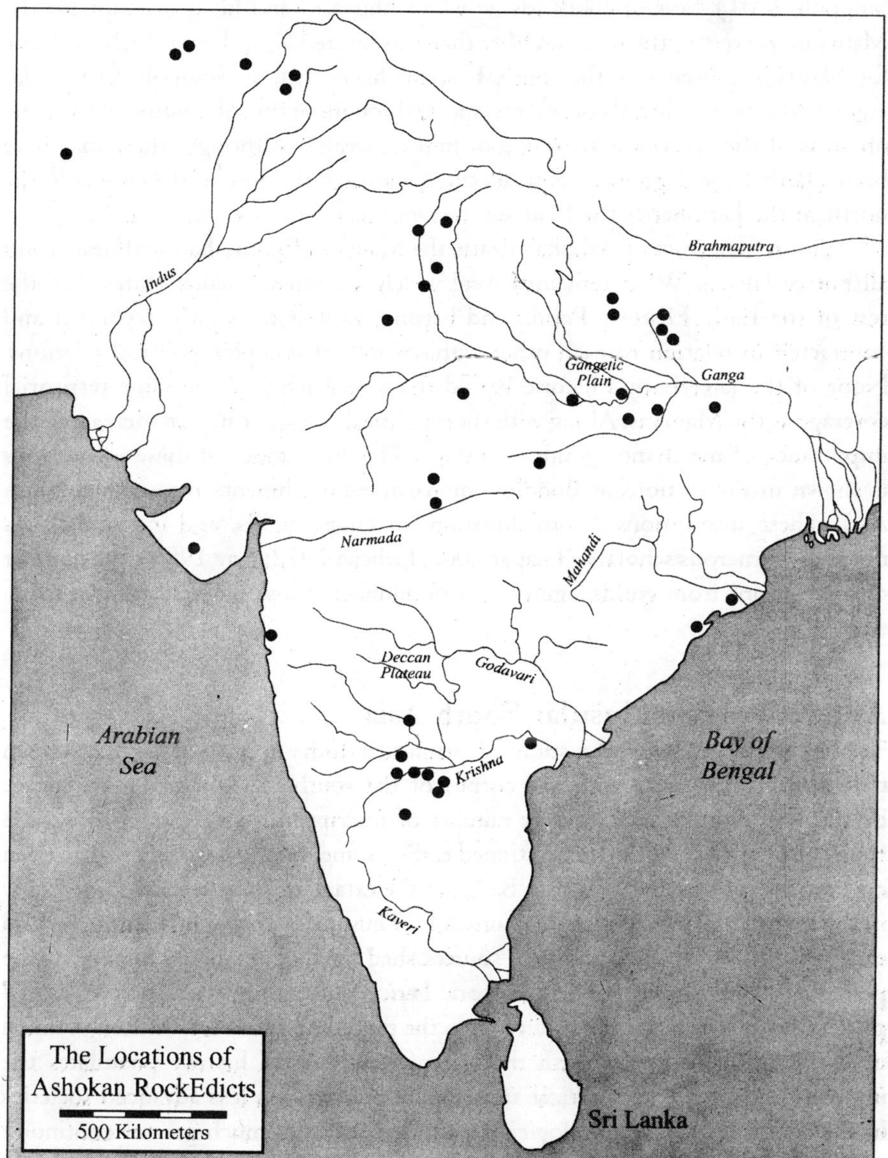

Figure 2.2. Map of Ashokan inscriptions.

The locations of Ashokan inscriptions in the subcontinent have been interpreted to claim direct Mauryan control over a substantial portion of the peninsula (see figure 2.2). More recently, some writers have noted that the distributions of the southern inscriptions are tightly circumscribed in the Deccan Plateau and Krishna River valley (Ray 1986; Thapar 2002; Fussman 1988; Habib and Habib 1990:

Sinopoli 2001). Several goldfields lie within this area and likely account for the Mauryan interest in the region. Other than this limited area, there is little evidence for Mauryan presence in the south. It seems likely that, as Sinopoli (2001) has argued, Mauryan political control was spotty throughout the subcontinent, focusing on areas of the greatest agricultural or mineral wealth. Althought there may have been a fairly large degree of political centralization in the core of the empire in the north, at the peripheries the Mauryan presence may have been less dramatic.

Within fifty years of Ashoka's death, the Mauryan Empire had withdrawn and all but collapsed. What remained were widely scattered, smaller states. For the rest of the Early Historic Period and beyond, rival states slowly expanded and contracted in relation to each other within a web of complex political relations. None of the later Early Historic Period states ever achieved the same territorial coverage as the Mauryas. Along with these political changes came an increase in the importance of merchants, guilds, and trade. The importance of these institutions is shown in inscriptions at Buddhist monastic establishments throughout South Asia. These inscriptions record donations of kings, guilds, and individuals. As noted by numerous scholars (Thapar 2002; Dehejia 1972; Ray 1986), the number of inscriptions from guilds significantly outnumbers those of the royalty at many sites.

Antecedents: Peninsular South Asia

The textual sources for the study of peninsular India appear, at the earliest, in the third century B.C. with the corpus of the southern Ashokan inscriptions. By the first century B.C. a larger number of inscriptions were carved by people from the peninsula itself. As mentioned earlier, some Tamil sources have also been credited to the first few centuries B.C., but the extant versions were recorded only in the first half of the first millennium A.D. Thus, prior to the first through third centuries B.C., only archaeological sources shed light upon the prehistory of the peninsula. The advent of Early Historic Period cultural practices was a gradual process, with significant continuity from the preceding Iron Age. Although much of the traditional north/south rhetoric of South Asian history postulates the imposition of Gangetic political and cultural practices on less advanced societies in the peninsula, the archaeological record demonstrates much greater continuity and overlap.

The Iron Age in Peninsular South Asia

The South Indian Iron Age is known, for the most part, from a large number of megalithic tombs and the grave goods found within them (Krishnaswami 1949; Brubaker 2000–2001; Moorti 1994). Other than the megaliths, few Iron Age archaeological remains have been identified or excavated (but see Nagaraja Rao 1971; Sastri, Bai, and Rao 1984). The earliest megalithic cemeteries date to c. 1000 B.C. A fourth-century A.D. Roman coin found in a megalith in Tamil Nadu is usually cited to mark the end of widespread megalithic construction (Srinivasan and Banerjee 1953, 112). During this period many different forms of megalithic burials were constructed throughout the peninsula, ranging from standing stones to large cairns and stone-carved tombs. Common to most of them is the presence of a burial in the center, often interred within a large urn. Graves contained many iron objects, including plow tips and other agricultural implements, swords, spearheads, knives, fishhooks, adzes, spindle whorls, needles, and bits for horses. Other grave goods included bangles, beads, and pendants, all made of shell, glass, gold, and semiprecious stones. In some cases the semiprecious stones were quarried in northern South Asia, demonstrating trade with the north from at least the mid-first millennium B.C. (Rajan 1994).

Grave goods are found in vastly different quantities in different tombs. In locations where there are large numbers of megalithic burials in close association, some of the tombs are significantly larger than the others. Within the graves, some have far more grave goods than others. Studies of the remains of those interred within the graves, though based on small sample sizes, demonstrate that most are males between the ages of seventeen and thirty-five (Moorti 1994, 45–112). Together, this suggests that there may have been marked rank distinctions between different members of Iron Age society.

In sum, the evidence from the megaliths and graves suggests that Iron Age society focused on agriculture and herding, but people continued to hunt and fish. At least part-time craft production of textiles, pottery, wood, and metal seems to have been practiced and, given that tools were interred in graves, prized to some degree. The differential degree of mortuary elaboration in graves and grave goods suggests that these societies had some social ranking, with chiefs and other leaders. That almost all of those interred were men reinforces this claim. Finally, the presence of swords and other weapons suggests that there was conflict between social groups.

The relative lack of archaeological investigations of Iron Age settlements makes a more complete picture of Iron Age society difficult. Using the size of megalithic cemeteries as a proxy for settlements, Brubaker (2001–2002) has conducted an interesting analysis of the settlement patterns in the Iron Age.[6] Following Johnson's (1980, 1981) study of settlement patterns in Mesopotamia, Brubaker analyzed the size distributions of megalithic cemeteries in the peninsula as a whole and in discrete geographic regions. In all cases, he found the size distribution of cemeteries followed a pattern typical of a weakly integrated settlement system or multiple weakly integrated settlement systems (Brubaker 2001–2002, 28–49). Combining this analysis with what was already known of Iron Age society from megaliths and grave offerings, Brubaker (2001–2002, 45–46) argued:

> At the smallest and least complex . . . chiefs with limited decision making prerogatives probably presided over single settlements. In larger examples, more powerful leaders based in larger centers likely exerted varying degrees of control over multiple and varying numbers of settlements. Finally, at the most complex end of this continuum, paramount chiefs ruling from large regional centers with lesser chiefs as political subordinates dominated even larger polities containing numerous settlements and substantial populations. In the present context it seems very likely that chiefdoms of the first type were prevalent during the earlier phases of the Iron Age, with those of the latter two types developing with increasing frequency as time passed.

The Early Historic Period in Peninsular South Asia

As in the Gangetic Plain, the advent of the Early Historic Period in the peninsula is determined by the date when textual sources become available—either the third century B.C. with the southern Ashokan inscriptions, or the first century B.C. with the more widespread evidence for donation inscriptions at Buddhist establishments. As stated earlier, megaliths were widely constructed from the first millennium B.C. through roughly the fourth century A.D. The Satavahana polity, often depicted as the first northern-style state in the peninsula, emerged in the first century B.C. Depending upon whether the advent of the Early Historic Period is dated to the third or first century B.C., the megalithic tradition and South Asian Iron Age overlap with the Early Historic Period from four to seven centuries.

Rather than northern social and political traditions replacing the preceding cultural traditions of the peninsula, there was substantial overlap and continuity in South Indian cultural practices. This continuity substantially blurs the traditional prehistoric/historic divide that has oriented much of the historical interpretations of the peninsula. Further, as shown by the presence of semiprecious stones quarried in northern South Asia in megalithic tombs in South India (Rajan 1994), connections with the peninsula substantially predate the epigraphic evidence.

North coastal Andhra Pradesh lies to the north of the greatest concentrations of megalithic cemeteries. As will be discussed in greater detail in chapter 5, only a few Iron Age burials have been found in the region. In general, little is known of the archaeological remains predating the Buddhist monasteries that are the focus of this research. Nevertheless, Thotlakonda dates to the time of overlap between the Iron Age and Early Historic Period in peninsular India. Later megaliths in the peninsula are contemporary with Thotlakonda. Buddhist monasteries and monuments in the peninsula did not replace megalithic traditions, but existed with them. The obvious similarities between Buddhist *stupas* and Iron Age megaliths suggest that Buddhism was integrated within an existing mortuary pattern in the peninsula rather than simply replacing it. Buddhism undoubtedly developed in the Gangetic Plain and spread southward, but indigenous cultural practices in the peninsula continued to play a central role in its adoption. This issue will play an important part of subsequent analyses of the mortuary pattern of cairns found on the hills surrounding Thotlakonda.

Contemporary States: The Kalingas and Satavahanas

To the north and south of north coastal Andhra Pradesh were two states contemporary with Thotlakonda and the other Buddhist monasteries in the region (see figure 2.3). To the north was the Kalinga state, the same polity whose conquest led Ashoka to religious contemplation and pacifism. To the south was the Satavahana, or Andhra, state of the Krishna and Godavari River valleys and the Deccan Plateau. Both polities claimed control over north coastal Andhra Pradesh at some point. It seems likely that at least nominal political control in north coastal Andhra Pradesh alternated between the two during the Early Historic Period, depending upon their relative power. In either case, it was on the periphery of both states, with limited control exacted by the center. At other times, it may have been independent of both states. Given the lack of historical data, the precise relations between the north coastal Andhra Pradesh, the Satavahanas, and the Kalinga cannot be established at this time.

The Kalinga

Despite the prominence of the Kalinga state in Ashokan rock edicts, little is known of its history. Ashokan inscriptions record that it was a relatively wealthy and powerful kingdom at the time of its conquest. The capital was Tosali, believed to be located near the modern city of Bhubaneswar in Orissa. Buddhism and Jainism were both practiced in the kingdom. The territory of the Kalinga state included coastal Orissa and at least part of coastal Andhra Pradesh. Once the Mauryan Empire collapsed, the only information on the Kalinga comes from a few vague references in Ptolemy and a single eroded royal inscription in a rock-cut Jain temple (Udayagiri) near Bhubaneswar, Orissa. As for the references in Ptolemy, they only reiterate that Kalinga was a kingdom in coastal Orissa (McCrindle [1927] 2000; Das 1977). The inscription, in contrast, provides a chronicle of one king's exploits for the first thirteen years of his reign.

The Hathigumpha inscription consists of seventeen lines, several unreadable, recording the life of King Kharavela, who likely lived during the first century B.C. (Sahu 2000; Das 1977). Overall, it presents an image of a king much like Ashoka.

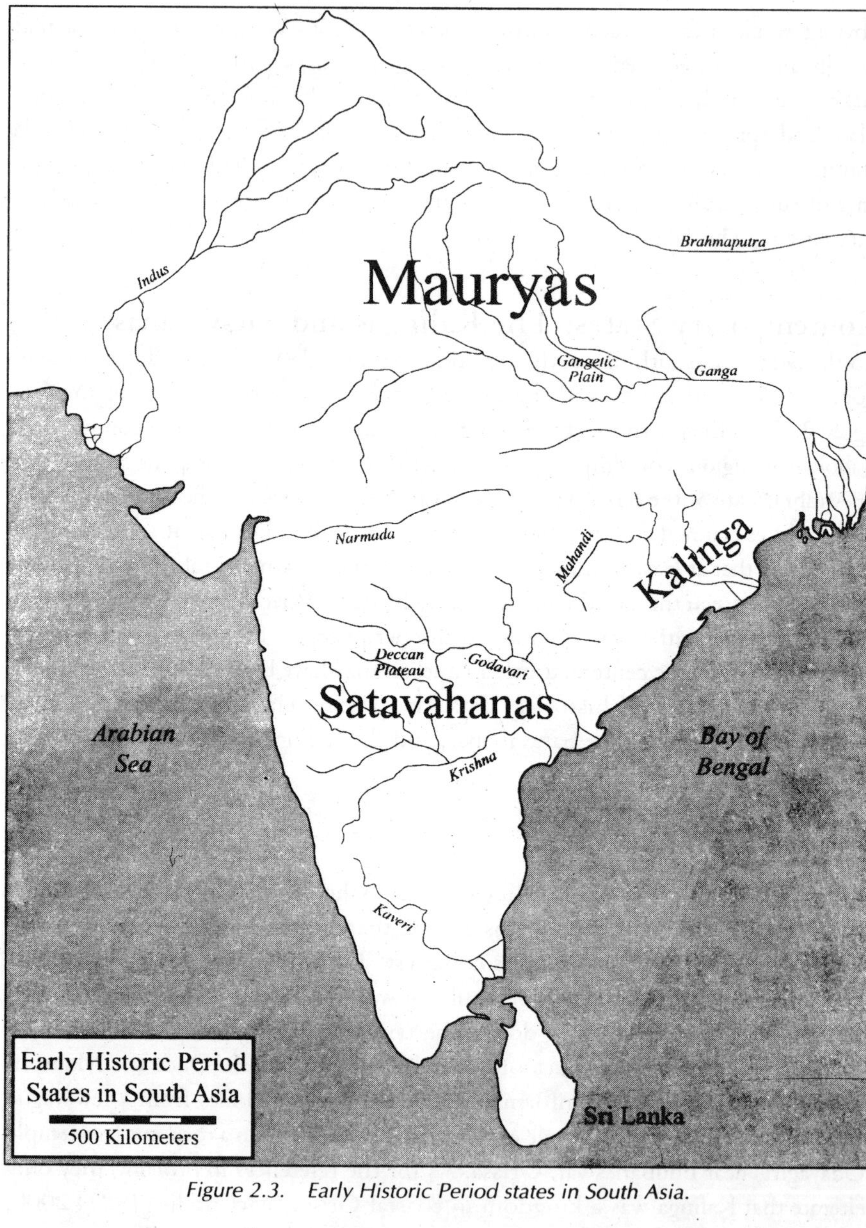

Figure 2.3. Early Historic Period states in South Asia.

It records his education as a young man in governance, finance, law, and sports. It lists his good acts of supporting religious institutions, with particular references to Jainism. It continues by recording successful military campaigns, principally to the north and west of Kalinga, with only one reference to campaigns southward. It is unclear how far this southern campaign traveled, or if north coastal Andhra

Pradesh was already within the Kalinga territory, or if it was added with this campaign. The inscription ends with Kharavela's thirteenth year, when he redirected his efforts to peace and erected a Jain monastery. The only other Early Historic Period inscriptions that mention the Kalinga record the names of either princes or rulers of Kalinga without dates or other additional information. No other historical information is available on the Early Historic Period Kalinga.

Despite a recent upsurge in the archaeological study of Orissa (see Basa and Mohanty 2000), the archaeology of the Early Historic Period is still relatively poorly understood. While two Early Historic Period rock-cut Jain temples (one containing the Hathigumpha inscription) attest to the practice of Jainism in the Kalinga state (see Mitra 1975; Sahu 2000), the role of Buddhism is far less clear. Two Ashokan inscriptions state that Buddhism was practiced in the Kalinga state (Luders 1912), but no definitive Buddhist monuments or monasteries have been identified from the Early Historic Period. The only exceptions to this are several poorly documented Buddhist monasteries and *stupas* near the Early Historic city of Radhanagar (Mishra 2000).

The *Chronicles of Xuanzang* note that Buddhism was extensively practiced in Orissa in the seventh century A.D. (Beal 1908; Liu 1988). In support of this claim, several Buddhist monasteries and monuments have been identified in Orissa dating to this time (see Basa and Mohanty 2000). Excavations at one of these later Buddhist monastic sites, Lalitagiri, has revealed what the excavators believe to be Early Historic Period ceramics, but no architectural remains were found to demonstrate that the site was a Buddhist monastery at that time (Chauley 2000; Patnaik 2000). Still, most historians and archaeologists believe that, despite the absence of strong literary or archaeological evidence, Buddhism was practiced in Early Historic Period Orissa.

In contrast to the lack of Early Historic monasteries, several urban centers have been found and partially excavated in Orissa. These include Sisupalgarh (Lal 1949; Smith 2002), Manikapatana (Pradhan, Mohanty, and Misra 2000), Radhanagar (Mishra 2000), and Jaugada (I.A.R 1956–1957, 30–31). All are walled settlements located on the banks of large rivers. Sisupalgarh, believed to be a capital of the Kalinga state, was occupied from the third century B.C. to the middle of the fourth century A.D. The city was surrounded by a square wall, one kilometer on a side. Within these walls were brick and stone structures laid out in an orderly grid. By the standards of the Early Historic Period, Sisupalgarh was a very large urban center.

The Satavahanas

In contrast to the Kalinga, a great deal more historical information exists concerning the Satavahanas. Nevertheless, the Satavahanas remain enigmatic, with contrasting and contradictory information permeating the historical literature. For some scholars (Sastri 1966; Mirashi 1981) the Satavahanas are a successor state to the Mauryas in the south. In this argument, the Satavahanas were central to the process of Aryanization of Dravidian areas in South India. Further, the Satavahanas are portrayed as a strongly centralized and territorially expansive empire modeled closely on the Mauryas. This view is strongly influenced by the north/south narrative discussed earlier. In contrast, more recent research (Ray 1986; Parasher-Sen 1993; Shastri 1987; Sinopoli 2001) has presented the Satavahanas as emerging c. 100 B.C. as a more loosely organized empire combining northern and southern traditions. For the next three centuries, the Satavahanas went through periods of greater and lesser power and centralization until their decline by the second century A.D. This newer view, followed here, is based upon a combination of historical, archaeological, and numismatic evidence.

The *Puranas* provide two dynastic chronologies for the Satavahanas (see Ray 1986). The longer (460 years) is employed by those who argue for more direct Mauryan influence. The shorter chronology is supported by those who favor the later development of the Satavahanas. In either case, several of the kings listed in the *Puranas* are named on coins and inscriptions found throughout the Deccan Plateau and Krishna River Valley. In addition, several inscriptions record the existence of systems of taxation, territorial officials, and other signs of imperial authority. That said, there is also ample evidence that the Satavahanas never had highly centralized imperial control over their territory. First, royal names on several coins are not present in the *Puranic* lists and may represent local rulers. The tight geographic circumscription of the distribution of these coins supports this claim (Dutta 1990; Sarma 1980). Second, no single capital existed during the Satavahana reign. At different times, and perhaps even at the same time, several cities were considered the seat of Satavahana rule. This suggests that Satavahana kings rose from powerful regional rulers rather than through the more typical process of hereditary ascension. In terms of broader characterizations of the Satavahanas, Sinopoli (2001, 177) states that

> the presentation of imperial status in inscriptions and monuments far surpassed any political, military, or economic infrastructure of empire that existed during the [Satavahana] period.... Nonetheless, the empire was characterized by brief periods of greater political centralization and more effective administration that correlated with the reigns of particularly capable rulers who were able to both achieve and consolidate military successes.

Throughout the Satavahana period it appears that the rulers supported a variety of religious sects and followed some Dravidian cultural practices. The first is illustrated in an inscription found within a Buddhist monastery at Nanaghat in the Western Deccan (Fergusson and Burgess [1880] 1988, 264). This inscription not only records a donation to the Buddhist monastery, but also celebrates the performance of several Vedic sacrifices by Satakarni I. The persistence of Dravidian practices among the Satavahana rulers is also shown in the continued preference for cross-cousin marriages (Trautmann 1981). This marriage pattern, expressly forbidden in Vedic texts, was the preferred marriage system of Dravidian speakers in the peninsula. Together, the evidence for religious heterodoxy and Dravidian kinship systems suggest that the Satavahanas were flexible in their use of northern and southern cultural traditions. Thus, the Satavahanas blur the north/south distinction portrayed in much of the historical literature.

One final question that should be addressed is the geographic origin and territorial control of the Satavahanas. The Satavahana territory covered the Deccan Plateau in the west through the Krishna and Godavari River valleys in the east. The arguments over origin derive from the two names that are used in the primary literature referring to the Satavahanas. In contemporary inscriptions and coins, the term Satavahana is used. In the *Puranas* the Satavahanas are called the Andhras. The Puranic term has been used to argue for origins in the Krishna River Valley and modern Andhra Pradesh (Shastri 1987; Goyala 1995). Thus, the modern location for the Andhra ethnic group is read backwards to place the origin of the Satavahanas (Ray 1986). Others point toward the earliest numismatic and inscriptional evidence in the Deccan Plateau to place the origin of the Satavahanas (Dehejia 1972). Like Sinopoli (2001, 170), I lean toward the Deccan. However, at this point I do not believe that sufficient evidence exists to answer the question definitively. This is important, since it casts into doubt the dates during which the Satavahanas occupied the Krishna and Godavari River valleys. This in turn makes it more difficult to assign a period when they would have had the greatest influence in north coastal Andhra Pradesh, the focus of this research.

Conclusion

In this chapter a narrative of Indian history has been presented in the broadest strokes. Given the paucity of historical data concerning north coastal Andhra Pradesh, this was necessary. Nonetheless, it should be remembered that this larger narrative conceals variations in beliefs and cultural traditions found throughout South Asia. In the discussion of the Satavahanas I provided some evidence that a blending of traditions occurred, challenging the traditional divide between the north and the south, the Aryans and Dravidians. Aloka Parasher-Sen has argued (1996) that Indian history must begin to focus more upon regional concerns rather than the sweeping narratives that have dominated much of the literature and debate. It is my intention to follow her advice, but not before presenting another broad discussion, this time focusing on Buddhism during the Early Historic Period.

Notes

1. Smaller excavations were also carried out at Kausambi (Sharma 1960, 1969), Hastinapura (Lal 1955), Rajghat (Narain and Roy 1976; Narain and Singh 1977), Nagarjunakonda (Ramachandran 1953), and numerous other locations. See Chakrabarti 1995 and Allchin 1995 for an overview of archaeological studies of the Early Historic Period.

2. More modern archaeological examinations of the Early Historic Period archaeological sites can be found in Sarkar 1966; Mitra 1971, 1965; Sastry 1983; Smith 1997, 2002; Sastry, Subrahmanyam, and Rao 1992; Prasad 1994; Barua 1979; Begley 1996, 1993; Shaw 2000, 2002; Ray and Sinopoli 2004.

3. For example, see Dirks 1993, 2001; Guha and Spivak 1988; Breckenridge and van der Veer 1993; Inden 1990; see also Said 1978.

4. The recognition of pre-Aryan cities at Harappa and Mohenjo-Daro in the early twentieth century muddied this picture but did not cause significant changes to the Aryan framework promoted in European histories. Rather, the Aryans were credited with destroying the preexisting civilizations of South Asia, creating a strong break between pre-Aryan and post-Aryan civilizations. The preexisting civilizations of South Asia were then reduced to an interesting historical oddity, without any direct impact upon the later historical developments. More recent archaeological research (see Shaffer 1984; Kenoyer 1998) has asserted much greater continuity between the Indus Valley civilization and later historical periods, rejecting many of the assumptions of the Aryan explanation.

5. Modern studies of skin-color variation in South Asia show that existing variation is completely explained by the latitude of the populations. People in the south are darker for protection from solar radiation. Skin color throughout the subcontinent parallels the skin color of populations at similar latitudes in the Old World (Jaswal 1990; Lukacs 1984).

6. The difficulties inherent in using cemetery size as a stand-in for settlement size are fully explored by Brubaker (2001–2002). He notes that the current knowledge of the distribution and nature of megalithic cemeteries is widely variable. For this reason, and others, his conclusions are still somewhat tentative. However, his study provides a valuable new understanding of the South Asian Iron Age and, I suspect, will guide a great deal of new archaeological research in the peninsula.

Buddhism in Early Historic Period South Asia 3

UNTIL RECENTLY, A GENERAL outline of early Buddhist history was largely accepted by most scholars (Davids 1910; Basham 1967; Lamotte 1988; Chakrabarti 1995b). The Buddha lived from 563 to 483 B.C. Over the course of the next few centuries, Buddhism was adopted by growing numbers of followers, with the establishment of religious monuments at the principal sites in the life of the Buddha and at *stupas* containing his relics. In the third century B.C., Buddhism was adopted by the Mauryan king Ashoka after he witnessed the loss of life caused by his own conquest over the Kalinga on the eastern coast of South Asia. After this, Ashoka promoted Buddhism across South Asia through inscriptions and the expansion of existing monuments. Ashoka's support of Buddhism was the catalyst that propelled Buddhism from its place as an important religion in South Asia toward a path that would eventually lead to its expansion throughout most of Asia.

In the last decade, almost every point of this historical outline has been challenged. Many researchers now suggest that the Buddha lived as much as a century later than previously believed (see Bechert 1995). Coningham (2001) has convincingly argued that currently there is no archaeological evidence that any of the major pilgrimage sites associated with the Buddha existed prior to the Mauryas in the third century B.C. Finally, even the centrality of Ashoka in the spread of Buddhism has been questioned. Recent interpretations of Ashokan inscriptions have led some to argue that, while Ashoka did support Buddhist institutions, his rock edicts were actually intended to promote his own personal religion and glory (Strong 1983, 1994; Thapar 1997). The similarities with Buddhist doctrine are explained as the product of more generalized religious orientations common in multiple religious traditions throughout Early Historic Period South Asia.

A common element in all of these reinterpretations of early Buddhist history is that they reject earlier, literal readings of Buddhist textual sources as well as archaeological studies that applied these readings uncritically (Schopen 1997; Coningham

1998, 2001; Ray 2004). Among the central complaints of all of these scholars are two issues of historical credibility. First, the versions of the texts available to modern scholarship significantly postdate the Early Historic Period, many by several hundred years. Second, the available texts are the product of a limited number of Buddhist monks writing in specific social contexts. Even if their greater antiquity could be accepted, it is unclear to what degree these texts reflect the actual practice of Buddhism by the majority of monks, much less those of wider Buddhist communities. In this chapter I will examine these texts, with the goal of evaluating their usefulness for my archaeological investigations.

Throughout this book I rely heavily upon the work of Gregory Schopen (1994, 1995a, 1995b, 1997, 2000). In his writings he has challenged many of the previous understandings of Early Buddhism derived from studies based almost exclusively on religious texts. While trained in a textual tradition, Schopen also employs inscriptions and archaeology to address the actual practice of early Buddhists. Through archaeology, I also focus on the practices of early Buddhists rather than on their larger philosophical and cosmological principles. It should be noted that Schopen is only one of several scholars who have recently redirected their focus toward more mundane aspects of early Buddhism (see, for example, Trainor 1997; Carrithers 1983; Strong 1983, 1994; Tambiah 1984, 1976; Obeyesekere 1978). Although useful for my studies, much of this work is focused on the development of Buddhism in Sri Lanka and Southeast Asia rather than mainland South Asia. In contrast, most of Schopen's writings focus on the Gangetic Plain and peninsular South Asia, increasing its value to my own archaeological investigations.

Textual Sources for the Study of Early Buddhism

Traditionally, studies of Early Buddhism have relied heavily on contemporary and historical accounts of Sri Lankan and Southeast Asian Buddhism (see Davids 1900, 1910; Coomaraswamy 1927; Frauwallner 1956; Lamotte 1988). This practice is predicated on the belief that these schools of Buddhism have remained significantly unchanged over the years, retaining the traditions and practices of *Hinayana* Buddhism more faithfully than those traditions that adopted *Mahayana* and *Vajrayana* practices. As stated in the introduction, I avoid the term *Hinayana* because of its somewhat derisive character, preferring instead the term *Early Buddhism*. Following from the work of several recent scholars, I also object to the assumption that Sri Lankan and Southeast Asian forms of Buddhism are appropriate proxies for Early Buddhism in mainland South Asia (Collins 1990; Schopen 1997; Trainor 1997).

The differences between Sri Lankan Buddhism and mainland Buddhism are best illustrated by the different treatments of the Mauryan king Ashoka, as discussed by John Strong (1983). In Sri Lankan Buddhism, Ashoka is remembered as a great *chakravartin*, critical to the widespread adoption and spread of Buddhism. Ashoka is described in glorious terms as the model Buddhist ruler. On the mainland, in contrast, other than the inscriptions he erected himself, Ashoka is little more than a historical footnote (see Thapar 1997). Finally, in the *Asokavadana*, a fifth or sixth century A.D. Sanskrit text from China, Ashoka is described as a more flawed ruler (Strong 1983). While still considered a *chakravartin*, Ashoka is depicted as engaging in extreme acts of cruelty, both before and after his adoption of Buddhism. It seems possible, if not likely, that these different representations of Ashoka reflect the manner of their importation into different social contexts. In Sri Lanka, Buddhism was initially adopted and promoted by the political and religious elite (Collins 1990; Smith 1978; Bechert 1978; Strong 1983). Thus, the greater emphasis on the glories of Ashoka in Sri Lankan Buddhism can be viewed as legitimizing elite power and authority (see Smith ed. 1978).

The movement of Buddhism into Sri Lanka is less a tale of export from the mainland than the import and modification of Buddhism by the Sri Lankan elite—with, unsurprisingly, numerous modifications to suit their own concerns. This was followed by more than two millennia of well-documented change and development of Buddhist doctrines in Sri Lanka. These developments not only diverged from the doctrines of the mainland, but also differed between Buddhist sects within Sri Lanka itself. The historical narratives reported in the Pali Canon of Sri Lanka refer to activities that would have occurred in the third century B.C. However, the chronicles available to modern scholars date only to the fifth or sixth century A.D. (Bechert 1978; Collins 1990). The texts themselves note a previous redaction dating to the end of the first century B.C. Given this, there is no good reason to assume that Sri Lankan Buddhism resembles Early Buddhism in the mainland, and there are numerous reasons to argue that it does not. While Sri Lankan historical sources are employed in subsequent analyses, they are not given any more weight than Chinese, Tibetan, or Sanskrit sources. All serve to provide possible explanations of the material remains of early Buddhism, but all must be applied with great care and substantial independent evidence from other sources.

In chapter 2, I discussed issues concerning the chronology and value of different historical sources. Here I will continue that discussion, focusing on Buddhist textual sources. It is not possible to assign a date when Buddhist textual sources accurately testify to the nature of early Buddhism. The available sources are found in a variety of languages and Buddhist sects from throughout Asia. Within each tradition, each text has its own history and context. The fragmentation of Buddhism and its dissemination throughout Asia resulted in numerous Buddhist sects. Though they shared many texts, each sect added its own interpretations and modifications. The result is that almost all texts can be found in multiple versions. In some cases the differences are minor. In other cases they are wholly different works. In and of itself, this progressive fragmentation of Buddhism is neither surprising nor problematic. The difficulty emerges because the "originals" upon which all of these texts are based are no longer available. This may be due to the natural decay of early manuscripts and the eventual displacement of Buddhism in South Asia. It is also likely that for many generations after the Buddha, his words were preserved only orally, suggesting that the existing documents are among the earliest written sources.

While Buddhism emerged and initially developed in the Gangetic Plain, the earliest textual sources are all found outside of modern India. As discussed above, the Sri Lankan texts available to modern scholars date to roughly the fifth century A.D. The earliest Chinese sources also appear to date to the fifth century A.D. (Schopen 1995a, 475–76). Still later are Tibetan (seventh century) and Sanskrit (fifth to seventh centuries) sources. It is important to note that the latter are found, for the most part, in Central Asia rather than South Asia. The Sanskrit sources have pride neither of place nor of time. Just as the Pali Canon was modified to fit the Sri Lankan social context, we can assume that sources from Tibet, China, and Central Asia were similarly manipulated.

Given this variety in sources, and the lack of "original" texts, many Buddhist scholars have employed "higher criticism" in order to reconstruct early Buddhism (Bareau 1974; Frauwallner 1956; Lamotte 1988). The method, on the surface, is both simple and compelling. Those textual and doctrinal elements that are shared by the disparate existing sources are most likely to have the greatest antiquity. Thus, if a specific sermon or concept is found in both the Chinese and Sri Lankan texts, it is likely to have a common origin in India. Given that these sources date to the fifth century A.D. and are believed to have been current for at least a few centuries before that, proponents of higher criticism postulate that their reconstructed Buddhism dates to the first few centuries B.C. Some proponents even claim that they are reconstructing the form of Buddhism preached by the Buddha himself (see Bareau 1974).

The actual practice of higher criticism is much more complicated than the simple outline presented above (critiques of higher criticism can be found in Schopen 1997 and Trainor 1997). First, since the existing sources have all been translated into different languages, the identification of similar phrasing or concepts requires reverse translation of the texts back into their original Sanskrit. This is not an easy or self-evident task. Second, higher criticism does not determine an actual date for the common, ancestral text that underlies its offspring. Despite claims by its proponents, commonalities in Chinese and Sri Lankan texts only demonstrate that the common text existed at an unspecified time prior to the existing texts in the fifth century A.D. There is no reason to believe that this reconstructed Buddhism resembled anything propounded by the Buddha.

The final difficulty in higher criticism lies in its assumption of independence between the different Buddhist traditions. If there was contact and borrowing between traditions, many of the assumptions of higher criticism crumble. For example, if one sect developed a new monastic code or interpretation of a sermon and another sect simply copied it, no earlier common text is implicated. Commonalities can be the product of communication and contact rather than common origin (Schopen 1997, 25–29). This problem would have been most pronounced in the earliest periods, when different sects were located in close proximity to one another. Over time, as Buddhism spread throughout Asia, the different schools would have been in progressively less communication. Thus, by the fifth century A.D. and beyond, the method of higher criticism becomes progressively more robust. Unfortunately, this is also the period in which Buddhist texts become common, obviating the need for higher criticism at all.

Higher criticism and the study of later Buddhist texts provide possibilities for the investigation of Early Historic Period Buddhism—possibilities of how and why certain practices were followed, and possibilities of historical development that require independent confirmation. For some Buddhist scholars, Early Historic Period inscriptions have cast doubt on many of the interpretations of higher criticism. The value of inscriptions is well summarized by Schopen (1997, 30): "The inscriptional material has at least two advantages. First, much of it predates what we can definitely know from literary sources. Second, and perhaps of greater importance, this material tells us not what some literate, educated Indian Buddhist wrote, but what a fairly large number of practicing Buddhists actually did."

As discussed previously, the earliest readable inscriptions in South Asia were carved at the direction of Ashoka in the third century B.C. While they attest to the existence of Buddhism in the Early Historic Period, they do not provide significant detail on the forms that Buddhism took at that time. A much larger number of inscriptions, found on the railings of Sanchi and Bharhut, can be dated between 120 and 80 B.C. These inscriptions record the donations of money and architectural pieces to the *stupas* by devout laity, guilds, monks, nuns, and royal families. Over the succeeding centuries, Buddhist donation inscriptions were carved at monasteries and pilgrimage sites throughout the subcontinent. While they are often short, they provide a great deal of information on Buddhism that dates well before the surviving textual sources. In subsequent discussions of Buddhism, I will employ information gathered from these inscriptions whenever possible. Typically, inscriptions will be discussed where they diverge from the textual sources. However, for the most part, textual and inscriptional sources agree on many of the basics of Buddhist thought. Often, inscriptions show that practices once thought to be later corruptions of Buddhism had greater antiquity than previously supposed.

Whether the Buddha lived in the sixth, fifth, or fourth centuries B.C., none of the currently available literary or inscriptional sources are contemporary with his life. A close reading of the texts and inscriptions in conjunction with higher criticism may be able to lead a reconstruction of the actual teachings of the Buddha—or it may not. As for archaeological evidence of Buddhism prior to the Mauryas, Coningham (2001) has convincingly argued that none currently exists. This should come as no surprise. Even assuming the biography of the Buddha to be true, only a small number of followers would have been present at the time he lived, leaving only limited traces of their presence. Only later, with the adoption of Buddhism by greater numbers, should we expect to find material traces of their practices. It is this later period, beginning in the second century B.C., where my research focuses. Rather than reconstruct an "original" Buddhism, I investigate what is known of the actual practice of Buddhism in the earliest periods for which we have direct evidence.

An Introduction to Buddhist Thought

In prayers and rituals in many Buddhist sects, worshippers were encouraged to take refuge in the three jewels: the Buddha, the *dharma*, and the *sangha*. The Buddha served, through his sermons and biography, as the exemplar of the proper Buddhist life. Buddhist literature relies on the Buddha's authority for almost every doctrinal question. His teachings are usually presented in the form of dialogues in which specific questions are answered, often creating new rules of conduct or ritual. *Dharma* is more difficult to translate. While often glossed as "law," it also refers to the body of sermons, and the principles that underlie them, as spoken by the Buddha. *Sangha* has several, nested meanings. Most broadly, it refers to the entire community of Buddhists, both laity and clergy. More narrowly, it is used to refer to the community of monks and nuns. At its most specific, it is used as a label for a regional group of monks or nuns who assemble each fortnight. Given these multiple meanings and the importance of the distinction between the clergy and laity in this book, this term will be avoided. Rather, to avoid confusion, I use the Western terms *laity*, *clergy*, and *monastery*.

To varying degrees, elements of the three jewels are embedded within every Buddhist text, though different elements dominate. *Vinaya* texts, while presented as dialogues with the Buddha, are mainly monastic codes of conduct. Other texts report on the life, and previous lives, of the Buddha, interlacing the *dharma* within his larger biographical narrative. In this section I will focus on the Buddha and the *dharma*, followed by a more focused examination of the *vinaya* texts. This will be a brief introduction into a large and complex religious tradition. More complete introductions to Buddhism can be found in Lopez (2001) and Lamotte (1988).

The Life of the Buddha

The biography of the Buddha is found in a variety of sources and traditions. As with other portions of the Buddhist literary material, all of it postdates the presumed historical Buddha by several centuries. Further, many differences, both minor and major, exist in these materials. What follows is a simplified abstract of the Buddha's life, consisting of elements common to many of the biographies of the Buddha, but not all.

The Buddha was born Siddhartha Gautama, a prince in what is now Southern Nepal. His birth was accompanied by numerous auspicious signs, leading his father to consult astrologers on his fate. They stated that Siddhartha would become either a great king or a great ascetic. To prevent the latter, his father shielded his son from all things that would make him unhappy. To this end he placed Siddhartha in opulent palaces surrounded by wealth and beautiful women. He was not allowed to see or hear of sickness, old age, or death. At age sixteen he married a princess and continued living his sheltered life until age twenty-nine. At this point, Siddhartha demanded to be allowed to explore the city in which he lived and, despite the efforts of his father, saw an old man. Further investigations and questions revealed to Siddhartha additional examples of misery, sickness, and death. Finally he saw an ascetic sitting beneath a tree and determined to leave the palace and take up such a life.

Leaving his wife and son, he wandered, begging for his food and studying meditation for several years. He then joined a group of five ascetics who practiced extreme fasting and other forms of self-mortification. Six years after he left the palace, he concluded that neither meditation nor self-mortification was useful. He resolved to sit under a tree until he knew the correct path. That night, after overcoming numerous demonic challenges, Siddhartha became enlightened. He first remembered all of his past lives. Next he understood the law of *karma* (see below). Finally, in many accounts, he understood the four noble truths (see below). With this knowledge Siddhartha became the Buddha and was freed from the cycle of rebirth.

The Buddha's first sermon was to the five ascetics who had abandoned him when he gave up self-mortification. The first sermon consisted of the *dharma,* focusing on the four noble truths. Over the next forty-five years, the Buddha continued to preach sermons to both humans and gods and performed numerous miracles. He established the orders of monks and, reluctantly, the order of nuns. As he lay dying at the age of eighty, surrounded by gods and five hundred disciples, the Buddha asked if they had any last questions. When they did not, he passed into *nirvana.*

The Dharma

The basic principles of the *dharma* were contained in the first sermon that the Buddha preached to the five ascetics in the deer park near Sarnath, on the Ganges River. Accounts of the content of this sermon vary to some degree, depending on the particular sect in which they have been recorded. That said, underlying many of the different Buddhist traditions is the concept of the four noble truths. The first noble truth states that life is sorrowful. A person can only expect disease, suffering, and death, followed by an equally sorrowful reincarnation. Even pleasure is transitory, making the inevitable sorrow that follows even worse.

The second noble truth is that all sorrow stems from craving and attachment. It is desire (e.g., for wealth, happiness, or pleasure) that causes people to engage in nonvirtuous actions. The accumulated actions of past lives (*karma*) determine the forms of suffering that must be endured in the present life.

The third noble truth identifies a state without suffering, *nirvana.* While a complex term, *nirvana* can be translated as "blowing out" or "becoming extinguished." In common use, it refers to the extinction of desire, hatred, ignorance, and, ultimately, rebirth.

The fourth noble truth specifies the actions required to attain *nirvana.* This is achieved through the combination of ethical behavior, the practice of meditation, and the gathering of wisdom. Together, these practices confer merit on the individual, speeding the journey to *nirvana.* A person who successfully enters the state of *nirvana* becomes an *arhat,* or "worthy one." Lopez (2001) describes two paths that Buddhists recognized for becoming an *arhat.* The first is a *shravaka,* or "listener." These are people who have heard the Buddha's words and have acted upon them appropriately. In contrast, *pratyekabuddhas* achieve enlightenment in solitude.

The identification of two forms of *arhats* in the Buddhist literature underscores a central issue in early Buddhism. With its emphasis on the individual's attainment of *nirvana,* the creation and maintenance of a cohesive Buddhist congregation was exceedingly difficult. With the widespread adoption of Buddhism in the first and second centuries B.C., the individualizing aspects of the religion needed to be tempered with practices that promoted group cohesion. Thus, it is not surprising that at this time an extensive body of literature developed that described the rules and obligations that early Buddhists employed to overcome the individualizing tendencies of their religion (Lopez 2001). This tension between the group and individual is illustrated in the two forms of *arhat* and the different paths toward enlightenment. Solitary meditation is the individualizing path of the *pratyekabuddha.* The concept of *shravakas,* on the other hand, emphasizes the need for learning in a more formal manner from the Buddha, his disciples, or a leading monk.

Karma and Merit

In terms of the actual practice of Buddhism, few concepts are as important as *karma* and merit. The law of *karma* states that every event that occurs in life, good or bad, is caused by an action, good or bad, in a previous life. As discussed above, the attainment of *nirvana* is predicated on breaking the cycle of rebirths and *karma.* However, in practice, it appears that the focus of the laity and the clergy was directed at achieving a better rebirth through virtuous actions in the present. The flip side of this, of course, was avoidance of rebirth as a "hungry ghost" or other similarly tortured being.

It is here that merit comes into play. Actions that were believed to improve one's rebirth conferred merit. Demerit, in contrast, weighed against the individual. Thus, for a typical Buddhist, the goal was to accumulate merit and avoid demerit. Assisting another being (either human or animal) or promoting Buddhism conferred merit. Listening to a recitation of the *dharma* conferred merit. Pilgrimage to the Buddha's birthplace (Lumbini), the location of his enlightenment (Bodh-Gaya), the location of his first sermon (Sarnath), and the place where he died (Kushinagara) all provided merit (see figure 2.1 on page 16). Death while on pilgrimage was said, in some traditions, to automatically result in rebirth in heaven (Schopen 1997).

Hurting another being, lying, and denigrating the Buddha resulted in demerit. The amount of merit or demerit depended upon the quality of the action. For example, killing an insect conferred only minor demerit, while killing another human was much more serious. Causing injury to either the Buddha or the *dharma* resulted in the highest penalties of all. The recitation of a Buddhist prayer was beneficial, but the repetition of that prayer a thousand times was a thousand times more meritorious. In Chinese Buddhism the interest in merit and demerit became an exercise in careful accounting, where people were advised to keep a daily ledger of their *karmic* actions (Lopez 2001). While this accounting was almost certainly looser in the Early Historic Period in South Asia, contemporary inscriptions demonstrate the importance of merit in Buddhist ritual.

The transfer of merit consisted of reassigning the merit gained through a ritual or donation to another (see Gomez 1996). Many Buddhist scholars have claimed that the transfer of merit was a late development in Buddhism, rising with the advent of *Mahayana* Buddhism after the second or third centuries A.D. (Lamotte 1988; Holt 1981). Often, the transfer of merit occurred between a child and his or her deceased parents. Like merit obtained by individual action, transferred merit improved the recipient's position in his or her next life. Inscriptions at numerous Buddhist sites across South Asia provide definitive evidence that the transfer of merit was practiced in the first few centuries A.D. (Schopen 1997, 56–67). Typically, these inscriptions end with a statement that a particular donation "is for the benefit of [the donor's] parents." Other inscriptions transfer merit "for the good of all beings." Inscriptions with phrases demonstrating the transfer of merit have been found at Amaravati, Bharhut, Bodh-Gaya, and numerous other monasteries in the Gangetic Plain (see figure 2.1). The importance of these inscriptions is not just in demonstrating that the transfer of merit has greater antiquity than previously thought, but also in demonstrating that the concept of merit, transferred or otherwise, had currency in the Early Historic Period. Thus, the many other donation inscriptions can be interpreted as recording merit-making activities as well.

Records of donations line the railings of major Buddhist pilgrimage sites and the walls of monasteries throughout South Asia. Each donation contributed to the support of the clergy and promoted Buddhism. Further, worship at these sites was itself meritorious. The large ritual spaces at many pilgrimage sites suggest that many Buddhists engaged in merit-making ritual (see Fogelin 2003a). Thus, it appears that Early Historic Period Buddhist monasteries were, as Lopez describes them, "factories for the making of merit" (Lopez 2001, 136). Buddhist pilgrimage sites and monasteries served as locations for merit-making, creating binding ritual ties between the Buddhist clergy and laity. As will become clear, the concept of merit infuses almost all of the analyses in this book, from the economic ties that supported Thotlakonda to the mortuary landscape that surrounds it.

Life in a Buddhist Monastery

Discussions of religious principles are surprisingly absent from most *vinaya* texts. Rather, they contain lists of rules and practices that govern the interactions between monks. The minutiae of daily life, and the possible offenses between monks, are covered in exacting detail. While not the most exciting of texts, they provide a window into the operation of Buddhist monasteries in the Early Historic Period. When combined with knowledge gained from inscriptions, they allow for a nuanced understanding of how large groups of men lived together communally. The *vinaya* texts also provide descriptions of the interactions between the monastic and lay communities, though from a monastic perspective.

Monastic Life

Life in a Buddhist monastery was rigidly ordered. A hierarchy of monks was recognized, ranked by the length of time each monk had been ordained. The order of nuns followed a similar hierarchy, though even the longest-serving nun was considered subordinate to the most recently ordained monk. At the top of the monastic hierarchy was the abbot. Below him were arrayed an assortment of different monastic positions. The *vinayas* of different sects list a wide variety of activities that monks may perform; a partial list includes monks who memorized a variety of texts, monks who were experienced in astrology, monks who specialized in meditation, and monks who served as kingly advisors (Lopez 2001). Some monks were also given more mundane administrative tasks, such as overseeing bathrooms, refectories, or monastic properties. The existence of a division of monastic labor in the Early Historic Period is demonstrated, to some degree, in inscriptions at Bharhut. Of the thirty-eight donation inscriptions recorded by monks and nuns, six call themselves "reciters," and three more refer to themselves as specialists in a variety of religious texts (Schopen 1997, 30–31).

The daily round at the monastery was rigidly ordered, with monks rising early to bathe and perform morning rituals. As presented in the *vinayas*, each action was to be performed in a precise manner, punctuated by prayers at specific points. As the day progressed, the monks alternated between ritual and mundane tasks, separated by periodic naps. The main meal was taken at noon. The day ended with another series of rituals near midnight. Monks were expected to act in a respectable manner at all times. Though the specific vows that monks took varied among the different sects and traditions, several general ones seem common. Monks were forbidden to have sex, steal, kill any living being, lie, or cause any harm to the Buddha or *dharma*. In addition to these more general rules were hundreds of smaller rules prohibiting all manner of activities, including sleeping in high beds, eating after the noon meal, or attending musical performances. Transgressing any of these rules had various penalties, ranging from public chastisement to expulsion from the order. In addition to these rules were elaborate codes of etiquette. What follows is a selection of monastic rules found in one section of the Pali *vinaya* (Horner 1957, 128–51).

> One should eat almsfood attentively. Whoever eats out of disrespect eats almsfood inattentively, there is an offence of wrong-doing....
>
> One should eat almsfood thinking of the bowl. Whoever eats out of disrespect eats almsfood looking about here and there, there is an offence of wrong-doing....
>
> One should make up a piece of food into a round. Whoever out of disrespect makes up a long piece of food, there is an offence of wrong-doing....
>
> One should not eat shaking the hands about. Whoever out of disrespect eats shaking the hands about, there is an offence of wrong-doing....

These precepts serve as small examples of the detail in which everyday activities were prescribed in *vinaya* texts. It is difficult to know to what degree any of these rules or codes were followed. The texts may present an ideal form that few, if any, monks ever followed.

Monastic Property Rights

Though Buddhist texts suggest monks should eat only what was placed in a begging bowl and that their material possessions should be limited to only the simplest of necessities, it is clear that by the second century B.C. many monks lived in well-appointed monasteries with a retinue of servants. Both *vinaya* texts and early inscriptions demonstrate that monks and nuns had access to significant wealth, both individually and communally. At Sanchi, Bharhut, and other monasteries throughout South Asia, a sizable proportion of donations, as explicitly demonstrated in the inscriptions, were given to monasteries by monks and nuns. Despite the vows of poverty they took upon entering a Buddhist order, it seems unlikely that monks could make substantial donations unless they had access to substantial wealth. Numerous passages within Buddhist texts, particularly the *vinaya* texts, define elaborate rules governing the accumulation and disbursement of wealth. While a full analysis of these rules is not possible here, a few key elements should be presented (more complete discussions of monastic and clerical property rights can be found in Schopen 1995a, 1995b; 1997).

The rules governing monastic property fall into two general categories. The first establishes the property rights of the individual monk in relation to other monks and the monastery as a whole. The second set covers the rights of the monastery in relation to the laity. This latter category focuses on the obligations that the recipient of a donation incurs. Individual monks were allowed to accept donations well beyond their begging bowls and robes (Schopen 1995b). Examples of such donations include *viharas*, perfumes, and even entire villages. Anything given to an individual monk or nun was considered his or her property. However, at death the property of a monk or nun was redistributed among the clergy. Those monks who took care of a dying monk and those who assisted in the funeral were given a greater share. Several *vinayas* clearly state that monks could not make wills or designate who should receive their possessions (Schopen 1995b, 115–16). In contrast, wills of the laity that designated monastic heirs were accepted. Thus, if the father of a monk died, the monk—and eventually the rest of the monastery—could receive his share of the inheritance. Similarly, if a man or woman took vows late in life, all of the goods he or she brought to the monastery remained there after his or her death. Once money entered the monastery, it rarely left.

Donations could also be given to the monastery as a whole. In this case it was communally held, though controlled by the abbot. All types of donations were viewed as conferring merit on the donor, but only if they were actually used. If, for instance, a *vihara* was donated but not used, the donor gained nothing. For this reason, donation created obligations on the monks or monasteries that received them. It was not sufficient for the monks to simply accept gifts; they had to use them in an appropriate manner. In one example, a particularly large monastery became underpopulated. The Buddha declared that individual monks must rotate through several *viharas* to fulfill their obligations to donors (Schopen 1994, 20–22). Continuing with this logic, the longer a donation benefited the monks, the greater the merit that was conferred. Buildings age and become decrepit, cloth becomes dirty and worn, food is eaten, but endowments last forever. Monasteries accepted money donations, lending it out at interest for maintenance and upkeep of the monastery (Schopen 1994). As this endowment could be expected to provide benefits to the monastery in perpetuity, the merit conferred on the donor was similarly perpetual.

Ritual Obligations

As stated earlier, donations established obligations between the donor and recipient. But this was not the only obligation that existed between the monks and laity in the Early Historic Period. Some *vinaya* texts contain references to obligatory ritual functions that monks were required to perform for the laity. Early Pali and Chinese *vinayas* state that monks were required to perform "life-cycle" rituals for the laity (Schopen 1995b, 105–6). These obligations are found in sections of the *vinayas* that list the reasons a monk could leave the monastery during the rainy season. Widely divergent *vinayas* state that a monk must leave the monastery to perform specific ritual obligations if he can return in seven days or less. The events listed include receiving gifts or donations, reciting the *dharma* at weddings, reciting the *dharma* for the sick, reciting the *dharma* at a funeral, and attending house dedication rituals (Schopen 1995b, 105–6). It is important to note that these events were the exceptional cases in which a monk could leave the monastery despite the normally restrictive policies during the rainy season. It should be expected that during other portions of the year monks were expected to perform even more ritual services for the lay community. These passages suggest that beyond being the simple recipients of donations for the accumulation of merit, monks played an active ritual role in their communities.

The existing *vinaya* texts present elaborate rules for etiquette, monastic law, and ritual obligations that every monk or nun was to follow. Using these texts alone, it is not possible to state to what degree these practices were followed by the majority, or if they were only an idealized model of behavior followed by a select few. While it forms only a small part of the textual record of early Buddhism, monastic participation in life-cycle rituals is central to my archaeological investigations at Thotlakonda. However, much of the archaeological material at Thotlakonda, if not in most Buddhist monasteries in South Asia, centers on a single life-cycle event—death.

Death in Early Buddhism

With the exception of the funeral of the Buddha himself, little was written in any of the Buddhist texts on the proper way to dispose of, and memorialize, the dead. Those sections that do concern themselves with mortuary ritual and memorialization are typically found in sections dealing with property and inheritance. The remaining instances are reserved for particularly prominent monks, whose memorialization closely follows the pattern established for the Buddha. No mention is made of the proper funeral or memorial of the laity. As will be discussed at greater length below, mortuary ritual and memorialization largely focus on the corporeal relics of the

Buddha. Who should worship the Buddha, for what purpose, and in what manner? In the scholarly literature, a great deal of emphasis is placed on the meaning and role of relics in Early Buddhism (see Trainor 1997). The same tendency holds in discussions of prominent monks. To these concerns I will also add the mortuary ritual of ordinary monks and the laity. For these followers of Buddhism, there is no question about the status of their remains. They were never worshipped. Rather, they were placed in locations where they could continue worship of the Buddha in death. The mortuary rituals performed over their remains propelled them toward a better rebirth and, eventually, enlightenment.

The Death of the Buddha

According to Buddhist textual sources, after the Buddha's death his body was cremated and the remains were divided into eight equal parts and enshrined in *stupas* across the Gangetic Plain. Later, Ashoka is credited with redistributing the Buddha's remains from seven of the *stupas* to eighty-four thousand new *stupas*. Traditional interpretations of Buddhist texts led Buddhist scholars to conclude that Buddhist monks did not worship these *stupas*, or the relics contained within them (Coomaraswamy 1927; Lamotte 1988; Oldenberg 1882). *Stupa* worship was viewed as the domain of the laity. Monks were to avoid worshipping the Buddha directly, while the laity, with their poorer grasp of Buddhist principles, required the aid of direct worship to ease them toward the path to enlightenment. The establishment of *stupa* worship, and eventually the worship of Buddhist images, by monks and nuns was believed to have been the result of the clergy becoming contaminated by the vulgar practices of the laity.

This understanding of *stupa* worship is principally derived from a single passage in the *Mahaparinibbana-sutta* (Schopen 1997; Trainor 1997; Davids 1910). In this passage the Buddha is asked twice by his disciple, Ananda, what should be done with the Buddha's physical remains upon death. The Buddha's first reply was that Ananda should not concern himself with the mortal remains of the Buddha, but focus on meditation and *nirvana*. When asked again, the Buddha directed that his physical remains should be treated just as if they were the remains of a *chakravartin*, a ruler with religious sanction. The Buddha specified that his remains should be handed over to devout lay worshippers, cremated, and placed in a large earthen mound, a *stupa*, where his remains (e.g., ashes, bone fragments, personal articles) could be worshipped. Traditional interpretations of this passage state that the first response was intended for monks, with the latter for the laity (e.g., Irwin 1980; Coomaraswamy 1927; Lamotte 1988).

This perspective has recently come under strong criticism by Buddhist researchers who focus upon inscriptions rather than literary sources (e.g., Schopen

1997; Trainor 1997). In evaluating inscriptional evidence for both the accumulation of wealth and worship of the *stupa* by monks and nuns, Schopen states (1997, 31–32):

> None of this accords very well, if at all, with the received views on the matter, with views that maintain that there is a sharp distinction between the kinds of religious activities undertaken by monks and the kinds of religious activities undertaken by laymen, and with the view that cult and religious giving were essentially and overwhelmingly lay concerns in the Indian Buddhist context. In fact, if we stick to what we actually know, it would appear that something very like the opposite was the case: we know for certain from inscriptions that from ca. 150 B.C.E.—that is to say, from our earliest knowable donative inscriptions and well before we can have definite knowledge of the textual tradition—monks and nuns formed a substantial proportion of those involved in donative, merit-making activities connected with the *stupa* cult.

Schopen continues this argument by noting a ubiquitous association between Buddhist monasteries and *stupas* from the second century B.C. onward. When combined with the later inscriptional evidence, Schopen (1997, 34) concludes that "from the very beginning of our evidence, [the *stupa* cult was] both monastically controlled and monastically dominated." Schopen concludes his analysis by rejecting the traditional monk/laity distinction that earlier, textually focused, Buddhist scholars had taken as a fundamental premise of their analyses. While I also identify differences between monks and the laity in this work, I fully accept that both monks and the laity were engaged in the *stupa* cult. The distinction I make between the two concerns the manner in which *stupa* ritual occurred and the different attitudes that monks and the laity brought to this worship.

The mortuary procedures for prominent monks described in various texts follow closely that of the Buddha. As with the Buddha, the remains were handed over to the laity for washing, cremation, and commemoration. Construction of a *stupa* was again left to the laity. In one case, the remains of a prominent monk were claimed by one of the Buddha's disciples and a lay devotee of the monk (Schopen 1995a). The Buddha determined that the remains should go to the lay devotee who promptly installed the remains within his home. However, when other laity arrived to worship the remains, they found the man away on business. When this was reported to the Buddha, he declared that the remains should be placed in a *stupa* in the monastery, but constructed by the lay devotee. Thus, the remains of the monk were memorialized by a member of the laity, no doubt with the accumulation of significant merit, but only in a location where the monks could maintain free access and control. An important point is that in this example, and several others (see Schopen 1995a), the claim to the remains was predicated on the status of a lay devotee. This suggests that those monks with the greatest ties outside the monastery were, conversely, the most likely to be enshrined within it. Further, if monks were placing *stupas* within monasteries to allow for continual access, the implication is that the laity had free access to at least that portion of the monastery that contained the *stupa.*

Mortuary Practices for an Ordinary Monk

The mortuary patterns discussed above concern those people who merit worship after death—the Buddha and prominent monks. A different pattern was practiced for the vast majority of monks and nuns who were not recipients of posthumous veneration. Here funerals were the responsibility of other monks and nuns. One account of a monastic funeral is found in the *Mulasarvastivada-vinaya* within the context of an exposition on the proper manner to redistribute the belongings of a recently dead monk (Schopen 1995a). After a monk's death, he returned as a hungry ghost, forbidding his fellow monks to redistribute his belongings until they had performed the correct funeral procedures. What follows is an abstract of the mortuary ritual based primarily upon this passage. However, a few details have been added from other passages within the same text (see Schopen 1995a, 1997).

Upon the death of a monk, a gong was sounded to announce his departure. The monks entered his cell and carried his body to the cremation grounds. At the cremation grounds the monks "worshipped the body." This consisted of washing the body and, perhaps, wrapping it in cloth and oil. Next, the body was cremated. This was followed by a recitation of the *dharma,* with particular emphasis on portions relating to death and rebirth. It is possible that this recitation occurred at a *stupa* or *chaitya* rather than the cremation grounds. At the conclusion of the recitation, the merit accumulated was transferred to the recently deceased so that he would be reborn in a higher position. Finally, those who handled the body cleaned themselves and their clothes, while those who observed washed their hands and feet. Those who were present at the funeral had the greatest rights to the deceased's belongings.

It is interesting that there is no reference in this passage of placing the remains in a *stupa.* In fact, no mention is made concerning what should be done with the remains at all. In other portions of the *Mulasarvastivada-vinaya,* the Buddha is credited with describing an elaborate hierarchy of *stupas* depending upon the relative status of a particular monk (Schopen 1995a, 481). The remains of prominent monks were to be placed in *stupas* within the monastery, while the small *stupas* of ordinary monks could be placed outside the monastery walls. Though derived from a fifth century A.D. Chinese text, this passage provides one possible interpretation of the large mortuary landscape surrounding Thotlakonda. The cairns were erected as memorials for ordinary monks, those not prominent enough to warrant burial within the monastery itself. Another possible explanation for these cairns can be derived through an examination of the mortuary practices of the laity.

Mortuary Practices of the Laity

Buddhist monastic texts do not report on the procedures for funerals of the Buddhist laity beyond the occasional references to rituals that monks performed for the dead and the dying. What is known of these rituals is derived exclusively from inscriptional and archaeological sources. Surrounding the *stupas* at major Buddhist pilgrimage sites—the four identified with moments of the Buddha's life (birth, enlightenment, first sermon, and death) and others containing his corporeal remains (e.g., Sanchi, Amaravati, and Dharmarajika)—are found hundreds of small votive *stupas* (Schopen 1997, 118–20). Votive *stupas* are typically carved from stone to resemble larger *stupas* that were the focus of veneration. Each usually contained a small chamber where the ashes of a devotee could be interred. Inscriptions on some of these stupas document that they contained the remains of Buddhist monks, while others memorialize the laity. These small *stupas* lie haphazardly in the courtyards around a larger, central *mahastupa*. For example, at Bodh-Gaya subsequent votive *stupas* were built atop the old votive *stupas* as the floor of the courtyard slowly was raised (Cunningham [1892] 1998). As mentioned earlier, worship or circumambulation of a *stupa* was a meritorious act. Schopen (1997) has suggested that burial near a *stupa* was similarly meritorious, allowing the perpetual worship of the Buddha.

Using inscriptional and literary evidence, Schopen (1997) argues that relics, and the *stupas* that contained them, were seen as the living Buddha, not simply the Buddha's remains. Thus, worship of the Buddha's relics was equivalent to worship of the Buddha himself. The large number of small *stupas* that surrounded the major Buddhist pilgrimage sites and the inscriptions found on them suggest that some devout Buddhist laity were enshrined within the walls of these pilgrimage centers. Interestingly, none of the monastic sites excavated so far in South Asia show anywhere near the same number of votive *stupas*. Further, in those cases where inscriptions are available, all of the votive *stupas* found within Buddhist monasteries memorialize monks or nuns. Thus, the mortuary population within monastic sites appears uniformly monastic. At pilgrimage sites, it is likely that the mortuary population included both monks and laity.

To the best of my knowledge, the mortuary landscape of Thotlakonda is the first assemblage of votive *stupas* to be identified and mapped outside the walls of a monastery or pilgrimage site. As with other monastic sites in South Asia, a small number of votive *stupas*, most likely erected for prominent monks, are present within the monastery. Given the lack of an archaeological equivalent, the nature of the votive *stupas* lying beyond the monastery is less clear. They could, as discussed above, be the memorials of ordinary monks. Alternatively, they could be the memorials of the laity or, as in the pilgrimage sites, a mixture of both monks and laity. Existing textual and epigraphic sources do not provide sufficient detail to address this question. It is here that archaeological study can add to, and modify, our existing knowledge of early Buddhism by giving a voice to those who are mute in the textual sources. Rather than rely on monastic claims concerning the laity, archaeology permits the study of the laity directly.

The Social Role of Buddhist Monasteries

The goal of my research at Thotlakonda is the investigation of the role of ritual in Early Buddhist monasticism, principally the role of ritual in the relationships between the Buddhist clergy and laity. In this research, I rely upon the developing anthropological field of practice theory (see chapter 4). However, where appropriate, I also rely upon Marxist and structural understandings of ritual. My emphasis on ritual practice and mundane ritual is founded upon my belief that both are insufficiently represented in current understandings of early Buddhist monasticism. Rather, studies of early Buddhism have focused either upon more abstract, canonical texts emphasizing the ascetic elements of Buddhist monasticism, or they have relied upon the legitimizing role of religion found in Marxism and its descendants.

All of the current understandings of early Buddhist monasticism are based primarily on textual and field research conducted from the nineteenth century to the mid-twentieth century. For the most part, the differences in the models are not the product of new information. Instead, differences in interpretation are the product of varying emphases placed on different aspects of the available data and changes in the general approaches to archaeological and historical interpretation that have occurred in the last century. Four major approaches have dominated research on the role of Early Historic Period Buddhist monasteries. Each of these models focuses primarily on a single dimension of monastic life. It is likely that they are not exclusive. Rather, individual monasteries were likely to blend these four aspects to varying degrees. Thus, I do not expect that any one model will fully explain the role of Buddhist monasteries in the social, economic, and political web of the Early Historic Period. These differing interpretive models serve only as a baseline for orienting and evaluating the data collected from my research.

Monasteries as Isolated Retreats

The earliest interpreters of Buddhist monasteries saw them as primarily isolated monastic retreats where monks could "conduct their observances undisturbed by the distractions of any human environment" (Brown 1965, 13). Thus, Buddhist monasteries were understood to have little or no significant contact with their immediate local context. Support for the monasteries was seen as coming from pious laity as an act of religious conviction. The only significant differences among earlier researchers were their understandings of who provided this support. Alexander Cunningham ([1854] 1966) emphasized the role of the Mauryan king Ashoka in founding and providing for monasteries. The withdrawal of Buddhism from India in the second millennium A.D. was viewed by Cunningham as the result of the loss of royal sponsorship. Like Cunningham, Fergusson and Burgess ([1880] 1988) also emphasized royal donations in their discussion of Buddhist monasteries in western South Asia.

If nineteenth-century researchers had a royalist approach, those in the early to mid-twentieth century were far more interested in the clergy. Brown (1965) and Basham (1967) accepted the importance of Ashoka in founding Buddhist monasteries and pilgrimage centers. However, after this *initial* royal push, "the form of Buddhism founded by Ashoka went through the process of changing its authority from the throne to the priesthood, the latter having been apparently organized with this in view" (Brown 1965, 13). Like Brown, Basham (1967) viewed monasteries primarily as retreats where monks could meditate away from the distractions of urban life.

Monasteries as Recipients of Gifts for Guild and Ruler Prestige

More recently, the analysis of Buddhism and Buddhist monasteries has focused on their economic roles (Ray 1986, 1989; Thapar 1966, 1997, 2002). Thapar has described in detail the apparent connections between the development of guilds and the support of Buddhist institutions. She noted many donation inscriptions at Buddhist monasteries as evidence for the patronage of Buddhism by merchants and artisans. She argued that Buddhism allowed trading partners to interact without the barriers of caste prohibitions. Another important aspect of Thapar's discussion was her recognition of the prestige given to donors for their gifts to the Buddhist clergy. While Thapar's analysis emphasized the economic role of Buddhism, it marginalized Buddhist monasteries by making them the simple recipients of gifts to provide merit for the kings and guilds. In Thapar's framework, monasteries primarily served a legitimizing function for economic and political institutions. Like earlier researchers, Thapar saw Buddhist monasteries as secluded retreats separated from the public and dependent upon the patronage of guilds and kings. While this interpretation shifted from the dominantly royalist and clerical perspectives of earlier researchers, others have pushed the economic interpretation even further.

Monasteries as Trade Centers

Ray (1986, 1989) has rejected the concept that monastic institutions were isolated "retreats." Her analysis of monastic institutions emphasized the proximity of Buddhist monastic institutions and *stupas* to trade routes (see also Lahiri 1992).

She argued that Buddhist monasteries actively facilitated trade. Ray also argued that, as the recipients of both land and money donations, monastic institutions were the purchasers of significant quantities of trade goods. Thus, the donations by merchants and guilds to monasteries were not only intended for prestige or merit, but helped provide "tangible benefits" (Ray 1989, 456). This point has recently been contested by Morrison (1995b), who argued that since monastic institutions do not have any large storage facilities, places to lodge traveling merchants, or other trade facilities, the monasteries were not involved directly with trade except as consumers. Morrison instead suggested that the locations of Buddhist institutions along trade routes facilitated the delivery of agricultural produce to the non-food-producing monks of the monasteries.

Monasteries as Agricultural Facilitators

In addition to Ray's trade-facilitator model, Ray and others (Heitzman 1984; 1997) have suggested that monastic institutions may also have served to organize and expand agricultural production into new areas. "Equally important was the fact that monastic establishments formed nuclei for the expansion of agrarian settlements and this is evident enough from land grants made by the ruling Satavahanas" (Ray 1989, 456). In this model, monasteries would have not only received the surplus production of village-based agriculture, but promoted it through active management and the adjudication of agricultural disputes. For example, in order to increase production, a monastery might underwrite the construction and maintenance of a reservoir. Evidence in support of this model is derived mostly from Heitzman's (1997) study of the Chola dynasty (A.D. 849–1279) in Southern India. Through a combination of historical, archaeological, and epigraphic evidence, Heitzman effectively demonstrates a similar role for monasteries in the Chola period as postulated for the Early Historic Period. Specific evidence in support of the same role in the Early Historic Period is less clear (but see Shaw 2002).

Conclusion

When comparing the newer and older interpretations of Buddhist monasticism, an interesting contrast is formed—religious disengagement versus economic engagement. This book is an argument for a third permutation—religious engagement. In this I do not mean engagement in terms of Buddhist doctrine, but in the practice and conduct of daily, mundane ritual. I argue that this ritual role in society has been underappreciated in the existing scholarship on Early Historic Period Buddhist monasticism. An element common to all of the previous discussions of Buddhist monasticism is that they are based upon a combination of Buddhist texts and archaeological excavations of the monasteries in isolation. Yet all previous interpretations of the social role of monasteries make claims to the broader social context in which monasteries were found. My research over the last two years in Andhra Pradesh has been oriented toward evaluating all of these potential models for Buddhist monasticism by directly examining the architecture of Thotlakonda Monastery and its position within a broader social landscape.

Through my investigations at Thotlakonda, I have come to realize that the differences in interpretations of Buddhist monasteries are not only a debate between historians—they were tensions that existed within the community at Thotlakonda. These tensions are manifested in the layout and organization of the monastery and in the larger landscape in which it is located. Different spaces were divided into distinct places for monastic isolation, ritual engagement with local lay populations, and economic concerns. All were elements in the contested role of monasteries in Early Buddhism.

Buddhist literary and inscriptional sources present a dynamic picture of Early Buddhism and early Buddhist monasticism in South Asia. Buddhist monasteries were actively engaged in their local communities through an elaborate set of ritual and economic obligations. Wealth, through merit-making donations, sustained the monasteries, but it created obligations in return. Monks were required to provide ritual services to their lay supporters at prominent points in their lives. Just as the monks were obligated to leave the monasteries to assist the laity, the laity made pilgrimages to prominent Buddhist sites and worshipped at the *stupas* of prominent monks within the monastery walls. The overall picture is of steady traffic between the monasteries and surrounding communities, with both the monks and the laity constantly moving from one to the other. This complex interaction is, perhaps, best shown in the complementary roles that the monks and laity played in mortuary ritual.

As should be clear at this point, I focus on the actual practice of Buddhism over the more philosophical teachings of the *dharma.* I do this because I have concerns about the late date of Buddhist textual sources and their applicability to the daily practice of typical Buddhists. That said, the texts do provide a window into the views of a small segment of influential Buddhist monks in the Early Historic Period in South Asia. While merit may be more useful in understanding Buddhist ritual than *karma,* the more scholastic teachings also have their value and place in studies of early Buddhism. Buddhist religious texts are an important part of a multilayered analysis of early Buddhism that combines literary sources, inscriptions, and archaeology.

Religion, Ritual, Architecture, and Landscape 4

THE GOAL OF MY RESEARCH at Thotlakonda is to determine the role of ritual in the relationships between the monks within the monastery and the laity living in the area immediately surrounding it. Previous studies of Early Historic Period monasticism in South Asia have had different orientations. Scholars of the late nineteenth and early to mid-twentieth centuries argued that monasteries were retreats, with little or no relations with local populations (e.g., Brown 1965; Cunningham [1854] 1997; Basham 1967; Lamotte 1988). Based upon readings of monastic texts, these scholars suggested that monastic ritual consisted, in the main, of private meditation. Later scholars focused on the role of Buddhism in legitimizing elite economic power and facilitating long-distance trade (e.g., Thapar 2002; Ray 1986, 1989; Lahiri 1992). In my research, I emphasize the role of ritual in building Buddhist communities at the local level. I do not suggest that ritual is primary. Rather, I argue that Early Historic Period Buddhist monasteries were engaged in all of these different activities—private ritual, public ritual, and trade—and that all of these can be identified in the architecture, landscape, and material artifacts of Thotlakonda.

My research at Thotlakonda is situated within broad anthropological approaches to ritual. In my investigations I examine religion, as it was practiced, within a dynamic social structure of competing concerns in daily life. The challenge of my work is to identify the material consequences of religious practice. To this end, I focus on architecture and landscape. In addition to religious symbolism, I also consider the implications of the physical layout of architecture on social interactions among ritual participants, interpreting these interactions through principles derived from Western and non-Western theatrical design. This approach links religious and other architectural spaces within a regional landscape of meaning and interaction. I employ architecture to derive the social implications of spaces, and landscape to link them within a larger social context. Below I review recent trends in the study of ritual, architecture, and landscape in order to orient my research at Thotlakonda.

Ritual

Given the centrality of religion and ritual in social life, both have received scholarly attention for centuries. Today the literature on religion and ritual is vast. Given its centrality in anthropological studies of religion, I begin with a discussion of Marxist approaches to religion. Here religion is understood as a mechanism for legitimizing elite power. This will be followed by a brief discussion of Emile Durkheim, Max Weber, Arnold van Gennep, and Victor Turner. I conclude with practice theory, the approach guiding much of my research.

Marxist Approaches to Religion

Marx's fundamental subject of inquiry was the economic basis of nineteenth-century European society. At the core of Marx's conception of capitalism are the dual concepts of infrastructure and superstructure. The infrastructure of society is described as the economic core upon which everything else, the superstructure, is dependent.

> The sum total of these relations of production constitutes the economic structure of society, the real foundation, on which rises a legal and political superstructure and which correspond to definite forms of social consciousness. The mode of production of material life conditions the social, political and intellectual life process in general. (*A Contribution to the Critique of Political Economy* [1859] in Elster 1986, 187)

In other texts, Marx places greater emphasis upon a dialectic between the infrastructure and superstructure, especially in regard to political and legal issues (in particular see *The Eighteenth Brumaire of Louis Bonaparte* [1852] 1964). However, while Marx does note the possibility of the superstructure conditioning the infrastructure, his writings on religion were generally unidirectional (Elster 1985, 504–10).

In a strict Marxist framework, religion and ritual are superstructural, and therefore secondary. The functions of ritual and religion are reduced to a legitimizing role in the establishment of elite power and coercion.

> The class that has the means of material production at its disposal, consequently also controls the means of mental production, so that the ideas of those who lack the means of mental production are on the whole subject to it. The ruling ideas are nothing more than the ideal expression of the dominant material relations. (*The German Ideology* [1845–1846] 1998 in Elster 1986, 302)

While Marx was consistent in his belief that religious ideology developed from the material realities of social relations, his writings are often contradictory about the mechanisms for the emergence and development of the ideologies. In the quote above, it appears that he sees ideology as forced upon the working classes. In other cases (see, in particular, the introduction to *Contribution to the Critique of Hegel's*

Philosophy of Law [1844] 1970), Marx argues that religious ideology is generated by the working class itself, as a means of coping with their subordinate social position. In either case, Marx saw religion, particularly Christianity, as supporting the interests of the elite, legitimizing their privileged status.

Cultural Marxism (e.g., Godelier 1978; Thompson 1963) is a response to the unidirectional focus, from infrastructure to superstructure, of traditional Marxism. Within this framework the distinction between the infrastructure and the superstructure is maintained, but equal, or relatively equal, emphasis is placed on both domains. In this view, there are several functions of the superstructure. The first is the organization of social life. For example, religion, kinship, or marriage rules organize the "thought and action" of a social group. But all ideologies must also play a part in organizing production. "In addition to [ideology's] own ostensible purpose and its explicit functions, [ideology] functions *directly and internally as a relation of production*" (Godelier 1978, 765, italics in original). Thus, cultural Marxism places greater emphasis on the ideological and recognizes that ideology and religion have functions beyond legitimizing economic exploitation.

Cultural Marxism still relies upon the duality of the infrastructure and superstructure, and the fundamental importance of economic relations. This is shown clearly by the varied and multiple superstructural functions of ideology when contrasted with the single infrastructural function as a relation of production. In cultural Marxism religion is downplayed as only one of many ideological systems. While this is still an improvement over the treatment by Marx himself, Godelier relegates religion to lesser importance than other ideological systems such as kinship. More importantly, cultural Marxism continues to hold the traditional hostility toward religion. While noting the role of religion in organizing society and possibly fulfilling some social needs, Godelier argues (1978, 767), "To my way of thinking, the monopoly of the means (to us imaginary) of reproduction of the universe and of life, must have preceded the monopoly of the visible material means of production."

This quote illustrates the continuing conviction that religion is an avenue toward, or a tool for, economic exploitation. In summary, cultural Marxism places greater emphasis upon the ideological components of society but continues to divide social phenomena into traditional Marxist categories. While they recognize numerous noneconomic functions of any given ideological system, Godelier and other cultural Marxists continue to place a heavy emphasis on the economic conditions of society. Even among ideological systems, religion is specifically given special treatment as a mechanism for elite economic control.

The continued centrality of the Marxist view of religion in subsequent theoretical approaches cannot be overstated, though most place greater emphasis on the dialectic between religion and the economic infrastructure. Modern anthropological interests in power, hegemony, and ritual practice follow from this premise. For example, Bloch (1989, 45) states that ritual is "the exercise of a particular form of power . . . [that makes] a power situation appear a fact in the nature of the world." Bell (1997, 82), in a summary of practice theory, argues that "ritualization is a way of acting that tends to promote the authority of forces deemed to derive from beyond the immediate situation. . . . Hence, rather than ritual as the vehicle for the *expression* of authority, practice theorists tend to explore how ritual is a vehicle for the *construction* of relationships of authority and submission."

In contrast to traditional Marxism, modern anthropological theories emphasize the role of resistance and authority in ritual and religion. Nevertheless, the dialectical framework developed by Marx remains the central explanatory device that illuminates most studies of religion. In studies of Early Buddhist monasticism, Marxist approaches influenced the interpretations of Thapar (1966, 1997, 2002), Ray (1986, 1989), and others (Heitzman 1984, 1997; Lahiri 1992). These studies focused on the evidence for monastic participation in long-distance trade, seeing religious beliefs and ritual practices through the lens of developing economic practices of the Early Historic Period.

Ritual as Solidarity

In the early twentieth century, Emile Durkheim suggested that a rise in the rate of suicides in France was the result of a diminishment of attendance in religious ceremonies ([1897] 1951). He argued that participation in religious ritual promoted a sense of belonging to a community, what he later labeled "social solidarity" ([1915] 1995). The loss of social solidarity, he argued, resulted in feelings of isolation leading toward an increase in suicides. Following this study, Durkheim continued his investigations of religion, developing many of the foundational concepts that remain to this day, including the "collective conscious" ([1915] 1955) and "mechanical" and "organic" solidarity ([1893] 1984). However, it is the concept of social solidarity, and recent modifications to it, that most directly concern my study.

As formulated by Durkheim ([1915] 1995), social solidarity was a relatively unproblematic and uncontested social process. Following from approaches that emphasize power and the negotiation of power (discussed below), I suggest that the form of social solidarity in Early Buddhism was an arena that was contested. Different forms of social solidarity can be formed by different types of ritual. In some cases, the form may foster elite power. In others, solidarity serves the interests of resistance. In the practice of forming a common solidarity, different social groups attempt to assert a form more appropriate to their own interests. The form in which solidarity is perpetuated is contested by the same social divisions it attempts to suppress.

In a previous article on Early Historic Period Buddhist religious sites, I identified three general types of ritual with direct implications on the forms of solidarity they fostered (Fogelin 2003a). These are individual, communal, and corporate ritual. Individual ritual corresponds with the more meditative and solitary aspects of Buddhism, and therefore does not significantly promote social solidarity. *Individual worship is defined as ritual that is direct between a single individual and the object of worship.* Individual worship does not require any other worshippers, but it does not preclude others from worshipping at the same time. In *stupa* complexes, the primary form of individual ritual was circumambulation of the *stupa*. Early Buddhists believed that by walking around a *stupa* individuals accumulated merit and ensured both a better position in their next life and a faster attainment of *nirvana*.

Given the individualizing tendencies of circumambulation and meditation in Early Buddhism, group ritual was important for maintaining a cohesive Buddhist community. However, not all group rituals are the same. Different methods and types of ritual foster different forms of solidarity. Two possibilities are rituals that promote egalitarian relationships between members of a group, and those that promote cohesion based upon the common identification with a single leader. I label the first "communal ritual." Communal ritual cannot be performed alone. *Communal ritual is a group phenomenon that has no ritual specialists or any other individuals leading worship.* All people are involved more or less equally. Communal ritual is worship between a group and an object or action. *Corporate ritual, on the other hand, is group worship of an object or action that is directed or mediated by a ritual specialist or other individual.* The important difference between communal and corporate ritual lies in the elevation of a person, or a small group of people, into leadership positions. These positions need not be permanent or hereditary for corporate worship to occur. In my original study (Fogelin 2003a), I concluded that in the Early Historic Period the Buddhist clergy focused on corporate ritual while the laity favored communal ritual. This issue will be expanded below in my discussion of methods for the archaeological investigation of architecture.

Ritual and Rites of Passage

For Durkheim and Marx, the study of religion focused on its function—the promotion of social solidarity, according to Durkheim, and the legitimization of authority, according to Marx. For other scholars, notably van Gennep (1960) and Turner (1966), the interest was more structural. These scholars documented common elements of ritual that mark the movement of individuals from one social status to another (i.e., child/adult, unmarried/married, alive/dead). Van Gennep identified three cross-cultural phases of ritual that affect the change from one social status to another. These three periods (separation, margin, and aggregation) make up what van Gennep labeled "rites of passage." The first phase of rites of passage removes an individual, both physically and metaphorically, from an existing social role. In the second phase, the liminal period, the change in status is effected. Finally, the third phase reintegrates the individual into society, with a new social role. Important to my research is the recognition by Turner and van Gennep that movement through these stages is often accompanied by spatial and architectural markers. In an archaeological study, these material symbols of rites of passage can serve to identify their practice.

While often tied to human biological changes such as birth, puberty, menstruation, and death, rites of passage mark changes in social status (Turner 1966, 94–95). While some generalizations can be made, not all societies mark the same biological changes with rites of passage. For example, in some societies menarche may be recognized as a significant change in social status for women and marked by a rite of passage, while in others it can be viewed as relatively unimportant. The main point is that rites of passage occur at transitions between socially constructed positions that may, or may not, be related to human biological development.

As defined by Turner (1966a, 93), the liminal period is an "interstructural situation" that lies at the heart of rites of passage. Individuals within the liminal period are neither here nor there, or as Turner (1966, 93) described it, "betwixt and between." Lying between two culturally sanctioned categories, people in a liminal period are unclassifiable, and thus not part of their society. With this foundation, Turner investigated the perceptions of liminality. Relying heavily upon Douglas's (1966) *Purity and Danger,* Turner argued that disorder and contradiction are considered unclean, polluting, and dangerous. Since people in the liminal period are outside any socially sanctioned category, they are themselves unclean and dangerous. This explains, in part, the typical pattern of separation and isolation of people going through rites of passage. Segregation limits the exposure of initiates to society and vice versa. Reintegration marks initiates' return to a classifiable social category.

As discussed in chapter 3, Buddhist monastic texts describe the procedures to be used in monastic funerals (Schopen 1995a). As presented in the Buddhist *vinayas,* they follow the tripartite division of rites of passage as defined by van Gennep and Turner—the ritual removal of the body from the monastery, cremation and burial outside the monastery, followed by ritual cleansing of the mourners prior to reentry into the monastery. These same texts state that monks were to perform life-cycle rituals for the laity. It is likely that these rituals also followed the patterns of rites of passage. As will be shown in later chapters, the tripartite division of ritual and perceptions of liminality have important implications in understanding the archaeological remains at Thotlakonda.

Ritual and the Routinization of Charisma

The routinization of charisma is a process by which a charismatic leader of a new social movement, such as the Buddha, operates beyond the traditional practices of everyday life, creating relationships with his or her followers that are "strictly personal" (Weber 1978, 246). Typically, the charismatic leader challenges the existing social norms and power structures of the society in which he or she lives. Further, the relationships between the leader and his or her disciples, by their very existence, challenge the existing power structures. These relationships, however, are unstable in the long run, since, with the death of the charismatic leader, the relationships inevitably deteriorate. Something must be done to reintegrate the radical social movement into broader social traditions in order for the community to persist. This, of course, necessitates changes in the community of people who follow the original leader, as well as modifications to the social order from which it originally diverged. For Weber, this was achieved primarily by various techniques that transferred the authority of charisma to a new person or group of people. Given that the original leader had often challenged an existing social order, the routinization of charisma was most often characterized by the development and imposition of a new power structure, often remarkably similar to that which existed previously.

As conceived by Weber (1968, 1978), the routinization of charisma is the process by which a subversive ideology and leader are transformed into a legitimizing ideology of authority. It is here that my approach extends beyond, and diverges from, Weber. The act of transferring the authority of a charismatic leader cannot be assumed to be either simple or uncontested. Different groups of followers have different attitudes toward the manner in which the community of followers should be perpetuated. Techniques to overcome resistance and the format in which resistance is practiced become part of the process of routinization.

Ritual Practice

My modifications to Durkheim and Weber are heavily influenced by the more recent emphasis on power and resistance that has percolated through the anthropological and archaeological literature in the last twenty years (e.g., Foucault 1977; Markus 1993; Zukin 1991; Miller, Rowlands, and Tilley 1989). Principally, this influence is shown in my rejection of a concept of society as a unitary phenomenon with a ubiquitous presence of social hierarchies. Rather, I place a greater emphasis on the competing interests of different social groups and the traces these factions (Brumfiel 1992, 1995; Crumley 1987, 1995; Brumfiel and Fox 1994) leave on the architectural and other material remains that survive for modern archaeological study. That said, the focus of this discussion is not an explication of the concepts of power, agency, faction, or resistance. These concepts are well explored in a wide variety of recent theoretically oriented articles and books (Ehrenreich, Crumley, and Levy 1995; Barrett 2001; Robb 1999; Dobres and Robb 2000). In this study I investigate the specific architectural and landscape patterns at Thotlakonda to identify the social and ideological tensions that existed within Buddhist monasticism and between the Buddhist clergy and laity. Central to this goal is the investigation of religion and ritual as practice.

Practice, as a label, covers a somewhat nebulous assortment of anthropological approaches. In general, however, practice is conceived in opposition to structure. Practice theorists argue that studies focusing on structural abstractions of culture lead to a picture of society that is inhabited by automatons who blindly follow some greater superorganic process. Beyond eliminating human intentionality and creativity, practice theorists argue that structuralism is incapable of explaining social change.

> In contrast to the static view of structuralism, which tends to see human activity as a matter of enacting cultural roles, practice theory claims to take seriously the ways in which human activity, as formal as a religious ritual or as casual as a midday stroll, are creative strategies by which human beings continually reproduce and reshape their social and cultural environments. (Bell 1997, 76)

Change, practice theorists argue, can only be derived from individuals acting to manipulate the system from within. By manipulating a variety of culturally specific social roles, practices, and beliefs, actors change the culture itself. Given these interests, practice theorists argue that change can only be understood within specific historical and social contexts. Explanations of change are contingent upon the conditions in which human actors are engaged.

The contextual aspects of practice theory are among its strengths. However, it cannot address commonalities between multiple social traditions. For instance, the common elements of rites of passage across many cultures cannot be explained as the product of any specific cultural or historical context. Likewise, explanations of change are explanatory only for the individual historical context for which they are constructed. Common patterns of change and development are not addressed. Despite these problems, practice theory is central to my interpretations of the archaeological remains at Thotlakonda. The use of practice theory in my research is possible, in part, because of my focus on a single monastery and its immediate geographic context. As I am not attempting to make cross-cultural comparisons, the inability of practice theory to address them is not a problem. In contrast, the emphasis on human action in practice theory is particularly amenable to the archaeological investigation of ritual.

A major contribution of practice theory is an emphasis on the experiential aspects of ritual. For example, Bourdieu (1973, 1977) has focused on the dialectical relationship between space and the people who create and inhabit it—arguing that people both manipulate spaces and their meanings and are also conditioned, or habituated, by them (see also Giddens 1984). In archaeology, with its focus on the material aspects of social life, practice theory elevates material remains from mere reflections of past culture, to former participants in a complex dialectical relationship between material, human action, and the complex ideological concepts of human experience.

Recently the terminology of practice theory has also been adopted by Buddhist studies, contrasting texts that focus on mundane activities with those that are more philosophical or cosmological. In his introduction to *Buddhism in Practice,* Lopez (1995, 11) states:

> Buddhism has a vast literature dealing with what we term logic, epistemology, and ontology—works that are (depending on one's perspective) as profound or as impenetrable, as rich or as arid, as anything produced in the West. However, like philosophical works in other cultures, Buddhist treatises are the products of a tiny, highly educated elite (largely composed of monks in the Buddhist case) and rarely touch the ground where the vast majority of Buddhists lived their lives.... The emphasis of this volume is Buddhism in practice, especially in the more quotidian sense of the term.

By focusing on the philosophical texts, traditional Buddhist scholars skewed understanding of Buddhism toward an overly scholastic version. By stressing practice, recent Buddhist scholars are attempting to generate a more balanced, more complete, understanding of Buddhism. By studying Buddhist practice, these scholars also hope to gain a greater understanding of Buddhist philosophy.

When compared to anthropology, the application of practice theory in Buddhist studies is more pragmatic. While Buddhologists accept and utilize many of the theoretical writings of anthropological practice theorists, the focus of research is oriented toward the ordinary practices of Buddhists. It should be remembered, however, that even the most mundane literary sources were almost entirely composed by Buddhist monks. While they may illustrate lay Buddhist practice, they are best understood as descriptions of the ordinary rituals and activities of the monastic community itself.

In my research, I stand somewhere between the anthropological and Buddhist studies approaches to practice theory. I feel that, at times, anthropological practice theorists spend so much of their energy arguing the theoretical importance of specific social contexts and historical contingency that they fail to examine any actual human society in detail. In comparison, I find that scholars within Buddhist studies accept their literary sources as evidence for lay practice too easily. For my research, the key element of ritual is its regularized, or habitualized, performance. Regularized human actions are likely to leave consistent patterns of material traces. These traces are themselves part of the action, part of the more abstract religious principles. The subsequent sections of this chapter address the specific methods

I employ to move from architecture and landscape into an investigation of ritual practice.

Architecture

Studies of religious architecture have a long history in archaeology. While a complete history of archaeological approaches to religion would be valuable, it is not my intention to present one here. Rather, I will review some of the more recent structural and practice approaches to architecture that guide my research. Like most archaeologists, I tend to blend different theoretical understandings of ritual in the study of ritual architecture. While this may lack theoretical consistency, I believe it allows the strengths of different theoretical understandings of ritual to be applied where they are most appropriate.

Symbolic and Structural Approaches to Architecture

The influence of structuralism has been profound in archaeological studies of domestic architecture (see Bourdieu 1973; Kent ed. 1990; Pearson and Richards 1994; Tambiah 1969; see also Rapoport 1982). Here archaeologists have identified oppositions (i.e., male/female, exterior/interior, east/west, etc.) in the use of space for the reconstruction of symbolic frameworks and deeper structural meanings. For example, in Richards's (1990) studies of late Neolithic houses in the Orkneys, he identified a right/left division of space. Since the doors of the houses enter toward the right side of the house, and provide greater illumination to that side, right/left can also be read as interior/exterior and light/dark. Finally, by identifying gendered activities in the two areas, a male/female dichotomy is also inferred. Richards continues by relating the organization of Neolithic houses to larger cosmological principles related to seasonal changes.

In a similar vein, other studies have attempted to read larger cosmological concerns into the layout of sacred architecture (see Carmichael et al. 1994; Bradley 1998). For example, medieval cathedrals in Europe have a ground plan in the form of a cross. The dominant religious ideology of Europe (Christianity) is manifested in the use of the primary religious symbol (the cross) as mapped into the architecture of the dominant ritual spaces (cathedrals). Similar studies have demonstrated the use of generalized South Asian cosmologies in the organization of space in Angkor Wat (Moron 1977) and Borobudur (Mus 1978) in Southeast Asia. Both sites are arranged as *mandalas*—maps of the cosmos with the sacred Mount Mehru at the center. Underlying these studies is the presumption that manifestations of cosmological principles in architecture condition the beliefs of an individual who enters the space.

The structural and symbolic studies of architecture have many of the same strengths and weaknesses as structural and symbolic approaches to religion generally. Architecture is viewed as the reflection of a disembodied concept of culture. Returning to the example of the medieval cathedral, it is unclear if someone within a cathedral would perceive that the building resembled a cross when viewed from above. A more important criticism is that the creation of the architectural space, or the cultural ideal that underlies it, is not addressed. Rather than a dialectic, architecture is interpreted as part of an overarching cultural abstraction dictating the beliefs and actions of its members. To be fair, many of those using structural approaches to architecture are also involved in examining the experiential aspects of architecture (see, for example, Pearson and Richards 1994). They combine their studies with the study of practice to balance their interpretations. The first step in this process is the realization that people choose to build a structure in some specific format. Further, every day people decide if they will continue to use a structure. Abandonment or modification is not simply an organic outgrowth from what precedes it but, rather, an active decision made by those who are enmeshed in an architectural environment.

Experiential Approaches to Architecture

In recent years, an emphasis on the experiential aspects of architecture has become an increasing focus of archaeological inquiry (e.g., Bradley ed. 1990; Carmichael et al. 1994; Garwood et al. 1991; Kowalski ed. 1999; Smith and Brookes 2001). This interest has also been extended into investigations of ritual architecture (e.g., Bradley 1998; Moore 1996; see also Tilley 1994). These studies emphasize issues such as patterns of visibility, sensory experiences, movement, and access in particular architectural forms. A valuable example is Moore's (1996) study of distance and elevation on the visual perception of ritual action in pyramid complexes in coastal Peru. He suggests that the form of ritual practiced in large pyramid complexes could be limited by the spectators' ability to perceive ritual at a distance. For example, a figure standing atop a large pyramid would have an extremely difficult time being seen and heard. Ritual in these contexts would most likely involve large movements with little emphasis on speech. Other portions of the book provide similarly rigorous analyses, with particular reference to the ability of architecture to promote elite power and authority. As I started my analyses, I expected to make extensive use of Moore's methodologies. Unfortunately, I soon found that the architectural layout of Thotlakonda resisted many of his methods. While the explicitness of Moore's methods is commendable, the architecture at Thotlakonda required other, more impressionistic, methods.

Hillier and Hanson (1984) have also emphasized the experiential aspects of spaces, focusing on patterns of access and movement through architectural complexes. Their method relies on plotting routes of access through an architectural space. By noting areas of constriction in the available routes of access (i.e., gates and doors), they identify areas and patterns of restricted access. While concealment and restriction are central to their arguments, for the most part, their analysis focuses upon a method for the identification of a spatial grammar that I do not employ in my research. While I employ Hillier and Hanson's methods for the study of restricted space (particularly in chapter 7), I also examine the patterns of *visibility* within Thotlakonda Monastery.

Buddhist Religious Architecture in Early Historic Period South Asia

In the synthetic chapters that conclude this book, I make extensive use of a methodology I developed in a previous study of Buddhist religious architecture (Fogelin 2003a). This earlier research focused on an analysis of the manner in which a primary ritual focus is presented. In particular, I contrasted the methods used for presenting *stupas* at monastic and pilgrimage sites in Early Historic Period South Asia. To this end, I compared rock-cut monasteries of the Western Ghats (see figure 4.1) with large open-air pilgrimage sites (see figure 4.2) favored by the laity. I concluded that the laity favored communal ritual and meditative individual ritual

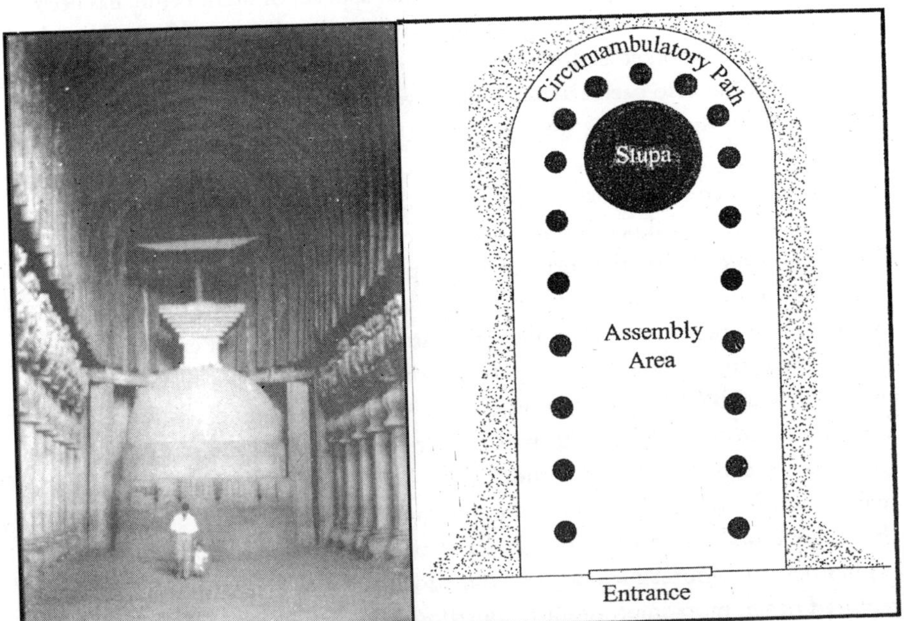

Figure 4.1. A schematic diagram of a typical rock-cut Buddhist monastery and photograph of the main chaitya at Karla.

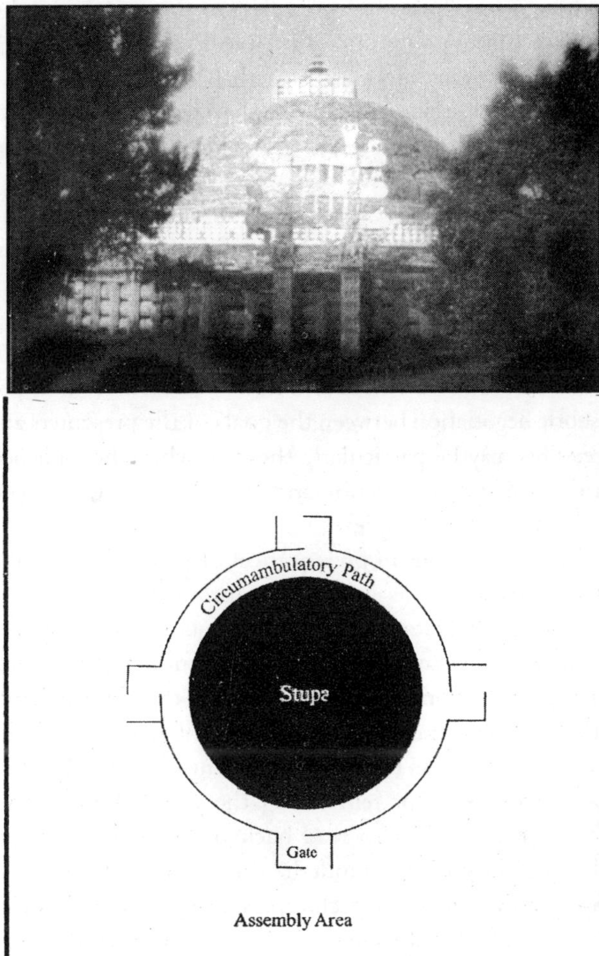

Figure 4.2. A schematic diagram of a typical pilgrimage stupa *complex and photograph of the main* stupa *at Sanchi.*

in the circumambulatory path. Early Historic Period monks, in contrast, downplayed circumambulation in their own worship spaces, focusing upon corporate ritual. Based upon these differences, I argued that the monks were attempting to routinize the charisma of the Buddha through the promotion of a particular form of hierarchical group ritual. During the Early Historic Period the laity successfully resisted this attempt at authority. Below, I outline the methods employed in my original analysis and briefly summarize my results. I begin with a discussion of presentation, the underlying concept on which the methodology rests.

In the most basic sense, "presentation" refers to the manner in which an object or action is shown to a person or group of people. Presentation is not synonymous with viewing. While it can be safely assumed that, for the most part, objects that are presented are also viewed, presentation emphasizes the intentions of the person or people who are showing an object or performing an action. Viewing focuses upon the reactions of those who see the object that has been presented. Thus, *presentation* refers to the *intended* effects on viewers that need not be the actual effects. By examining the forms of presentation within *stupa* complexes, this method of analysis focuses upon the intentions of the people who designed and built *stupas*. That said, not all forms of presentation will be acceptable to the people to whom the presentation is directed. The audience of a presentation always enters with its own ideas of what should be presented and how. The final form of presentation is the result of a subtle negotiation between the goals of the presenters and the desires of the audience. This may be particularly the case when the audience is partially responsible for the costs of construction and maintenance of a presentation space, as was the case for many *stupa* complexes.

Different goals or intentions in presentation often result in different architectural forms of presentation. This initial assumption must be modified by some pragmatic concerns. The final form of presentation is always a negotiation between the intended goals of presentation, the specific cultural and historical context in which it occurs, the expectations of the audience, and the physical limitations of architecture. Within these constraints, a large amount of architectural variation exists. In ritual spaces, presentation can take many different forms, each with corresponding strengths and weaknesses for reinforcing the goals of the rituals conducted within them. Thus, it is possible to read back from the range of presentational forms of ritual spaces the goals that underlie their construction.

The following analysis relies on techniques derived from theatrical set design (see Payne 1993, 37–51). Set designers work within theatrical spaces—halls and arenas—that roughly correspond to the forms of ritual space in early Buddhist religious structures. Modern set designers note that halls foster more formal actor/audience relationships, while arenas are more participatory. While the terminology of halls and arenas is derived from Western theater, the same concepts are found in the *Natyashastra,* an early Indian treatise on theater and dance (Muni 1986; Sharma 1987). It should be noted that, while valuable, the *Natyashastra* dates to the second or third century A.D. and cannot be used for direct interpretation of the early *stupa* complexes discussed here. The *Natyashastra* has large sections devoted to the design of nine different types of theaters, including several types of halls and arenas. In relation to presentational forms, it states that formal plays concerning the gods should be presented in halls, while circuses, dancing acts, and comedies should be presented in arenas. Like Western theatrical traditions, the *Natyashastra* recognizes that more participatory forms of theater belong in arenas, while more formal religious plays and instruction belong in halls. Taken as a general statement of early South Asian views on presentation, the *Natyashastra* demonstrates that the principles of presentation in Western set design are relevant to an analysis of early Buddhist *stupa* complexes.

An analysis of sightlines—what can and cannot be seen from any given point within a theater (see Payne 1993)—is a valuable technique to determine the nature of theatrical presentation. Sightlines can also be used to address the likely forms of presentation for individual, communal, and corporate ritual discussed previously. Individual ritual should emphasize the object of worship and minimize the distraction of other individuals. Thus, if the goal of presentation is to facilitate individual ritual, the layout of the architecture should limit the viewing of anyone or anything other than the object of worship. In contrast, communal participation in ritual requires that the audience see other audience members and interact with them while still maintaining the ritual focus. Finally, corporate participation in ritual places the focus on the object of worship and the intermediaries who direct worship.

The most obvious form of presentation for individual ritual is a small room adjacent to, or containing, the object of worship. The walls of the room would block from view all other potential distractions while the ritual focus would be clearly visible. In fact, in later Buddhist periods, this format was adopted for individual ritual. But, during the period addressed here, pragmatic concerns forced a modification of this ideal form. At many *stupa* complexes, large numbers of people engaged in individual ritual simultaneously. A small room, or even several small rooms, could not accommodate all worshippers. Rather, individual ritual occurred in circumambulatory paths that allowed large numbers of people to engage in individual worship simultaneously. The railing surrounding the path visually and spatially separated worshippers from outside distractions, serving to promote individual engagement with the *stupa*.

Two presentational forms that closely relate to communal and corporate worship are arenas and halls. An arena is a presentational space in which the audience surrounds the object or action being viewed, while a hall places the audience on only one side of the object or action. This basic difference in layout creates fundamental differences in the sightlines of these spaces. In an arena, the faces of other individuals are visible as a backdrop to the action or object on which the presentation is focused. While actively viewing this object or action, each individual cannot avoid seeing how other audience members are reacting. The sightlines in an arena highlight both the object and the audience, promoting communal participation in ritual. Arenas also allow more audience members to be physically close to the central focus than halls do.

Along with fostering communal ritual, arenas also hinder the performance of corporate ritual. In an arena, there is no place where a ritual specialist could stand

and command the attention of the entire audience. The ritual specialist would always have his or her back toward half of the audience, no matter which way he or she faced. In an arena in which the ritual focus is elevated, such as a *stupa,* this problem is even more pronounced. Unless the ritual specialist stood upon the top of the *stupa,* which was almost certainly prohibited, most of the audience could not have even seen the back of the ritual leader. As the ritual mediators would have been at the same level as the worshippers, those who did not want to listen could vote with their feet by walking around to the other side of the *stupa.*

In contrast, halls promote ritual mediators. Unlike arenas, halls downplay interaction between audience members. While the principal object or action is clearly visible, only the backs of fellow audience members' heads can be seen. Without the ability to see other peoples' faces, only the grossest of reactions can be gauged from body language and some vocalization. The sightlines of a hall help direct attention toward a specific focus, allowing an individual or group of individuals to command the attention of the audience. By standing between the ritual focus and the entire audience, a ritual specialist can establish himself or herself as a ritual mediator, both physically and metaphorically. Thus, the hall form of presentation is most appropriate for corporate ritual.

The ubiquitous association of *stupas* with almost all monasteries suggests that the people who designed and controlled them were monks and nuns (Schopen 1997). In rock-cut *chaityas,* the audience was clerical. In open-air pilgrimage *stupa* complexes, the audience was a combination of both the clergy and laity, with the latter most likely comprising the majority. Presentational forms are the result of a negotiation between the people who design and build a structure and the audience that is expected to frequent and support that structure. Since the clergy controlled both forms of *stupa* complexes, the differences between the presentational forms of open-air and rock-cut *stupa* complexes are the product of the different audiences that frequented them. Thus, the differences in presentational form can be attributed to the different expectations of worship among monastic and lay audiences.

Using the layout and forms of presentation in rock-cut *stupa* complexes as indicators of monastic expectations of worship, several conclusions can be drawn (see figure 4.1). First, the hall form of the assembly area indicates that the clergy favored a form of ritual that elevated certain individuals into roles as ritual mediators. Second, using proximity to the *stupa* as a measure of relative importance of different worship spaces, the clergy saw corporate worship in the assembly area as more important than individual worship in the circumambulatory path. This is shown by the placement of the circumambulatory path along the exterior walls of *chaityas,* with the assembly area interposed between the path and the *stupa* (see figure 4.1). Since the circumambulatory path was the more solitary form of ritual, it seems that monks and nuns were less interested in individual *stupa* ritual than in corporate, directed worship. The clergy also worshipped the Buddha symbolically, as shown by the lack of relics within many monastic *stupas*.

In contrast, the form of worship at open-air pilgrimage *stupas* can be used to address the expectations of the laity (see figure 4.2). The laity privileged more individualized worship within the circumambulatory path over group worship practiced in an assembly area with less direct contact with the *stupa*. Even the form of group worship was different. The arena format of the assembly area fostered communal ritual, deemphasizing the potential for ritual specialists acting as mediators between the laity and the Buddha. Finally, the *stupa* in open-air complexes always contained a relic, suggesting that the laity did not accept the worship of a symbolic representation of the Buddha in the form of the *stupa*. In sum, the laity preferred to worship the Buddha directly, without the imposition of a ritual specialist, in both the circumambulatory path and assembly area. In fact, ritual leadership was effectively limited by the presentational forms of open-air *stupa* complexes.

This discussion illustrates how an investigation of the manner in which objects are presented can inform upon religious ritual. In this case, the forms of presentation have illuminated two underlying tensions in early Buddhism. First, the organization of *stupa* complexes into two distinct ritual spaces demonstrates how early Buddhists promoted social solidarity within a highly individualistic religious tradition. Second, the layouts of the spaces designated for group ritual illustrate differences in the systems used to promote solidarity between the laity and the clergy. The construction of spaces designed to foster hierarchical or corporate forms of ritual by the monks can be understood as an attempt to routinize the Buddha's charisma. However, this authority had not yet been fully recognized by the laity. The continued use of communal ritual spaces by the laity was the successful resistance to that attempt. During the Early Historic Period this tension remained unresolved, with monks and laity each asserting their own interests. Social solidarity among the two groups was achieved while a common solidarity between them was not. In later chapters, I will use the methods presented here to analyze the layout of Thotlakonda Monastery. As is the case in this earlier study of Buddhist religious architecture, my analysis of the architecture and landscape at Thotlakonda demonstrates that the monks and laity had a somewhat ambivalent relationship.

Landscape

Recent trends in the archaeological study of landscape mirror many of the concerns that have developed in the study of architecture. This is most evident in the developing interest in the way that people perceive, and move through, a landscape. As argued by its advocates, modern landscape approaches stand in direct opposition to earlier studies that emphasized the environment and resource use. Rather, modern landscape theorists focus upon the way that conceptions of landscapes shape worldview and human/nature relationships. Given the new emphasis on ideology, it is not surprising that a great deal of attention has been placed on the study of sacred landscapes (see Bradley 2000; Carmichael et al. eds. 1994; Ashmore and Knapp 1999; Tilley 1994). It is this latter work that serves as the foundation of my research at Thotlakonda. However, while I employ landscape approaches in my research, I do have some concerns over its application.

With the movement away from a more static view of the landscape as a backdrop to human action to a view that emphasizes the perception of landscape by people in the past, several theoretical and methodological issues arise. Most of these issues rest on one simple question—whose perceptions are we talking about? Just as different people in the present have different perceptions of a landscape, we can expect that there was no single monolithic view of landscape in the past. For example, men and women may have very different perceptions of the landscape based upon where they typically spend their time or perform ritual observances (Ashmore and Knapp 1999). Different social classes may also have different attitudes—for instance, differing views of a golf course by those who are members of the club versus those who are not. When addressing the perceived landscape in an archaeological analysis, it is necessary to specify who exactly we think was doing the perceiving. Better yet, archaeological analysis should try to determine variations in perceptions of the same landscape by different people. This latter approach would serve to illustrate what some have termed nested landscapes (Ashmore and Knapp 1999, 16–17), but might better be described as blended landscapes. For my own part, I attempt this through a comparison of monastic and lay perceptions of the landscape surrounding Thotlakonda.

The difficulty with this approach, however, is that perception is not easily identified in the material remains available to archaeologists. It is a truism to state that something with no material implications cannot be identified through studies of material remains alone. A number of different archaeological approaches have emerged to address this problem. Among the most problematic of these is the recent appropriation of phenomenology from religious studies by Christopher Tilley and others (Tilley 1994; Thomas 2001, 1996; see Insoll 2004 for a more detailed comparison of religious studies and archaeological approaches to phenomenology).

Phenomenology

In its original formulation in religious studies, phenomenology assumed a high degree of similarity in the ways that people think about and perceive the world.

This was necessary given the primary method employed by phenomenologists—imagining what they would think if they were in the context being investigated (see Moran 2000 for a critical review of phenomenology in religious studies). At first glance this would seem to be a rather sloppy approach, allowing pretty much any interpretation to be advanced with only the barest of evidence. In practice, traditional phenomenologists used a variety of methods that attempted to remove some of these biases. It is precisely these methods that were abandoned in the archaeological appropriation of phenomenology. Rather, phenomenology was adopted by archaeologists who had an even stronger commitment to the position of social constructivism—that no objective world exists outside of our own individual perceptions of it. By rejecting any commonalities in perception or ways of thinking, archaeological phenomenologists accepted that their conclusions were entirely subjective, relating only to their own emotive responses to landscapes. This is not the place to argue over the nature of reality. It is sufficient to state that, where the goal of archaeological research is an understanding of how people in the past understood and perceived the world, archaeological phenomenologists have argued themselves into a position of irrelevance. This is all the more frustrating since many of their specific observations and conclusions are both insightful and compelling.

For my part, I support the practice of phenomenology inasmuch as it involves sitting on a rock and looking at stuff. Some of my best insights concerning Thotlakonda—not to mention many really bad ones—occurred in the early evening as I sat on the main stupa looking out across the hilltops, picturing what it must have been like two thousand years ago. My criticisms of phenomenology are not intended to be criticisms of imagination. It is possible to think yourself into the past; you just cannot have too much faith in your conclusions. Imagination must be tempered with rigorous investigation. A good example of a more balanced approach can be seen in Tilley's own recent work on Bronze Age sites in southwest England (Tilley et al. 2000).

In recent research at Leskernick Hill, Tilley and others (2000) came across a landscape consisting of human-modified or moved boulders within a landscape dominated by naturally occurring boulders. While recognizing that both the human-modified and natural stones in the region would have had varied meanings to the inhabitants of Leskernick Hill, Tilley and his co-authors argued that determining which stones were which could serve to help understand the social meanings of both. Methodologically, they employed precise geomorphological criteria to differentiate natural and human-modified stones. In their case, the primary geomorphological mechanism creating the boulder fields related to periods of heavy frost upheaval. By carefully examining the effects of frost, they developed specific criteria for evaluating each stone they encountered. Thus, the specific angle of stones and their distribution across the face of the hill were used to identify those stones that had been modified or moved by human action.

Tilley would certainly object to the suggestion that the geomorphological methods he employed allowed for a more objective understanding of Leskernick Hill. That said, this study demonstrates that Tilley and his co-authors see little value in calling a natural conglomeration of stones a house. In other words, phenomenology is improved by more rigorous forms of observation and recordkeeping. It is important to differentiate between natural and cultural features to allow for a better understanding of past perceptions of each. While this type of research does not achieve certainty in any epistomological sense, the conclusions seem much more informative than the results of more vulgar formulations of archaeological phenomenology.

I have faith that as archaeologists we can determine the landscape perceptions of people in the past. That said, I do not think it is easy. The meanings of landscapes in the past must be inferred from material remains that do not have obvious meanings affixed to them. Two concepts that help bring this difficulty into focus are the opposed terms of space and place.

Space and Place

Space refers to the physical world in which people live, work, and exist. Place refers to the meanings conditioned by, and imposed upon, spaces. As stated by Tilley (1994, 14–15):

> The key concern in this approach is the manner in which places *constitute* space as centers of human meaning, their singularity being manifested and expressed in the day-to-day experiences and consciousness of people within particular lifeworlds.... Space is a far more abstract construct than place. It provides a situational context for places, but derives its meaning from particular places.... Geographical experience begins in places, reaches out to others through spaces, and creates landscapes or regions for human existence.

As archaeologists, most of our data concerns space. We find temples, houses, and other remains. Their meaning, their *place,* must be interpreted through reference to specific material remains. This creates the first difficulty in the archaeological application of landscape studies. Material remains are only one-half of the dialectic being investigated.

As in the example of Leskernick Hill, a major emphasis in landscape studies is the recognition that unaltered natural places may have an important role in the ideology of a particular society. For example, in the modern United States some spaces have been designated as wilderness areas. By design, it is the absence of human modification that defines these places. By analogy, archaeological identification of similarly unmodified places in the past is exceptionally difficult. Attempts toward overcoming this problem have followed two paths. The first, followed by Tilley and his colleagues (2000), is the identification of smaller, more ephemeral material indicators and their use in constructing interpretations of the broader landscapes in which they are found (see also Alcock 1993; Bradley 2000; Shaw 2002). I refer to this approach as "specific landscape." Alternatively, archaeologists have tried to create more generalized landscape understandings of particular societies through studies of architecture, iconography, and historical sources (e.g., Cosgrove 1984; Cosgrove and Daniels 1988; Barnes 1999). For example, pyramids are interpreted as representations of sacred mountains, and thus mountains, in general, are considered sacred (Townsend 1982). I refer to this approach as "generalized landscape."

Generalized Landscape

Interpretations of generalized landscape are generally informed not by landscapes themselves, but by representations of landscape in art, literature, or architecture. A Buddhist example is Gina Barnes's study of Buddhist landscapes of East Asia (Barnes 1999). Through analyses of architecture, *mandalas* (artistic representations of Buddhist cosmology), and even ceremonial cups depicting mountains, Barnes identifies a continuity in Chinese conceptions of sacred mountains and caves in the generalized landscape of later East Asian Buddhism. She then ties this sacred landscape to the production of Buddha images through the use of specific raw materials. She concludes her analysis of the images by stating that "they make every landscape of their occurrence a Buddhist landscape, facilitating a meta-physical awareness as persons go about their daily business" (Barnes 1999: 121).

Undoubtedly, Barnes's analysis has value in addressing specific East Asian Buddhist landscapes. Future studies can use her conclusions to interpret specific archaeological materials. Her work also exemplifies the strengths and weaknesses of generalized landscape approach. By using representations of landscape in art, literature, and architecture, researchers avoid the problem of moving from space to place. However, these same sources often lead to more static, overarching, structural interpretations of landscape. By using disparate sources from large geographic regions and long time periods, the product of analysis is often highly abstract. This tendency can be best seen in the emphasis on continuity in many of these studies—for example, Barnes's identification of continuity between pre-Buddhist and Buddhist landscapes in all of East Asia.

Braudel (1969) developed the concept of *longue durée* to describe historical continuities lasting centuries or even millennia. In anthropology and archaeology, the *longue durée* is often understood in terms of the long occupation of certain monuments or landscape features (see, for example, Bradley 1998; Rowlands 1993).

The relative permanence of these structures is interpreted as a product of the relative stability of these structures' social meaning. Thus, interpretations employing the *longue durée* of monuments often identify relatively unchanging principles underlying long-lived archaeological phenomena. By their persistence, these principles are assumed to be at the core of landscape perception. It should be noted that those who employ the *longue durée* note that significant changes in the social context must have occurred. However, most also rely upon Bloch's (1977) suggestion that ritual is a particularly unchanging form of social behavior—that ritual is expressly concerned with perpetuating ties with the past, with memory, through its anachronistic format (see Van Dyke and Alcock 2003 for a review of recent uses of memory in archaeology).

As described here, generalized studies of landscape have many of the same strengths and weaknesses as structural studies of ritual. The breadth of its application and usefulness is balanced by its abstraction and detachment from actual historical processes. The interpretations are often somewhat ahistorical, with persistent landscape understandings shaping the beliefs of those who live and operate within spaces. Specific landscape, in contrast, follows more closely the ideas of ritual practice, focusing on the particularities of specific landscapes and histories to develop specific meaning in relatively smaller regions.

Specific Landscape

Studies of specific landscapes can benefit from studies of general landscapes. General landscape perceptions derived through art, iconography, or other sources can illuminate specific archaeological landscapes. However, the sources used for the study of general landscapes (e.g., art, literature, and monumental architecture) often represent the views of one segment of society (i.e., literate people or the elite). In comparison, studies of specific landscapes examine the distribution of archaeological material across a landscape. Often this results in the identification of both elite and non-elite landscape use and perception (see Alcock 1993). Thus, studies of specific landscapes allow for a more practice-centered investigation of landscape rather than the more structural, elite-centered examination of general landscapes.

Among the best examples of the effective study of specific landscapes is Richard Bradley's (2000) *An Archaeology of Natural Places.* In this book he analyzes site location, patterns of access, and patterns of visibility of votive deposits, rock art, production sites, and monuments to address the landscapes of prehistoric Europe. By staying "close to those areas where there is archaeological material available for study," Bradley (2000, 43) focuses on specific landscapes.

Like Tilley (1994), Bradley sees the interpretation of landscape less as a methodological shift than an interpretational shift. In an evaluation of his own previous research on votive deposits, he states:

> These were largely concerned with discussing how the deposition of wealth may have been used in prehistoric societies in northern and western Europe: an enquiry that I thought of at the time as a contribution to 'social archaeology.' . . . The main role of natural places in my work was as 'receptacles' for this kind of material. Despite the use made of distribution maps, their wider significance as places was not a major issue. Instead I emphasized the more abstract properties of *space*. (Bradley 2000, 43)

For Bradley, the interpretation of a particular landscape is the result of the interpretation of specific archaeological remains toward understanding those areas of a landscape where remains are not found. In essence, this is no different from the approach used more generally in archaeology, where material remains are used to infer human actions and cultural patterns.

My analysis of the landscape surrounding Thotlakonda employs both general and specific landscape approaches. Using Buddhist literary sources, I develop generalized landscape perceptions of Early Buddhism. As these are based upon Buddhist monastic texts, they represent the views of Buddhist monks and nuns. Using archaeological remains, I construct specific landscape models for my survey area. As I demonstrate in the synthetic chapters that conclude this book, much of what I found illustrates the landscape perceptions of the laity. The analysis consists of a comparison of the two, identifying points of similarity and disjuncture. This approach produces a more dynamic understanding of landscape, allowing multiple social meanings to be identified in the landscape surrounding Thotlakonda.

Conclusion

In practice, the approaches I take to landscape are more or less the same as those I use for architecture, only bigger. Just as people often construct architecture to achieve certain ends, people often alter the landscape either to reflect their view of it or to more closely approximate their understanding of it. Returning to the example of wilderness areas, a fence not only demarcates the space that is deemed wilderness, but serves as a barrier that reinforces the meaning of wilderness in regard to the rest of the landscape. Walls, buildings, temples, and other more ephemeral archaeological remains can similarly mark or modify the landscape. When investigating specific landscapes, these modifications serve as the foundation for analysis. Archaeological remains are the spatial half of the dialectic that exists between space and place, serving as the basis for inferences concerning the meanings of past landscapes.

Similarly, the methods used for the analysis of architecture—sightlines, routes of access, and proximity—can be applied to landscape studies as well. The major difference between my architectural and landscape analyses concerns the role of intentionality. In my examinations of presentational architecture, I argued that the intentions of those who built and designed the spaces were more apparent than the reactions of those who used them. While the same can be said of many landscape modifications discussed in subsequent chapters, in numerous other cases intentionality is less clear. For example, a path or road might be shown by a linear pattern of debris—the result of years of people discarding trash as they walked along the path. In this case intentionality does not play a part in the creation of the archaeological signature. However, the route the path takes (e.g., connecting two villages) might well inform upon broader landscape concerns.

This final point is best illustrated in my specific analyses of the architecture and landscape of Thotlakonda Monastery, the focus of the remainder of this book. All of the remaining chapters are intended to serve as a case study, providing a specific illustration of theoretical and methodological perspectives presented here. These chapters reverse the argumentative arc that this chapter has taken—moving from broader theoretical issues regarding religion toward more direct methodologies for their investigation. In chapter 6 I combine a discussion of the specific field methodologies that guided my research and a description of the results of two seasons of fieldwork. This is followed by two synthetic chapters that focus on the architecture and landscape, respectively, of Thotlakonda. I conclude in chapter 9 with a discussion of the implications of my research on the broader understandings of religion that began this chapter. Before all of this, I review previous archaeological research conducted in north coastal Andhra Pradesh in general, and Thotlakonda Monastery specifically.

Thotlakonda's Archaeological and Environmental Context

5

PRIOR TO MY SURVEY IN the areas surrounding Thotlakonda, the APDAM had conducted several years of excavations at the monastery and several other Early Historic Period archaeological sites in the local area (Sastry, Subrahmanyam, and Rao 1992; Prasad 1993, 1994). In this chapter I review the information gathered from their reports in order to situate my research. I begin with a discussion of local environmental and geological conditions. This summary is important for understanding some of the problems encountered during fieldwork and Thotlakonda's environmental context during the Early Historic Period. The bulk of this chapter, however, is devoted to a discussion of the APDAM excavations at Thotlakonda and other archaeological sites in north coastal Andhra Pradesh.

Thotlakonda Monastery is located in north coastal Andhra Pradesh, near the modern city of Visakhapatnam (see figure 5.1). It sits on a low hill overlooking several coastal valleys leading to the Bay of Bengal. In addition to Thotlakonda, the area around Visakhapatnam is home to several other Early Historic Period Buddhist monasteries. These include Bavikonda, Pavuralakonda, Sankaram, and Dharapalem. Three of these monasteries (Thotlakonda, Bavikonda, and Pavuralakonda) were excavated by the APDAM. For the most part, this chapter relies exclusively upon the information gathered from their excavations. If it were not for the high quality of their initial research, my own investigations in the area would not have been possible. I thank the APDAM for supporting my research and making their collections available for reanalysis.

Local Environment and Geology

Geographically, north coastal Andhra Pradesh is a narrow strip of land lying between the Bay of Bengal and the Eastern Ghats (see figure 5.1). These mountains, with their irregular peaks and dense forest cover, serve as an effective barrier to movement into the area from the west. The southern border is defined by the

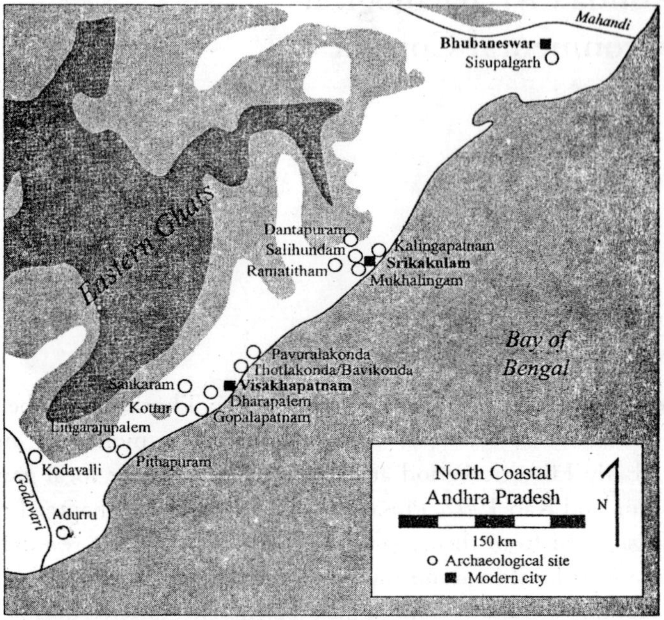

Figure 5.1. Early Historic Period archaeological sites in north coastal Andhra Pradesh.

Godavari River, with the northern border around the Vamsadhara River in the Srikakulam district of Andhra Pradesh. Between the two rivers are numerous coastal valleys and small floodplains defined by ridges originating in the Eastern Ghats that reach all the way to the ocean. There are no large rivers in the area. Even the Vamsadhara is small when compared to the much larger Godavari River to the south and Mahanadi River farther north in Orissa.

The coastal zone between the Eastern Ghats and the Bay of Bengal is primarily underlain by khondalite, a coarse-grained basalt with prominent veins of quartzite (Reddy, Prasad, and Harindranath 1996). As shown by the heavily worn columns and sculptures at Thotlakonda, khondalite erodes easily. Hilltops and hillsides throughout the area are also heavily eroded, with loose khondalite boulders in dense clusters. The valleys and floodplains of the region are filled with red sediments ranging from clay to sandy loam (Reddy, Prasad, and Harindranath 1996, 51). Most sediments contain a significant portion of gravel. The dominant erosion regime of the region is causing a gradual expansion of the coastal plain into the Bay of Bengal (Reddy, Prasad, and Harindranath 1996). The rates of sedimentation vary tremendously along the coast, and there are no estimates for the region immediately around Thotlakonda. It can only be stated that the modern coastline is likely to be farther into the bay than it was during the Early Historic Period.

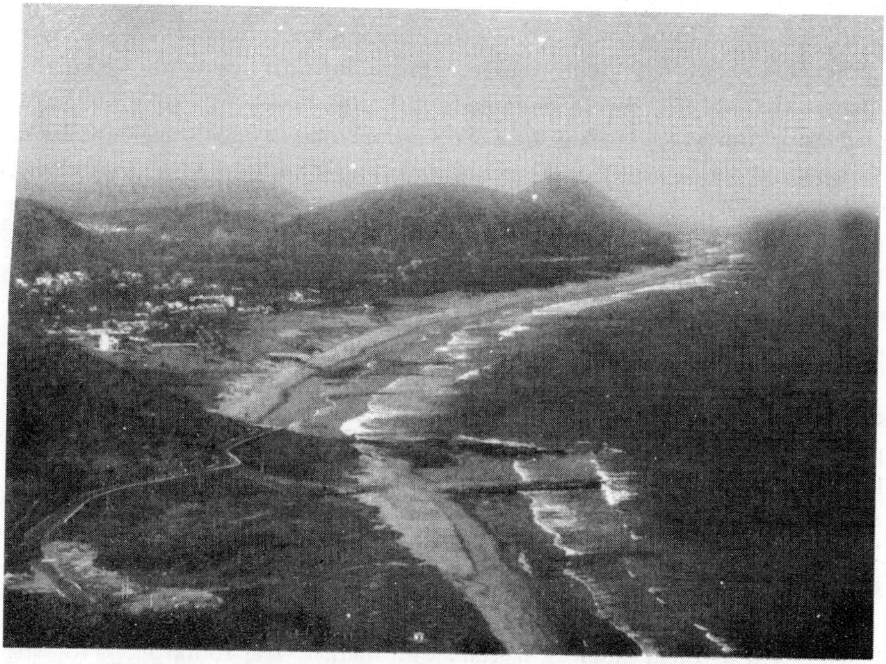

Figure 5.2. A view of the coastline of north coastal Andhra Pradesh.

The climate of north coastal Andhra Pradesh is hot, with a mean high temperature of 33°C in May and mean minimum temperature of 19.6°C in January (Eliot 1906). The average annual rainfall in Visakhapatnam is 1,050 mm, most of which falls between June and September during the southwest monsoon.

Between 1945 and 2000, 490 cyclones formed in the Bay of Bengal (Cane 2002). Between 1970 and 1996, eight made landfall in north coastal Andhra Pradesh (Indian Meteorological Department 2002). While most were mild, three were strong storms that caused significant damage and loss of life. Damage from cyclones is caused by high winds, flooding, and the storm surge. While usually only a few meters, the storm surge that accompanied the landfall of a cyclone in Orissa in 1999 was as much as six meters above normal sea level (Indian Meteorological Department 2002). The storm surge pushed up rivers, flooding areas up to nine miles inland. The accompanying rain caused massive flooding even in rivers unaffected by the storm surge. It should be expected that storms such as this, and more typical smaller cyclones, would have had profound effects on settlement patterns and building methods during the Early Historic Period. Coastal settlements should be located on higher ground, while those in the interior should be located to avoid flooding and mudslides.

The modern natural vegetation of the coastal areas consists of a wide variety of thorny bushes. These grow on the hilltops and hillsides beyond the agricultural zones in the valley bottoms. Dense stands of thorny shrubs cover some hills, completely preventing access to large areas. This proved to be one of the major problems encountered during survey of the area surrounding Thotlakonda. Moving inland, there is progressively more forest cover, with the Eastern Ghats covered in dense forests of teak and other tropical hardwoods (Reddy, Prasad, and Harindranath 1996). Extensive forest clearance over the last several hundred years has dramatically reduced the coverage of the forests. During the Early Historic Period these forests may have extended well into the coastal valleys.

The area immediately surrounding Thotlakonda is currently planted in several crops. The lowest, best-irrigated areas are planted in rice. Surrounding the rice paddies are fields of chilies, bananas, millet, and pulses. In the drier, rain-fed fields at the bases of the local hills are cashew orchards. Although small streams and reservoirs are used to irrigate a few fields, wells provide most of the water. Measurements taken in several of the wells in February 2001 show that the dry-season water table is roughly three meters below the ground surface. The use of wells allows the local farmers to grow two crops of rice a year and produce a small but steady year-round supply of vegetables for market. Year-round access to water allows the local farms to remain economically viable despite relatively poor soils and moderate yields (Reddy, Prasad, and Harindranath 1996).

In the coastal villages below Thotlakonda, many of the residents focus on fishing rather than farming. The beaches and waters of Timmapuram, a village one kilometer north of Thotlakonda, provide safe anchorage for local fishing vessels. The local fishermen leave each night and fish the waters up to five kilometers out to sea. The waters of the Bay of Bengal deepen rapidly, limiting the value of fishing farther out to sea. While many of the local fishermen have switched to metal boats, numerous fishermen continue to use traditional sewn wooden boats. During the day fishermen repair boats and nets on the beaches. It is also common to see fishermen using small nets from the coast or from small, one-person boats. On several occasions I witnessed the use of large nets from the beach. These nets are deployed by small boats, and then pulled in to the beach by groups of twenty to forty men. Larger fish are sold for food, while the smaller fish are dried on the beaches and sold for chicken feed.

It is unclear to what degree the modern environment and resources reflect those that existed during the Early Historic Period. During the Early Historic Period local populations most likely farmed and fished, just as they do today. Of the specific crops that were raised or the specific fish that were caught, nothing is known for certain. Answers to these questions must await excavations that employ more precise methods that allow for the collection of botanical and faunal remains.

Similarly, local geomorphological studies could greatly aid in determining the local environment. In particular, if the coastline has moved outward since the Early Historic Period as believed (Reddy, Prasad, and Harindranath 1996), the area north of Thotlakonda Hill may well have been a protected bay (see figure 6.2). In turn, the presence of a bay could have had a dramatic impact upon the types of ocean resources available to local populations. The bay could have also served as an anchorage along the coastal trade routes.

Thotlakonda Monastery

Thotlakonda Monastery is named for the low hill on which it stands. Located sixteen kilometers north of the modern city of Visakhapatnam, it was discovered during aerial survey by the Indian navy and subsequently excavated by the APDAM between 1987 and 1991 (Sastry, Subrahmanyam, and Rao 1992). The excavations revealed several *viharas, chaityas, stupas,* and other Buddhist remains. The excavators dated occupation of the site between the second or third centuries B.C. through the second or third centuries A.D. Material remains found during the fieldwork included a variety of ceramics, Roman and Satavahana coins, roof tiles, nails, and other building materials. In addition, several inscriptions were found at the site. What follows is a closer examination of the archaeological remains at Thotlakonda, as published in the APDAM site report. In subsequent chapters I will revisit this material in light of the knowledge gained from my survey of the area immediately surrounding the monastery.

Site Layout

The architectural layout of Thotlakonda is the product of several centuries of development. In its final form, the monastery was divided into three general areas, linked by a system of stone paths (see figure 5.3). The first area was a central courtyard or cloister flanked on three sides by monastic cells (*viharas*). In the center of this courtyard were a large columned hall, several small votive *stupas,* and two circular *chaityas.* To the north of the cloister was the second portion of the monastery, containing the large main *stupa,* main *chaitya,* several smaller *stupas,* and several circular *chaityas.* Just north of these ritual structures were the remains of three cisterns cut into a large patch of sheetrock (see glossary). Together these structures formed the primary ritual area of the monastery. To the east of the cloister was the third portion of the monastery: a refectory and several storerooms.

Several building methods were employed at Thotlakonda. Throughout the complex, floors are plastered in lime concrete in both interior and exterior locations. Semicircular stone steps (moonstones) are inset into the concrete in front of most doors. Walls were often plastered with decorated stucco. Fragments of stucco

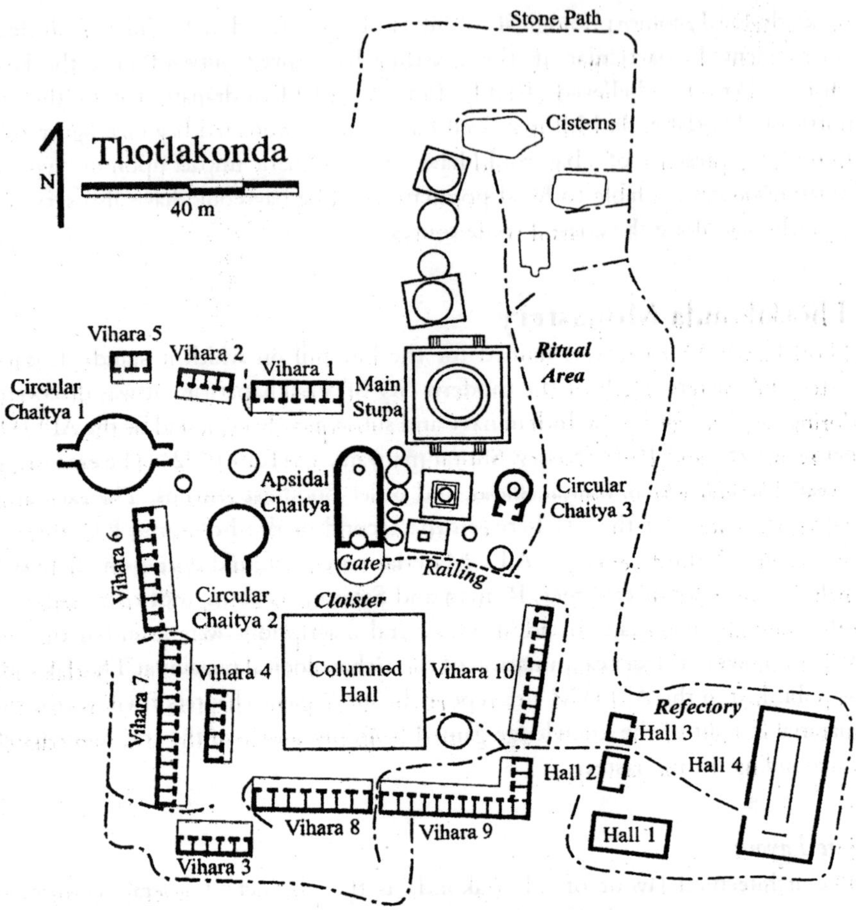

Figure 5.3. Plan of Thotlakonda Monastery.

lotuses and other flowers were found throughout the complex. As evident from the large number of tiles found in the excavations, many of the structures had wooden superstructures capped by terra-cotta tiles. Other buildings may have been capped with less permanent materials, such as palm fronds. All of the non-ritual structures were made of brick. Most of the ritual structures were also brick, though some were constructed of stone.

The Cloister

The cloister lies at the heart of Thotlakonda. This was the residential core of the monastery. The monks lived in brick *viharas* that flanked the cloister on three sides. They likely received religious instruction in the columned hall in the courtyard.

While the largest ritual spaces lie north of the cloister, smaller *stupas* and circular *chaityas* were present within the cloister as well. Each *vihara* in the cloister was divided into two to fourteen individual cells. In total, sixty-seven cells are found at Thotlakonda. Each cell is small (roughly 2.5 × 2.5 m), suggesting use by a single individual. *Vihara* 8 has evidence of a few brick benches that likely served as beds. Benches are also found in cells in other *viharas*, though the degree of preservation makes their identification difficult.

Evidence from other, contemporary Buddhist monasteries, particularly the well-preserved rock-cut monasteries of the Western Ghats (Dehejia 1972; Nagaraju 1981), suggests that monastic cells were typically furnished with simple benches. Each cell also had a wooden door, as shown by the presence of door sockets in areas of better preservation. Cells opened upon a common veranda running along the front of each *vihara*. This covered area provided protection from both the sun and rain. As noted by the excavators, the thicker, load-carrying rear walls of the *viharas* suggest that the tile roof sloped down toward the back of the *viharas*.

If all of the *viharas* were in simultaneous use, sixty-seven monks could have been housed with some degree of privacy at Thotlakonda. It should be noted, however, that several of the cells may have served as storerooms, reducing the possible monastic population. In addition, Coningham (2001, 71) has noted the use of temporary shelters for monks and nuns in modern Sri Lankan monasteries. The excavations at Thotlakonda did not identify these types of remains, but they cannot be ruled out. It is possible, for instance, that novitiates were housed in either common structures or temporary structures surrounding the monastery. At some times during the year additional monastic populations may have been forced to use other structures for housing as needed. The central columned hall, for example, could have easily accommodated a large number of visitors.

At the center of the cloister stood a large (23.5 × 23.5 m) sixty-four-columned hall. Laid out in an 8 × 8 grid, the columns, 4.25 meters high, were made of local stone (khondalite). The columns stood upon foundations 1.25 meters below the floor surface, creating a hall three meters high. Sockets in the tops of the columns suggest the hall was capped by a wooden roof. A small (2.4 × 2.0 m) brick platform stood at the center of the hall. Only two courses of brick were intact when excavated. This platform could have held ritual objects or may have been an elevated position for the presentation of sermons or lectures. The columns of the hall were carved with a variety of motifs, most of which are too poorly preserved to identify.

Two circular brick *chaityas* were found in the northwestern portion of the cloister. Both were poorly preserved, with only a few courses of brick remaining. While it is assumed that both contained a *stupa*, in neither case is evidence preserved. The smaller of the two has an entrance on its southern side, while the larger has entrances on both the west and east. The entrances to this latter structure are interesting, as the western entrance extends outside the cloister while the eastern entrance falls within it. As will be discussed in greater detail later, this *chaitya* may have served as a ritual entrance and exit to the cloister, defining a separation between sacred and secular space.

As mentioned previously, the cloister was defined on three sides by *viharas*. On the north, it was defined by a railing. Traces of this railing are poorly preserved, but the foundation stones and a few fragmentary vertical columns were found. Based upon the shape of the sockets on the columns, the cross-members were lenticular in section. This would conform to the general pattern for railings at Buddhist *stupa* complexes throughout South Asia (see Mitra 1971; Brown 1965; see figure gloss.1). As no intact columns were found at Thotlakonda, it is not possible to state the exact height of the railing. However, based upon similar railings at other contemporary archaeological sites, it is likely that it was at least a few meters high. As shown by the spacing between lenticular mortises carved into the railing columns, the vertical spacing between cross-members was not more than ten centimeters. Thus, the railing would have served, both physically and visually, as an effective barrier on the northern boundary of the cloister.

Ritual Area

The ritual area at Thotlakonda is dominated by a large *stupa*. The *stupa* rested upon a square platform (19.5 × 19.5 m, height 1.2 m) with stairs ascending the northern and southern sides. The *anda* (the central, stone tumulus) was 9.5 meters in diameter and consisted of a rubble core encased in several layers of brick. At the time of the excavation, nine courses of brick remained of the *stupa*. Encircling the *stupa* was a small brick platform 85 centimeters wide and only a single brick high. These bricks may have served to mark the circumambulatory path. There is no evidence for a railing surrounding the *stupa*, though a small railing may have been located on the stairs leading to the *stupa*. No relic chambers were found.

As a whole, the main *stupa* at Thotlakonda was neither particularly elaborate nor large when compared with contemporary *stupas* in peninsular South Asia or even the local area. It was a fairly simple structure, lacking *ayaka* platforms or a clearly demarcated circumambulatory path. As noted by the excavators, the simple rubble fill stands in contrast to more stable designs used in contemporary *stupas* in the peninsula (Sastry, Subrahmanyam, and Rao 1992, 27). In short, the main *stupa* at Thotlakonda does not conform to the patterns typical of the era. Instead, it seems more like a large votive *stupa* than the primary ritual space of a monastery—an interesting possibility, given the existence of a much larger and elaborate *stupa* found at the contemporary Buddhist monastery of Bavikonda (discussed below) only 2.25 kilometers away.

The second major structure in the ritual area is a large apsidal hall (18.35 × 5.7 m). Its entrance lies on the southern end, and it contained a small *stupa* (2.25 m diameter) in the north. It is a simple structure with no columns dividing the ritual space. The thick walls (1.2 m) result in a long but relatively narrow (3.3 m) interior space. In front of the entrance lies a large paved area in the form of a moonstone. It is from this paved area that the railing begins, separating the ritual area from the cloister. The orientation of the apsidal hall, and the presence of a gate in the railing, allowed the resident monks to move easily from the cloister into the apsidal hall.

Other structures in the ritual area include eleven votive *stupas*, two stone platforms, and a single circular *chaitya*. The larger votive *stupas* are found in a line north of the main *stupa* and are constructed of rubble and brick with their exterior surfaces veneered in stone. The remaining votive *stupas* and the circular *chaitya* are constructed of brick. Also north of the main *stupa* are three large cisterns cut into a patch of sheetrock. Steps leading into cisterns have evidence for grinding in the forms of slicks and mortars. A path leads from these cisterns directly to the refectory, so these slicks might be part of the processing activities that went into food preparation. However, these slicks may also be the product of ritual activities at the main *stupa*, apsidal hall, or other ritual structures in the area.

Refectory

The refectory lies on the southeast of the monastery. It is comprised of three storerooms (halls 1, 2, and 3) and a dining hall (hall 4). While no specific cooking area has been identified, a large midden of storage vessels, cooking pots, serving bowls, and ash was found immediately southeast of the refectory. As there is no evidence of a permanent cooking area, it is likely that cooking was done in temporary structures surrounding the refectory. Immediately southeast of the refectory was a large reservoir. As will be discussed in later chapters, archaeological survey identified several grinding slicks and mortars cut into the sheetrock surrounding this reservoir. The APDAM research also identified stairs and a path linking the refectory, the reservoir, and several cisterns located on the northern edge of the monastic complex. Slicks and mortars are also found on the steps leading into five additional cisterns located to the southwest of the monastery. These remains demonstrate that the reservoir and cisterns were used in the food processing and other domestic activities in conjunction with the work conducted in the refectory area.

The largest building in the refectory was the dining hall. This large (30 × 12 m) hall was directly connected to the cloister by an elaborate and well-made stone path (see figure 5.3). Upon arriving at the dining hall, the monks could sit around a large U-shaped brick bench for their meals. The bench was one meter across with a gap of 1.8 meters between the two arms of the U. The total length of the bench was roughly

45 meters. The APDAM report states that if people sat around both the interior and exterior of the bench, over two hundred people could be accommodated. This number assumes that each sitting person would require 45 centimeters of sitting space. This is rather tight.

Using an average-sized Indian friend as a guide, I estimated that the knees of a person sitting cross-legged are 60 centimeters apart. Allowing for an additional five centimeters between people sitting around the bench, each person would have required 65 centimeters of space. Using this figure, only 138 monks at a time could have sat around the U-shaped bench. If the interior of the U was reserved for food servers, this number would be reduced to 69 people, give or take. This latter figure is more in line with the presumed monastic population at Thotlakonda, as shown by the number of monastic cells in the cloister.

It is difficult to know who was responsible for cooking, cleaning, and other mundane activities at the monastery. They may have been conducted by the monks themselves, by non-monastic workers, or by some combination of the two. In any case, the refectory was the center of these domestic activities and was intentionally isolated from the rest of Thotlakonda. Subsequent chapters will address this architectural separation in greater detail, based upon information gathered from the survey of the surrounding area.

Architectural Sequence of Thotlakonda

In the original excavations at Thotlakonda, fairly small numbers of artifacts were recovered. Those found include pottery, Roman and Satavahana coins, sculptural pieces in stone and stucco, beads, nails, tiles, and bricks. Seven inscriptions were also found at the monastery. With the exception of the coins and inscriptions, the precise provenience of these remains was generally not specified in the excavation report. However, given the lack of carbon-14 dates, these artifacts provide the best means for dating the occupation of Thotlakonda and determining the sequence in which specific buildings were erected.

Ceramics

Excavations at Thotlakonda by the APDAM (Sastry, Subrahmanyam, and Rao 1992) revealed a wide variety of ceramics. Most of these were fragmentary sherds. Only a few miniature vessels were found whole. The excavators report on 116 sherds in detail (1992, 60–77). Overall, the excavators state that the ceramics consisted of 75 percent Red Ware and 15 percent Red-and-Black Ware, with the remaining 10 percent consisting of Black Ware, Tan Ware, and Gray Ware (1992, 60). Despite poor stratigraphic preservation due to erosion and soil deflation, the excavators developed a two-phase ceramic chronology of the site. This was based upon patterns of association between the ceramics with older and newer portions of the monastery and upon evidence from contemporary archaeological sites with better stratigraphic preservation.

Phase I at Thotlakonda (c. second century B.C.–A.D. first century) yielded Tan Ware, Red Ware, Black Ware, and Black-and-Red Ware. Decorations were generally simple incised grooves. Phase 2 (c. first through third centuries A.D.) is characterized by Red Ware, Black Ware, Rouletted Ware, Gray Ware, and "an inferior variety of Black-and-Red Ware" (Sastry, Subrahmanyam, and Rao 1992, 60). The later Black-and-Red Ware is distinguished by a medium to thick profile and coarser construction. Similar wares were found at numerous sites in north coastal Andhra Pradesh (Sastry 1983). In phase 2 a higher, but still low, percentage of decorated sherds were found. Decorations included appliqué chevrons, finger-impressed chain motifs (see figure 6.21), lotus medallions, and rope motifs.

As noted by the excavators, there was substantial continuity between the two phases, with many wares and forms persisting for the entire period of occupation at Thotlakonda (Sastry, Subrahmanyam, and Rao. 1992, 60). For example, appliqué rope and chain motifs are found in greater numbers in phase 2, but also occur in phase I (Sastry, Subrahmanyam, and Rao 1992, 61). Further, several of the wares assigned to phase 2 are known to occur at other sites on the east coast of the peninsula during the period assigned to phase I. For example, the few sherds of Rouletted Ware are assigned to phase 2 (c. first through third centuries A.D.), but at Arikamedu in Tamil Nadu (Begley 1986, 1988, 1996; Wheeler, Ghosh, and Deva 1946) Rouletted Ware is found in contexts dating as early as 150 B.C.

Many of the wares and lip forms recorded by the APDAM at Thotlakonda resemble those found at other contemporary sites in north coastal Andhra Pradesh and the east coast of the peninsula (see Sastry, Subrahmanyam, and Rao 1992, 61; Sastry 1983). The similarities between these sites include both general vessel forms and specific decorative elements. Of particular importance to my study is the widespread distribution of large storage jars with finger-impressed appliqué bands (see figure 6.21). Similar vessels have been found at Arikamedu (see Begley 1996, 209–11), Sisupalgarh (Lal 1949, plate XLIII), and Salihundam (Subrahmanyam 1964, 80–84). As discussed more extensively below, several sherds from similar vessels were found in the course of my survey beyond the monastery.

In addition to the storage vessels with finger-impressed appliqué bands, other decorative motifs at Thotlakonda are also found in other, contemporary, east coast archaeological sites (see Sastry, Subrahmanyam, and Rao 1992 for a more complete discussion). The report also identifies similarities in the forms of undecorated sherds. Taken together, the ceramics from Thotlakonda Monastery demonstrate that the monks at Thotlakonda were participants in a larger social network spanning the east coast of South India. However, as discussed in chapter 6, it appears that most of the ceramics at Thotlakonda were produced locally. The similarities in ceramic forms and decorations are the product of social contact, not necessarily extensive trade of the ceramics themselves.

Sculpture

The vast majority of the stone sculptural elements at Thotlakonda were made of the local poor-quality khondalite. For this reason, most are fragmentary and illegible, though they do seem to follow the general stylistic conventions of the second or third centuries B.C. through the second or third centuries A.D. Of the relatively intact sculptures, two are carved votive *stupas* (height 1 m). Each was carved in two pieces (drum and *anda*), with a hollow between them to accommodate a small urn. Similar votive *stupas* are found at Buddhist sites throughout South Asia (Schopen 1997, 118). It is likely that these were made to hold cremated remains of devout laity or prominent monks. The presence of these carved votive *stupas* at Thotlakonda will have important implications for subsequent discussions on the nature of *stupa* rituals at Thotlakonda.

Inscriptions

While twelve inscriptions were found at Thotlakonda, only seven fragmentary inscriptions are legible (see table 5.1). Of these, six were found on small *chhatras* (umbrellas) that are likely to have originally stood upon votive *stupas* in the ritual area. The last legible inscription was found on the rim of a large stone bowl, also located within the ritual area. The remaining inscriptions were located on moonstones leading into various *viharas* and are now too abraded to read. All of the inscriptions are fragmentary, providing little information beyond the names of the donors and, at times, the name of a city or town. None record royal donations, nor is it possible to reliably identify the locations of the towns mentioned. The primary value of the inscriptions for archaeological study is that they provide a means to date the occupation of Thotlakonda paleographically. They also demonstrate that lay support for the monastery was derived from at least three different towns.

Coins

A second line of evidence for the date of occupation at Thotlakonda comes from the identification of Roman and Satavahana coins. Of the fourteen coins found at Thotlakonda, five are silver coins issued by the Roman emperor Tiberius (A.D. 14–37); five copper and lead coins were issued by the Satavahana ruler Siriyana (first century A.D.); and four copper coins date to the Satavahana ruler Satakarni (first century B.C.). Dating site occupation from coins is problematic because of

Table 5.1. Inscriptions found at Thotlakonda (texts, translations, and dates from Sastry, Subrahmanyam, and Rao 1992, 84–85)

Inscription	*Text*	*Translation*	*Paleographic Date*
Fragment 1	POYADHI	"One who has gained knowledge of the POYA SUTTA"	3rd–2nd century B.C.
Fragment 2	HASA DANAM CHHATA KOTURU KIRI NIVA SINA	"A resident hailing from a place called Kottura Kiri who made the gift of. . . . "	1st century B.C.–1st century A.D.
Fragment 3	PIJURA HALIKO SILADA	"An agriculturist by the name of Silada of a place called Pijura"	1st century A.D.
Fragment 4	(GA) HA PATI	Name	2nd–3rd century A.D.
Fragment 5	HA PATI NO	Name	2nd–3rd century A.D.
Fragment 6	(SU) KECHI GAHA PA TI DANAM CHATA MALA (THA) PITA BHAGAVATO	"The donation of a string of *chhatras* (umbrellas) to (god) *Bhagavata* that is Buddha"	2nd–3rd century A.D.
Fragment 7	DONA DATTI CHIMAKA CHIKA MAYA 10 DA SA MA DI . . . MATA . . . SENAKA GIRI NI (Vasi) NA - BHA (RI) YA . . . CHINA	"The gift of a dona or trough on the 10th (day?) by the wife of Chikamaya son of Chimaka, the resident of Senakagiri for the longevity of. . . . "	2nd–3rd century A.D.

their inherent value and easy portability. Coins, particularly those that are made of precious metals, are often kept for several generations. Thus, coins can enter the archaeological record many years after they were issued, making later strata appear earlier. For this reason they can only be used to determine the earliest possible date for a particular strata, and then only if care is taken to rule out any post-depositional factors. At Thotlakonda, the precise strata from which the coins were recovered are not recorded in the site reports. It is not known if they rest in the lowest or highest strata. Thus, they cannot be used to date the earliest possible occupation of the site. That said, the dates of the coins do seem to straddle the A.D./B.C. divide, and are likely to have been deposited at that time or shortly thereafter.

Together, the chronological evidence from the inscriptions, sculptural styles, and coins suggests that the site was occupied between 250 years at the minimum and 600 years at the maximum. Of the fourteen coins, ten date to the first century A.D. Of the seven legible inscriptions, six are assigned paleographic dates of the second or third century A.D. Of the remaining two, one lies in the first century A.D., with the other straddling the A.D./B.C. divide by a century. In fact, with the exception of a single fragmentary inscription paleographically dated to the second or third century B.C., there is no evidence for occupation of Thotlakonda prior to the first century B.C. Even if occupation preceded this, it seems likely that the site reached its maximum extent only in the first few centuries A.D.

Bricks

Given that almost all of the dateable materials are portable objects found out of their original context, it is not possible to provide absolute dates for the developmental sequence of construction at Thotlakonda. Rather, only a relative architectural sequence can be constructed based upon changes in brick size among different structures. The construction phases produced, therefore, are of uncertain duration. Excavations revealed bricks of two sizes at Thotlakonda: 54 × 27 × 7 centimeters and 50 × 27 × 7 centimeters. Excavations at *vihara* 8 revealed that originally it had been an apsidal hall constructed of the larger bricks (Sastry, Subrahmanyam, and Rao 1992, 43–46). It was subsequently converted into a *vihara*, using both the larger and smaller bricks. This establishes that larger bricks are earlier, with the smaller bricks used in later periods.

Using brick size alone, it seems that almost all *viharas* and the two larger circular *chaityas* were constructed first, followed by the construction of *vihara* 8 and the main *stupa* (see figure 5.4). Several structures cannot be assigned a phase since they were either not made of brick (i.e., the cisterns and columned hall) or the brick sizes were not recorded in the excavation report (i.e., the apsidal hall, refectory, and votive *stupas*). The APDAM report provides a more specific construction sequence, perhaps based upon information not available in the publication (see figures 5.5, 5.6, and 5.7). In the APDAM sequence, Thotlakonda was established with four small *viharas*, two apsidal *chaityas*, and two circular *chaityas*. While no earlier remains were found below the main *stupa*, the report suggests that a large *stupa* was likely to have been present from the inception of occupation at Thotlakonda. Traces of the earlier *stupa* were completely removed with the construction of the main *stupa* in the late phase.

Both of the apsidal *chaityas* at Thotlakonda show evidence of abandonment. As discussed above, traces of an early apsidal hall were found under *vihara* 8. As *vihara* 8 was constructed of both large and small bricks, it seems likely that the original apsidal hall was disassembled, with the bricks reused in the construction of the *vihara*. This point should be emphasized, as it is possible that other structures may have also been disassembled at Thotlakonda. If late-phase buildings were constructed solely of robbed bricks, they would appear archaeologically as if they were from the early period. For example, *vihara* 4 and *vihara* 3 are similar in both size and number of cells. The excavators suggest that both date to the earliest phase at Thotlakonda. I believe that *vihara* 4 was moved, becoming *vihara* 3. While the

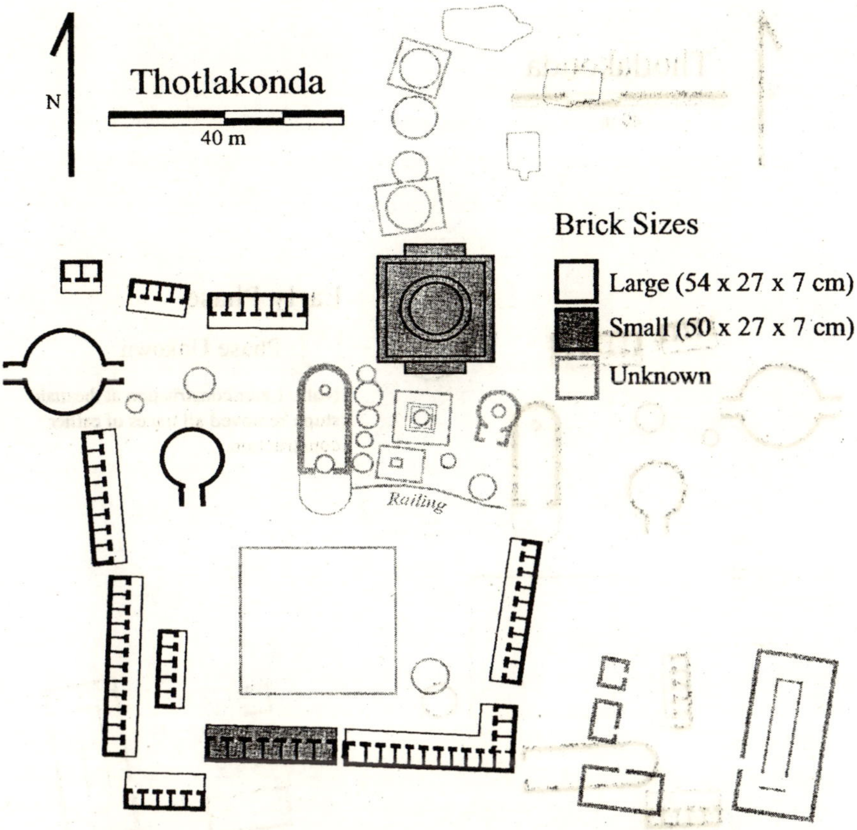

Figure 5.4. The distribution of large and small bricks at Thotlakonda.

foundation of *vihara* 4 remains, the bulk of the bricks were transferred to *vihara* 3. When *vihara* 7 was constructed, *vihara* 4 stood between it and the columned hall. For this reason, *vihara* 4 was disassembled and rebuilt as *vihara* 3. This would partially explain why *vihara* 3 stands outside the line of *viharas* defining the cloister.

The main apsidal hall adjacent to the main *stupa* seems to have been abandoned late in the sequence at Thotlakonda. This is shown by the presence of a votive *stupa* in what would have been the door to the apsidal *chaitya*. Construction of this votive *stupa* required the removal of foundation stones from the apsidal *chaitya*, demonstrating the later date for the votive *stupa*. The later votive *stupa* would have completely blocked access to the *chaitya*. Given this placement, it seems that the *chaitya* must have already collapsed when the votive *stupa* was made, or that access to the *chaitya* was intentionally sealed off while it was still standing. Given the available information, it is not possible to distinguish between the two possibilities.

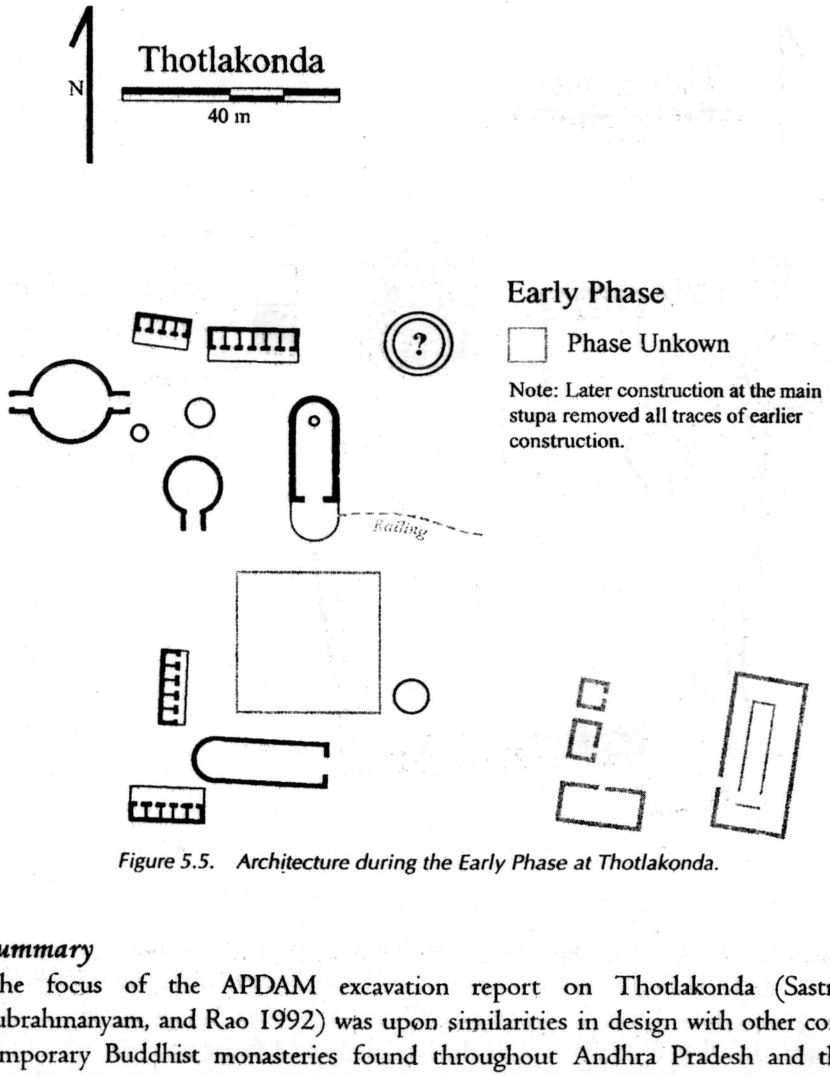

Figure 5.5. Architecture during the Early Phase at Thotlakonda.

Summary

The focus of the APDAM excavation report on Thotlakonda (Sastry, Subrahmanyam, and Rao 1992) was upon similarities in design with other contemporary Buddhist monasteries found throughout Andhra Pradesh and the monastery's place in the textually based narrative of early Buddhism. For example, in discussions of the refectory, the APDAM report (1992, 49–55) cites early Buddhist religious texts that describe the process by which the Buddha determined that a separate dining area was required. In those portions where the report addresses the broader social role of the monastery, it emphasizes its position in long-distance coastal trade (1992, 99–101). This position is supported by the numismatic evidence (1992, 78–84). In terms of the political context, the excavators rely upon the Hathigumpha inscription from Orissa (see chapter 2) that identifies north coastal

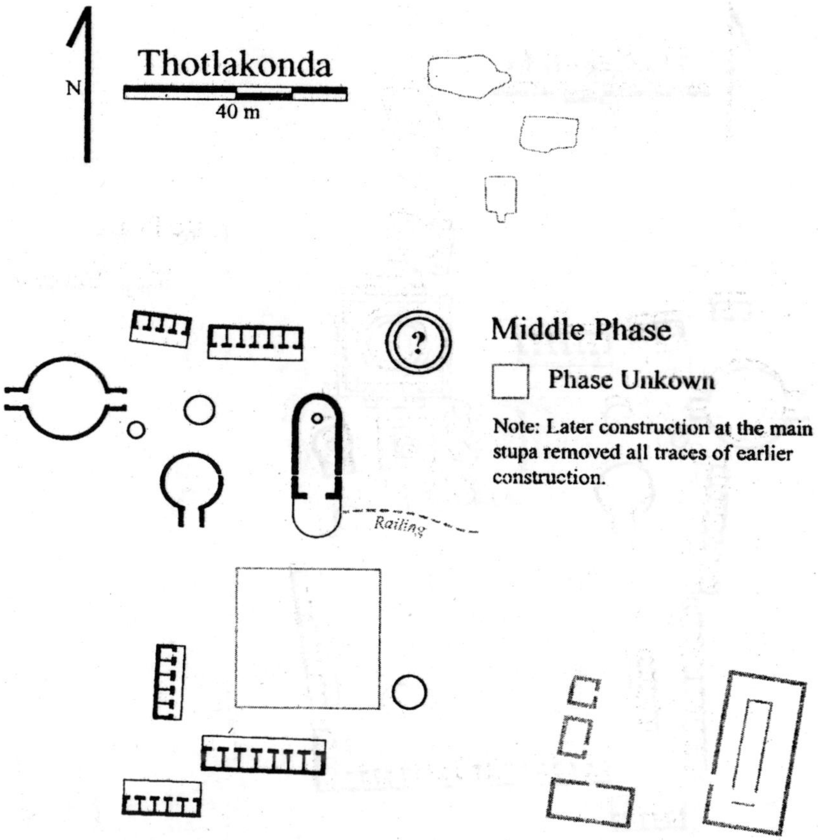

Figure 5.6. Architecture during the Middle Phase at Thotlakonda.

Andhra Pradesh as part of the Kalinga territory in the first or second century B.C., though the degree of control exerted by the Kalinga is not considered to be great. For the most part, Thotlakonda is presented as a retreat, with minimal relations with its immediate hinterland. I will question this view in subsequent chapters on the basis of my survey of the local area. However, if it were not for the high quality of the APDAM excavations and resulting publication, much of my research could not have been accomplished.

Bavikonda

The Buddhist monastery of Bavikonda is located on a hill 2.25 kilometers southwest of Thotlakonda. While a narrow hill lies between the two, both sites are easily visible to one another. Excavations at Bavikonda by the APDAM between 1982

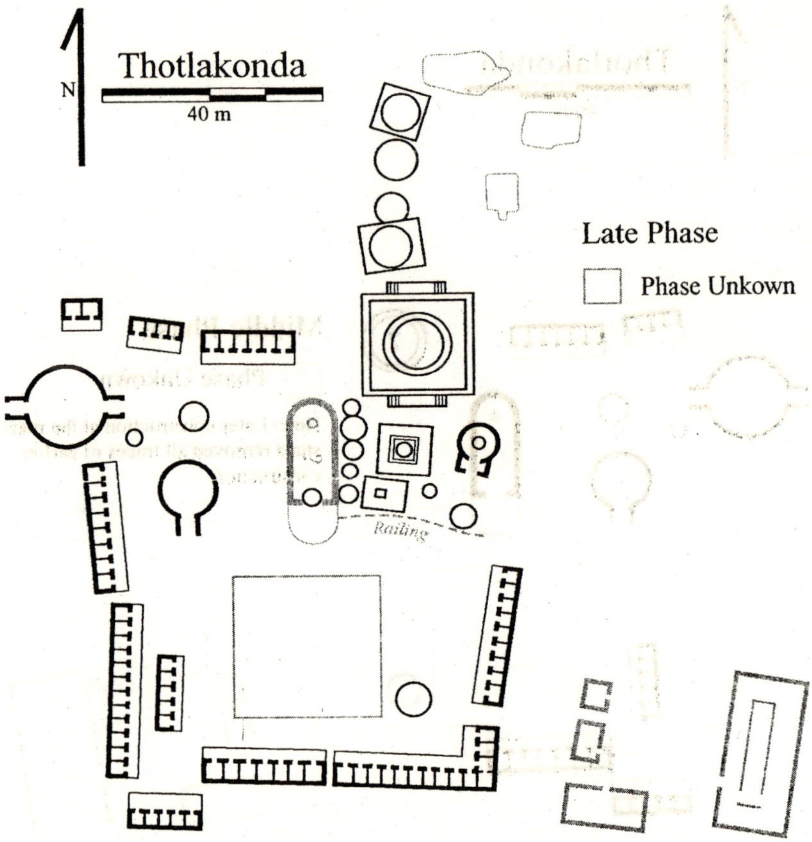

Figure 5.7. Architecture during the Late Phase of Thotlakonda.

and 1987 revealed an Early Historic Period monastery, strikingly similar in plan to the neighboring Thotlakonda (Prasad 1993, 1994). The principal similarity between the two is Bavikonda's division into cloister, refectory, and ritual area (see figure 5.8). Even the spatial arrangement of these divisions mirrors that found at Thotlakonda. Additional similarities in the material remains suggest that Bavikonda was contemporary with Thotlakonda. This is not to say that the sites are identical. A few key differences have important implications for the potential relationships that may have existed between the two complexes. This difference is most apparent in the size, elaboration, and layout of the main *stupas*. The *stupa* at Bavikonda is a large structure, with clearly demarcated and segregated circumambulatory paths. Within the *stupa*, excavations revealed five distinct relic caskets, several of which were made of precious materials. The following discussion is derived almost exclusively from the APDAM excavation reports (Prasad 1994, 1993).

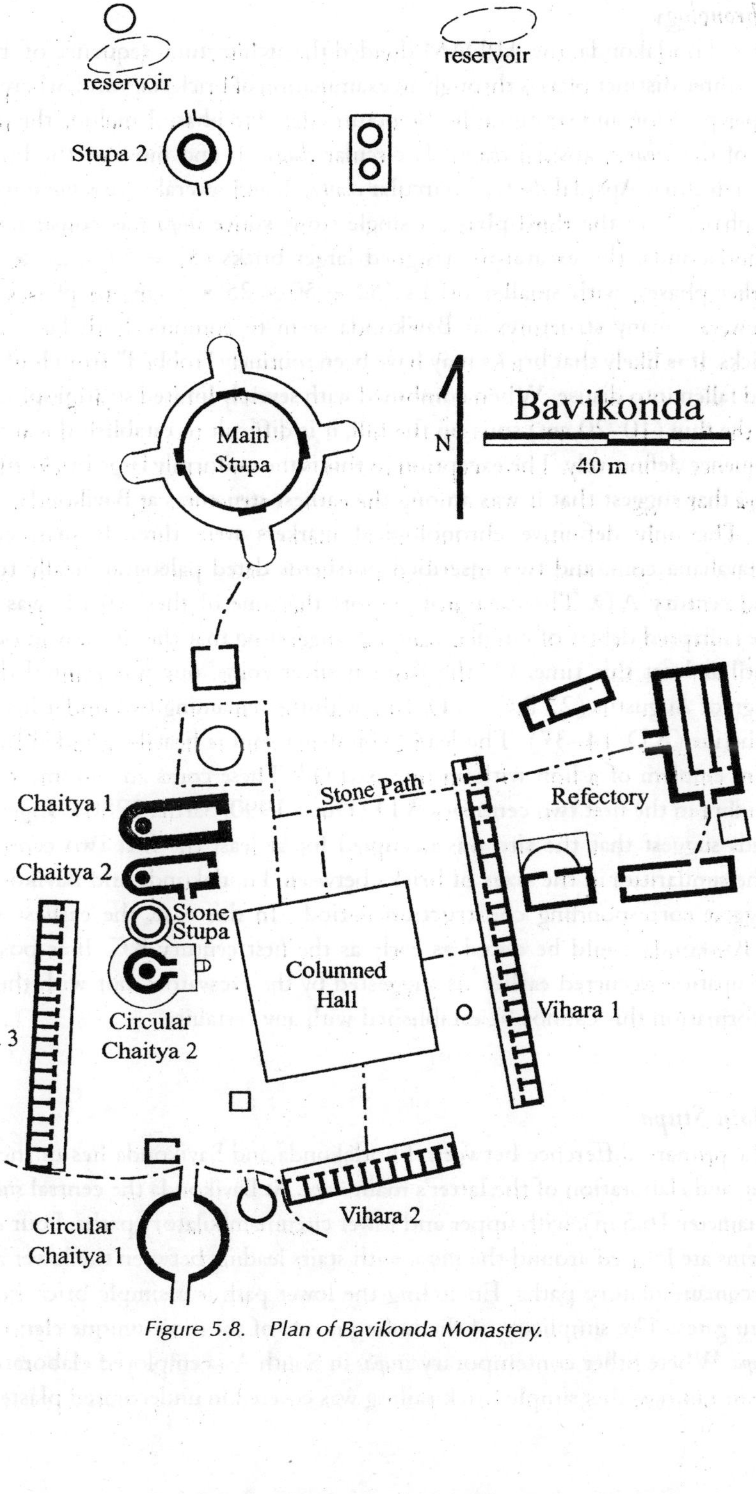

Figure 5.8. Plan of Bavikonda Monastery.

Chronology

As at Thotlakonda, the APDAM divided the architectural sequence of Bavikonda into three distinct phases through an examination of brick sizes and, where available, super-position and stratigraphy. Structures dated to phase 1 include the main *stupa*, all of the *viharas*, apsidal *chaitya* 1, circular *chaitya* 1, and most of the buildings in the refectory. Apsidal *chaitya* 2, circular *chaitya* 2, and several votive *stupas* were added in phase, 2. In the third phase, a single stone votive *stupa* was constructed. As at Thotlakonda, the excavators assigned larger bricks (57 – 54 × 27 × 7 cm) to earlier phases, with smaller bricks (52 – 50 × 25 × 7 cm) to phases 2 and 3. However, many structures at Bavikonda seem to combine both large and small bricks. It is likely that bricks may have been routinely "robbed" from buildings that had fallen into disuse. When combined with severely limited stratigraphic data due to the thin (10–20 cm) soils on the hill, it is difficult to establish the architectural sequence definitively. The exception to this is the uniformly large bricks of the main *stupa* that suggest that it was among the earliest structures at Bavikonda.

The only definitive chronological markers were three Roman coins, one Satavahana coin, and two inscribed potsherds dated paleographically to the second century A.D. The excavators report that one of these sherds was found in the collapsed debris of circular *chaitya* 2, suggesting that the site was in occupation until at least this time. Of the Roman silver coins, one was minted during the reign of Augustus (27 B.C.–A.D. 14), with the remaining two under his successor Tiberius (A.D. 14–37). The lead Satavahana coin is heavily abraded but has the faint emblem of a lion with an upraised tail. These coins are common in coastal Andhra in the first two centuries A.D. (Dutta 1990; Sarma 1980). Together, these finds suggest that the site was occupied for at least the first two centuries A.D. The similarities in the sizes of bricks between Thotlakonda and Bavikonda might suggest corresponding construction periods. In this case, the earliest structures at Bavikonda could be dated as early as the first century B.C. It is possible that occupation occurred earlier, as suggested by the excavators, but with the available information this cannot be established with any certainty.

Main Stupa

The primary difference between Thotlakonda and Bavikonda lies in the size, layout, and elaboration of the latter's main *stupa*. At Bavikonda the central *stupa* is large (diameter 16.5 m), with upper and lower circumambulatory paths. Four *ayaka* platforms are located around the *stupa*, with stairs leading between the lower and upper circumambulatory paths. Encircling the lower path is a simple brick railing with four gates. The simplicity of the railing is one of the more unique elements of the *stupa*. Where other contemporary *stupas* in South Asia employed elaborately carved stone railings, this simple brick railing was covered in undecorated plaster, with its exterior supported by an earthen berm. The *ayaka* platforms are similarly simple. At Amaravati, perhaps the best known *stupa* in Andhra Pradesh, the *ayaka* platforms were topped by five stone pillars. At Bavikonda neither pillars nor postholes for pillars were found. Excavators do report fragments of stucco lotuses in the debris near the *ayaka* platforms.

Excavations along the periphery of the *stupa* revealed relic caskets in each of the four cardinal directions. The caskets consisted of coconut-shaped ceramic urns containing silver and gold relic caskets nested like Russian dolls (see Prasad 1993). In the south there was an additional stone receptacle, similar in design to a votive *stupa*, found below the coconut-shaped reliquary. Nested within the stone receptacle were a coconut-shaped Red Ware urn, a silver relic casket, and a gold relic casket. At the heart of all of the reliquaries were ashes, bone fragments, and beads made of silver, gold, turquoise, and coral. The metal caskets were decorated with alternating, incised swastika and lotus motifs.

At the top of the stone receptacle were highly abraded Brahmi characters reading "POYA." While too abraded to be dated paleographically, the excavators note a similar inscription at Thotlakonda reading "POYADHI," dated paleographically to the second or third centuries B.C. The excavators also note the similarities between earlier megalithic burial traditions of the fourth and third centuries B.C. and Buddhist *stupas*. Given this, the excavators argue that the *stupa* at Bavikonda dates from at least the third century B.C. As discussed in chapter 3, in the Pali Canon Ashoka is credited with redistributing the remains of the Buddha from seven of the eight original *stupas* that housed his remains. Given the quantity of ash in the large, southern casket, the excavators suggest that this may be the "eighth part of the corporeal remains of the Lord Buddha" (Prasad 1993, 11). Whether these are the remains of the Buddha or not, it is sufficient to state that whoever is enshrined within the main *stupa* at Bavikonda was important enough to warrant a large, elaborate memorial. These issues will be revisited in subsequent discussions.

Other Local Archaeological Sites

Several other Buddhist monastic sites have been found within the Visakhapatnam district near Thotlakonda (see figure 5.1). The degree of research conducted at each of these monasteries varies greatly, as does the knowledge of their layout, chronology, and material remains. Here I will briefly summarize what is known of these sites in order to place Thotlakonda in its larger regional context.

Pavuralakonda

Pavuralakonda is located on a hill above the town of Bhimunipatnam, 7.5 kilometers north of Thotlakonda. Since the site is currently being excavated by the APDAM, no reports have been issued thus far. The information provided here is derived from discussions with Dr. B. Subrahmanyam of the APDAM (see also Sastry, Subrahmanyam, and Rao 1992, 10–12). At this time, it appears that Pavuralakonda is similar in date and plan to Thotlakonda and Bavikonda. There appears to be a spatial division into cloister, refectory, and ritual areas. The material remains and architectural forms also appear similar. The most notable features of the site are the large number of rock-cut cisterns. The large number of cisterns may be due to the narrow ridge upon which the monastery is constructed, which limits the potential for any large reservoirs. The ridge may also have forced a different spatial arrangement of the monastery, but confirmation of this must await the publication of the complete site plan by the APDAM.

Its height and position made Pavuralakonda the most visually prominent monastery in the area. From Pavuralakonda, both Thotlakonda and Bavikonda are easily visible across a large alluvial plain. Below Pavuralakonda is the town of Bhimunipatnam. It was here that the Dutch established a trading colony in the seventeenth century. The Dutch were drawn to the area by the presence of a river with excellent anchoring locations that runs along the foot of the hill on which Pavuralakonda is found. During this time, the Dutch built two houses atop the Buddhist remains on the hill above, robbing many of the stones and bricks from the former monastery.

Four inscriptions have been published from Pavuralakonda, one dated paleographically to the third century B.C. and three to the first through the second centuries A.D. (Subrahmanyam 1998). One of the latter documents the gift of a *chhatra,* cistern, and *mandapa* to the monastery from a village named Paula. The others record the names of monks. Several Roman and Satavahana coins were also found at Pavuralakonda.

Dharapalem

Preliminary excavations were conducted by Dr. B. Subrahmanyam in a small valley four kilometers northeast of Simhachalam temple in Visakhapatnam (Subrahmanyam, personal communicaton; Prasad 1994). Excavations revealed a possible Buddhist *stupa* and a stone sculpture of a five-hooded *naga* (cobra). Subrahmanyam also reports other, unexcavated, brick structures in the same area. It appears that this may be yet another Early Historic Period Buddhist monastery.

Sankaram

Located forty-five kilometers southwest of Thotlakonda, the Buddhist monastery of Sankaram was built on two stone outcrops rising above a large alluvial plain (Mitra 1971; Rea 1907–1908, 1–10). Unlike the monasteries discussed so far, Sankaram is located twenty-one kilometers inland. More striking is the radically different architectural layout and construction style. Much of the architecture at Sankaram is carved out of stone, with brick used only to fill in gaps. Almost all of the monastic buildings lie on the eastern outcrop, with the western outcrop reserved for several hundred rock-cut votive *stupas.* On the southern side of the eastern outcrop are four rock-cut caves. The largest has images of the Buddha carved above its entrance and a rock-cut *stupa* within its square, columned interior. Three rock-cut cells were carved in other portions of the outcrop. Two contain figures of the Buddha, but the last contains ninth-century images of Shiva and Ganesha.

An apsidal hall and large *stupa* are located at the pinnacle of the outcrop, the bases of both carved from the outcrop at identical heights. The bases of the structures are rock-cut, with the superstructures constructed of brick. Flanking the apsidal hall were two rows of *viharas.* Several rock-cut votive *stupas* also dot the hill. Over two hundred similar rock-cut votive *stupas* were carved on the western outcrop along with two small cells. One of these cells contains its own small, rock-cut votive *stupa.* The overall effect of the western outcrop is a jumble of votive *stupas* cut into almost every available piece of stone. They seem almost to be stacked, one upon the other, in a dense forest of *stupas.* The largest rock-cut *stupa* is almost ten meters high, with the smallest only thirty or forty centimeters.

In my visits to the site, I found dense concentrations of sherds in a small orchard at the base of the hills. These may suggest occupation in this area, or they may be middens created by the monks dumping refuse from the outcrops above. At the time the monastery was occupied, a small river flowed past the base of the hills. Based upon material remains and sculptural styles, the main occupation of the site seems to have occurred in the third to fifth centuries A.D., though initial occupation may have preceded this by a few centuries. The images of Shiva and Ganesha attest to use of the site until the ninth century, but not solely by Buddhists.

Other Early Historic Period Archaeological Sites in North Coastal Andhra Pradesh

Beyond the immediate vicinity of Visakhapatnam lie several other Buddhist monasteries and a few contemporary non-monastic settlements. Locations and summaries are provided in figure 5.1 and table 5.2, in lieu of detailed discussion. It should be noted that the information summarized in these tables comes from a wide variety of sources, and the quality and detail of the reports is highly variable. For this reason, the dates of occupation listed in table 5.2 should be treated as tentative. As shown above, even those sites that have been well excavated and reported still cannot be unproblematically assigned dates of occupation. In sites that were excavated early in the last century, insufficiently reported, or both, the dates are even less certain.

Table 5.2. Prominent Early Historic Period archaeological sites in north coastal Andhra Pradesh

Site	*Date*	*Description*	*References*
Gopalapatnam	1st–5th c. A.D.	A Buddhist monastery located on several terraces of a hill. Architectural remains include *viharas*, votive *stupas*, cisterns, and a main *stupa* at the pinnacle of the hill. Material remains include numerous sculptural fragments and early historic pottery.	Sastry [et al.] 1992,12–14; IAR 1990–1991, 2; IAR 1991–1992, 3; IAR 1993–1994, 5
Kottur	2nd c. B.C.– 2nd c. A.D.	A hilltop monastic complex with a *stupa* and *viharas*. A single inscription dates paleographically to the 2nd c. B.C. It lies on the left bank of the river Sarada near Elamanchili.	Subrahmanyam 1998,114; IAR 1953–1954
Lingarajupalem	1st–5th c. A.D.	This Buddhist monastery is located on a low hill adjacent to a good anchoring location at a small stream. Excavations by Rea revealed brick structures and sculptural fragments. These fragments include images of the Buddha as well as lotus wheel motifs. One Satavahana lead coin and two silver roman coins (Augustus and Tiberius) were also found.	Prasad 1994, 7–8; Rea 1907–1908; IAR 1959–1960
Pithapuram	Early Historic Period	Mound with brick structures, Rouletted Ware and Red-and-Black Ware.	IAR 1961–1962

Continued

Table 5.2. (*Continued*)

Site	*Date*	*Description*	*References*
Adurru	Early Historic Period	The site consists of a *stupa* (d. 17 feet) and the remains of a monastery. The *Stupa* has both a raised drum and *ayaka* platforms.	IAR 1985–1986, 1
Rajahmundry	2nd or 4th–18th c. A.D.	Limited excavations revealed a *stupa* and one wall of a brick monastery, Red Ware, and Arretine Ware. Later levels revealed Hindu bronzes and, later still, cannonballs.	IAR 1979–1980, 1
Timmavaram	2nd c. B.C.– 1st c. A.D.	This site was completely destroyed by brick robbing. It appears to be a monastery with a large *stupa.* Relic caskets found during brick robbing date to the 2nd c. B.C.–1st c. A.D.	Subrahmanyam 1999
Kodavalli	2nd or 3rd c. A.D.	The site consists of four cisterns, several *stupas,* and brick *viharas* on a low hill above a lagoon on the Bay of Bengal. One inscription is dated to A.D. 210.	Subrahmanyam 1988
Ramatirtham	1st or 2nd–9th c. A.D.	This monastery is built on the narrow ledge of a cliff face. The site contains several apsidal halls, a large main *stupa,* two lines of *viharas,* a large cistern, and several smaller structures. One inscription is dated paleographically to the 2nd c. B.C. A standing figure of the Buddha, similar in style to those found at Amaravati, was found. Jain images from the 8th–9th centuries are the latest dateable finds.	Mitra 1971; Rea 1907–1908

Continued

Table 5.2. ***(Continued)***

Site	*Date*	*Description*	*References*
Salihundam	2nd–6th c. A.D.	Located on a prominent hill overlooking the Vamsadhara River, the site consists of a monastery with several religious structures. At the peak of the hill lies a large circular *chaitya*. Less prominent structures include *stupas*, circular and apsidal *chaityas*, and several votive *stupas*. Later images show evidence of Vajrayana Buddhism. Limited remains of earlier brick structures and Rouletted Ware may hint at earlier occupation of the site. Numerous inscriptions date to between the 2nd and 6th c. A.D.	R. Subrahmanyam 1964; Mitra 1971
Kalingapatnam	c. 1st c. A.D.	Excavations revealed a large (d. 85 feet) *stupa* with *ayaka* platforms. The *stupa* is well constructed in a wheel format. Early Historic material remains were found in the area.	IAR 1958–1959, 68; IAR 1976–1977, 10; IAR 1977–1978, 14; IAR 1979–1980, 11
Mukhalingam	1st c. B.C.–9th c. A.D.	Adjacent to a modern Hindu temple of the same name, several brick structures, Early Historic pottery, and one Satavahana coin have been found. Several fragments of 9th c. Buddha images were also found.	Sarma et al. 2000; IAR 1957–1958: 64; IAR 1961–1962: 3
Dantapuram	3rd c. B.C.–2nd c. A.D.	This fortified settlement lies on the right bank of the River Vamsadhara. The settlement is surrounded by a mud rampart 60 feet wide and 35 feet high. A variety of Early Historic ceramics and other material remains were noted.	Sarma et al. 2000; IAR 1993–1994, 5

I have omitted references to sites that are either reported in name only or were not reported in sufficient detail.

Little is known of the archaeological landscape of north coastal Andhra Pradesh prior to the Early Historic Period. Earlier sites have been identified in explorations of the Visakhapatnam and Srikakulam districts by students from Andhra University in Visakhapatnam (IAR 1983–1984, 5–9). The explorations in Srikakulam focused on the upper portions of the Vamsadhara and Nagavali rivers, identifying thirteen sites. Descriptions of the sites are limited, but material remains include flaked and ground stone tools, carnelian beads, and simple Red Ware pottery, some of which has incised patterns. An Iron Age urn burial was found at one site, with possible megaliths at another.

Exploration in the Visakhapatnam district revealed twenty-four Iron Age sites. The material finds were broadly similar to those in Srikakulam. One site, Paradesipalem, contained an urn burial, a "cist-like burial," and rectangular and square stone alignments (IAR 1983–1984, 7). Two Iron Age sites, Rishikonda and Vadapelam, lie only six kilometers south of Thotlakonda. Unfortunately, the specific material remains of these sites are not reported. Given the paucity of information on the Iron Age in north coastal Andhra Pradesh, it is not possible to characterize the nature of Iron Age habitation in the area. However, these reports do demonstrate that the Early Historic Period occupation in the area surrounding Thotlakonda was preceded by Iron Age communities. The relationships between the two must await further research.

Local Historical Information

Earlier, I discussed the broader history of the east coast of India. It was shown that several different states claimed north coastal Andhra Pradesh as part of their territory at different times. The Hathigumpha inscription of the first or second century B.C. claims that Kharavela ruled a territory extending as far south as the mouth of the Krishna River (Das 1977; Sahu 2000). Likewise, the *Puranas* and inscriptions at the Buddhist monastic site of Nasik record that the Satavahanas ruled over the Kalinga sometime from the second century B.C. through the second century A.D. If this was the case, north coastal Andhra Pradesh would also have been under Satavahana control at this time. As discussed in chapter 2, north coastal Andhra Pradesh appears to have been a contested territory between the Satavahanas and Kalingas. It is likely that control of the area was often weak—and often shifting. Ideally, archaeological and epigraphic evidence from north coastal Andhra Pradesh could be used to identify these shifts in power more precisely. However, no strong evidence for either Satavahana or Kalinga political control is found at any of the Buddhist monasteries of the region.

Of all the Early Historic Buddhist monasteries found in north coastal Andhra Pradesh, only one, Ramatirtham, has an inscription that *may* record a royal donation. No other monastery has indications of royal favor or sponsorship from either the Satavahanas or Kalingas. As for the inscription at Ramatirtham, it records the name of a king (Siri Sivamaka Vijaya) and is found on a clay sealing (Subrahmanyam 1998). The legend of the sealing is dated paleographically to the second century B.C. The same name is also found in one inscription at Amaravati, though it is not clear that both inscriptions refer to the same person. In either case, this king is not prominent in either the Kalinga or Satavahana dynastic lists. Given that the inscription is on a clay sealing (an impression in clay used to mark goods for trade), it is not even certain if he comes from north coastal Andhra Pradesh, the Krishna Valley, or somewhere else entirely.

The presence of Satavahana coins at Thotlakonda, Bavikonda, and most other Buddhist monasteries in north coastal Andhra Pradesh has been cited by AP-DAM researchers as evidence for Satavahana domination of the area (Sastry, Subrahmanyam, and Rao 1992; Prasad 1994). Given coins' value and portability, it does not seem that a few stray coins can be used to clearly determine political sovereignty. In sum, there is only limited local evidence for either Kalinga or Satavahana rule over the area. This does not mean that one or the other did not periodically gain control; it only means that political control is not recorded in the existing epigraphic and archaeological evidence. It may be more valuable to view north coastal Andhra Pradesh as a border area—a region the armies and merchants of two rival states were forced to cross to reach the heartland of the other.

Conclusion

Taken together, the archaeological and environmental context of Thotlakonda suggests that while Buddhism and Buddhist monasteries flourished, political control of the area was weak during the Early Historic Period. The monasteries of north coastal Andhra Pradesh operated in a fluid political context. Similarly, there is no epigraphic evidence for donations by guilds. The location of several monasteries directly above the Bay of Bengal (i.e., Thotlakonda, Pavuralakonda, Bavikonda, Gopalapatnam, etc.) suggests that they may have been engaged in coastal trade, but the numerous inland sites (i.e., Sankaram, Salihundam, Ramatirtham, etc.) call this into question. Further, it appears (see table 5.2) that it was the inland sites that survived the Early Historic Period, some developing into either Hindu (e.g., Sankaram) or Jain (e.g., Ramatirtham) centers. In contrast, the coastal sites seem, for the most part, to date between the first century B.C. and the third century A.D. The apparent abandonment of the coastal sites stands in marked contrast to the expansion of long-distance trade with Southeast Asia that began in the second and third centuries A.D.

All of the Buddhist monasteries in north coastal Andhra Pradesh are built on hills, for several possible reasons. First, hilltop locations would have protected monasteries from cyclone-induced flooding. However, religious/ideological factors should not be discounted. The placement of Buddhist monasteries on hilltops is a common feature throughout South Asia. Shaw (1999) has examined the hilltop placement of Buddhist monuments at Sanchi in Madhya Pradesh in terms of the visual and symbolic prominence these positions would have provided. While I generally agree with this line of inquiry, many of the monasteries in Andhra Pradesh were not visible below the hills upon which they stood. Understandings of the underlying ideological reasons for the placement of hilltop monasteries requires a greater attention to the specific topography of the hills on which they are located and the social contexts in which they operated.

The APDAM research in north coastal Andhra Pradesh documented a high concentration of Buddhist monasteries in the Visakhapatnam area. As will be discussed in greater detail in subsequent chapters, during survey I identified a small (three hectares) settlement near Thotlakonda. While small, it is the only non-monastic settlement known in the immediate vicinity of Thotlakonda. What is missing at this time is any large Early Historic Period settlement. It seems likely, due to the high density of monasteries in the area, that some larger, non-monastic settlements must have also existed. Such settlements may be located under the modern cities of Visakhapatnam and Bhimunipatnam or, perhaps, in locations still accessible archaeologically.

Given the lack of evidence for financial support of the monasteries from either guilds or royalty in the area, understanding the relationships between the monasteries and local populations becomes critical. This is the focus of the remainder of this book.

Beyond the Monastery Walls

6

In chapter 4, I discussed recent perspectives on the study of archaeological landscapes. Here I review the method and theory underlying archaeological survey and summarize the results of my survey in the area surrounding Thotlakonda (see also Fogelin 2003b, 2003c, 2004, in press a). While the methodology of archaeological survey developed well before many of the recent theoretical approaches concerning landscape, it is nonetheless well suited to these concerns. In this chapter, I provide little analysis of the sites that I describe. Subsequent chapters will use the data presented here to address the broader social role of Thotlakonda Monastery. I conclude this chapter with a brief discussion of the pottery sherds collected in the course of survey. Several analyses performed on the ceramics provided critical insights into understanding the role of Thotlakonda in its broader social landscape. This chapter is not intended as an exhaustive presentation of the results of the Northeast Andhra Monastic Survey (NEAMS). Rather, it is intended to introduce only those elements that are critical for subsequent chapters. More complete discussions of this research can be found in Fogelin (2003c), including several appendices that provide almost all of the primary data on which the analyses are based.

The modern techniques of archaeological survey began to be formulated in the 1950s and 1960s. Given that all human societies exist in areas larger than any single site, the goal of archaeological survey is to identify the spatial relationships between sites within a geographic region and how those relationships changed over time. Underlying this is the assumption that spatial relationships can serve as a basis for inferences on the social relationships within and between past societies. Early surveys were conducted in a variety of archaeological settings, beginning in coastal Peru (Willey 1953), spreading to the Near East (Adams 1965, 1981; Wright and Johnson 1975), Mesoamerica (Sanders, Parsons, and Santley 1979; Blanton 1982), and the southwestern United States (Powell 1983; F. Plog 1974). Similar approaches were also independently developed in Europe and the Mediterranean

(Cherry, Davis, and Mantzourani 1991; Jameson, Runnels, and Van Andel 1994; Renfrew and Wagstaff 1982; see Ammerman 1981 and Bintliff 1991). Given this heavy reliance upon archaeological survey, a large body of literature has emerged concerning assorted methods and difficulties in its practice.

The Method and Theory of Archaeological Survey

While the modern practice of archaeological survey began in the 1950s, in the most general sense, survey has been a part of archaeology for as long as archaeologists have searched for the remains of ancient societies (see Cherry 1982 for discussion of the development of survey techniques). Exploration of this sort took many forms. In some cases, archaeologists traveled to an area and inquired in local villages about archaeological remains (village-to-village survey). At other times, archaeologists searched areas they felt had the greatest chance of yielding archaeological remains. Thus, if sites were known to occur on low hills above floodplains, archaeologists searched similar hills. These forms of exploration are still practiced, and still valuable, today. Particularly in areas that have limited prior research, exploration allows for some sense of the archaeological setting to be evaluated relatively quickly and cheaply.

Systematic archaeological survey was developed to address several problems with these earlier forms of exploration. In village-to-village surveys, for the most part, only those archaeological sites that are large or distinct enough to be recognized by someone untrained in archaeology are found. When searching only environments known to have sites, archaeologists tend to find sites similar to ones already known. The methods developed in the 1950s and 1960s were intended to reduce these biases by making exploration more systematic and more thorough. In a sense, the difference between systematic survey and exploration is the same as between archaeological excavation and simply digging up a site. The greater precision of systematic survey allows for more information to be recovered but, like careful excavation, it is much slower and allows for less area to be examined.

Survey Methodology

Systematic survey involves a small group of people lining up at specified intervals and walking across a landscape, recording all archaeological remains as they come across them (see figure 6.1). Using compasses, tape measures, GPS units, aerial photographs, and a good map, an area is systematically searched in an attempt to remove some of the grosser biases of earlier methods of exploration. Maps are carefully drawn to record the areas searched and not searched. While not strictly necessary, there is usually an attempt to cover areas where sites are expected, as well as those where they are not. In theory, these techniques allow for archaeologists to

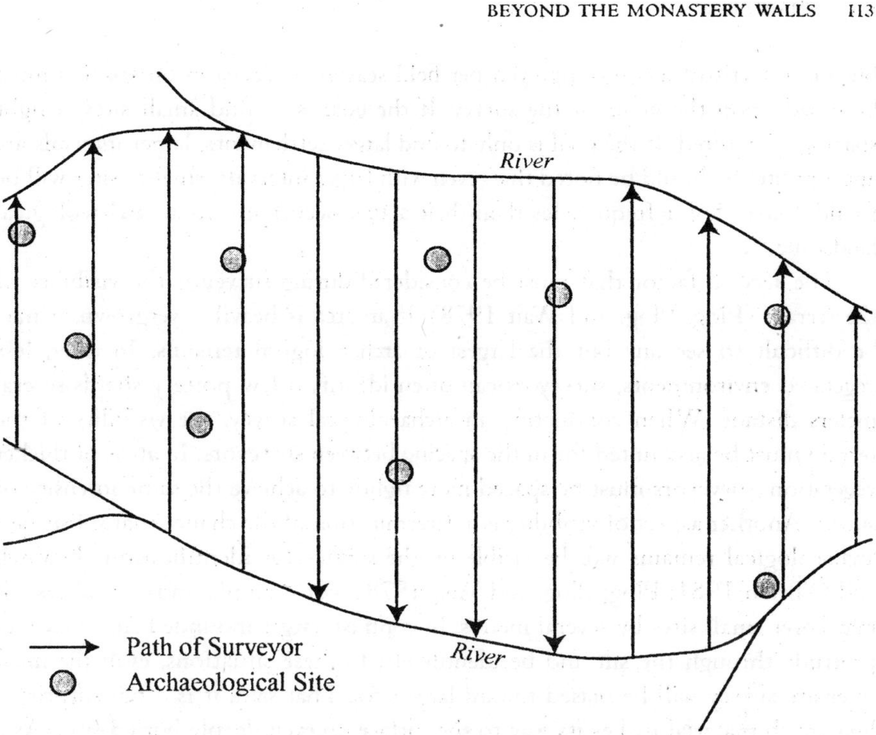

Figure 6.1. A schematic diagram of the method of archaeological survey.

identify sites themselves (overcoming the biases of village-to-village survey) in both expected and unexpected areas (overcoming the biases of only searching certain environmental contexts). In practice, with the adoption of systematic survey came a whole new set of methodological questions and concerns.

Since the 1960s, a large number of articles and edited books have focused on the methodologies of archaeological survey (e.g., Ammerman 1981; Plog, Plog, and Wait 1978; Dunnell and Dancey 1983; Fish and Kowalewski 1990; Sullivan 1998; Lewarch and O'Brian 1981). Several factors of critical importance to the practice of systematic archaeological survey have been identified. For the most part, these factors concern the implications of research design, environmental condition, and field methodologies on the identification of archaeological remains. Here I address three recurrent issues that most directly concern the field methodologies used in the survey at Thotlakonda—spacing, visibility, and crew training.

The first factor affecting the survey methodology is the spacing between surveyors (Plog, Plog, and Wait 1978). If surveyors are spaced tightly (e.g., 5 m apart), it is more likely that very small archaeological remains will be found, but tight spacing also decreases the total area surveyed in a single field season. As the interval between surveyors increases (e.g., 100 m) fewer small sites are encountered, but more territory can be surveyed per field season. A decision on spacing must be based upon the goals of the survey. If the goal is to find small sites, a tight spacing is required. If the goal is only to find larger settlements, larger intervals are appropriate. It should be noted that, even with larger intervals, smaller sites will be found, but in lower frequencies than their actual occurrence in an archaeological landscape.

The second factor that must be considered during survey is the visibility of the terrain (Plog, Plog, and Wait 1978). If an area is heavily overgrown, it may be difficult to see any but the largest of archaeological remains. In drier, less vegetated environments, surveyors can often identify a few pottery sherds several meters distant. When conducting an archaeological survey, the visibility of the terrain must be accounted for in the spacing between surveyors. In areas of thicker vegetation, surveyors must be spaced more tightly to achieve the same intensity of survey. Another aspect of visibility is a determination of the chance that subsurface archaeological remains will be visible on the surface for identification (Lewarch and O'Brian 1981; Plog, Plog, and Wait 1978). For example, in river valleys silt may cover small sites by several meters. In contrast, larger mounded sites may still protrude through the silt and be identifiable. In these situations, even the most intensive survey will be biased toward large sites. That said, it is often surprising how much material makes its way to the surface on even deeply buried sites. As a general rule, it is useful to do some survey of even the most unpromising areas, if only to establish that they are unsuitable for surface survey methodologies.

Another factor, somewhat related to visibility, is crew training. For sites to be identified, all crew members must be familiar with the types of remains in the area in which survey is conducted. Given varied knowledge of an area, different crew members identify sites differentially. To some degree, this bias can be addressed through careful training prior to the start of survey. Nevertheless, differential ability is never eliminated completely. Some surveyors are better at site identification than others. Even with extensive training, some variation will remain. There is no substitute for years of survey experience. Having spent time working with some "old hands" at survey, I have always been amazed by their ability to recognize archaeological features from what seems little more than a jumble of surface debris.

Intensive and Extensive Surveys

A final question that must be addressed in any survey is the area to be covered. The most important factor in this decision is the geographic dimension of the research question. If, for example, the goal of the survey is to investigate a regional site network, the survey must attempt to cover the entire network, or at least some representative sample of it. In either case, the survey area would likely need to be geographically extensive. In contrast, if the goal of the survey is to identify the peripheral and/or ephemeral sites associated with a single large site, the area surveyed might be substantially smaller. However, the smaller size and more subtle archaeological signature of these sites might require a greater intensity of survey through tighter spacing. The result may be that a more intensive survey of a smaller area would take the same amount of time as an extensive survey with less intensity.

Intensive survey of a large area is expensive, time-consuming, and labor intensive. It is often impossible, given the resources available to an archaeologist. Rather than attempting "full coverage" of a survey area, archaeologists have developed several sampling strategies for these situations (Fish and Kowalewski 1990; Plog, Plog, and Wait 1978; Nance 1983; Read 1986). Common to all of these strategies is the intensive survey of some sample of the survey area with the goal of adequately representing the whole. The most simple of these strategies divides an area into units and randomly selects some proportion of those units for survey. More elaborate systems divide the survey area into smaller discrete zones (e.g., by topography or other environmental factors, visibility, or the likelihood of finding sites) and then randomly select units within each (see Nance 1983; Read 1986). This eliminates the possibility that purely random selection will miss the full variation that exists within a survey area. Any of these methods allows for the relative frequency of sites in the entire survey area to be predicted. For example, if 25 percent of an area is surveyed, and twenty-five sites are found through random sampling, it should be expected that one hundred sites would be found if the entire area had been surveyed at the same intensity.

Archaeological surveys that employ sampling have one large drawback. Only those sites within the sampled areas are firmly located. The precise locations of predicted sites are unknown. Sampling is effective for providing the frequency of sites within a region, but does not fully illuminate the spatial relations between sites (Kintigh 1990). In studies such as my own, where identifying spatial relations across the entire survey area is central to the research goals, sampling is not effective. For this reason I employed "full coverage" survey, but from the outset it must be noted that no survey ever attains full coverage (Cowgill 1990; Lewarch and O'Brian 1981). No matter what strategies are employed, some sites will be missed, some areas unexamined. For example, a wide spacing between surveyors will, in effect, create its own sample of the survey area with some proportion of smaller sites passing unnoticed between surveyors.

Non-Site Survey

A concern in any survey project is what to record, and how to record it. This question has been subsumed under what are often called non-sites or non-site survey.

Two somewhat separate concerns fall under these general terms. The first involves very small or natural features and their value in understanding an archaeological landscape (Thomas 1975; Plog, Plog, and Wait 1978). The second is a broader concern with the nature of artifact scatters and the definition of a "site" (Dunnell and Dancey 1983; Foley 1981). In both cases, discussions typically focus on the identification of artifact scatters (dense concentrations of artifacts), though they are applicable to the identification of other features as well.

In many surveys, the identification of a site is determined by specified concentrations of artifacts (e.g., five pottery sherds per m^2). Thus, when searching an archaeological landscape, only those areas with ceramic concentrations higher than this are recorded. This establishes a systematic bias toward denser ceramic scatters. It also presumes that sites with fewer artifacts than this do not warrant full investigation. Given that some sites typically have very low artifact densities (e.g., butchering sites or agricultural fields), this can cause a systematic removal of sites that may be central to the archaeological questions being investigated. If, for example, subsistence patterns are the focus of research, the omission of butchering sites and agricultural features would adversely impact any conclusions drawn from the survey. The converse problem is that if every minor concentration of artifacts is recorded, the time spent on survey would dramatically increase. A balance must be made between these two extremes. Artifact density can serve as a guide, but it should not act as a limit. As stated by Plog, Plog, and Wait (1978, 389),

> Such a definition should never be absolute. On the one hand, it should be tied to the notion of interpretability in the specific context in which the survey is being conducted. On the other hand, it should be regarded by each member of every survey crew as a standard about which arguments are to occur and judgments are to resolve. The occurrence of such arguments and the focusing of such judgments are the most important effects of quantitative definitions of sites.

With a recent emphasis on meaning in the study of landscapes, many researchers have begun to address the problem of natural spaces (e.g., Bradley 2000; Tilley 1994; Shaw 2002). Unmodified large promontories, caves, or other landscape features may have had important meaning within past societies, just as they do today. The challenge is that, without evidence for human modification or the presence of artifacts, it is often difficult to state if a particular landscape feature had a significant meaning for people in the past. Solutions for this are usually highly contextual. Archaeological sites may be situated so that a certain landscape feature is consistently visible. In other cases, certain types of features may commonly show evidence of human modification, and it is assumed that others in similar contexts do as well. Finally, the modern inhabitants of an area may be asked about natural features. The social significance of the features is then postulated for previous societies in the region. None of these approaches is without problems, but given the highly contextual nature of the arguments, they can only be evaluated as the claims are made, within the specific contexts in which they are found.

In addition to these more practical concerns over site identification, there is a broader concern over the "site concept." Dunnell and Dancey (1983; see also Foley 1981) have suggested that the "site concept" is detrimental to archaeological study. As stated earlier, archaeological material is usually scattered across a landscape in pockets of greater density, with areas of lesser density between them. The "site concept," they argue, creates artificial boundaries unrelated to the real distribution of artifacts across a landscape. In Dunnell and Dancey's view, an archaeological landscape is best understood as "a more or less continuous distribution of artifacts over the land surface with highly variable density characteristics" (1983, 272). The arbitrary assignment of sites to certain concentrations obscures the variability in artifact distributions that Dunnell and Dancey see as the appropriate focus of archaeological inquiry.

The practical implication of this view is that areas between clusters of archaeological material must be systematically recorded in the same manner as the concentrations more typically recorded. This is accomplished either by collecting all artifacts within precisely measured units systematically placed across an entire landscape or by recording the specific position of every artifact encountered. Both of these approaches dramatically increase the amount of time and labor required to complete a survey. In areas with few artifacts, these strategies may be useful. In archaeological landscapes with large numbers of artifacts and features, such as the area surrounding Thotlakonda, this degree of precision is prohibitive.

While I sympathize with Dunnell and Dancey's criticisms of the site concept, I continue to use the term "site" in my analyses, for several reasons. First, as discussed in chapter 4, modern landscape theory differentiates between the dual concepts of space and place. Just as people understand some indistinct spaces today as discrete places despite the lack of definitive spatial boundaries (e.g., Los Angeles), it is likely that people in the past also created places from indistinct spaces. This does not mean that the recognition of past places is necessarily obvious or easy. As place is a culturally constructed ideological concept, the identification of places must be inferred from a wide variety of contextually specific material indicators. It is unlikely that these indicators can be adequately interpreted from concentrations of archaeological remains as they are encountered in the field.

I do not claim that any of the sites I have recorded during survey are necessarily discrete locations in either the present or the past. A site in my survey is no more than a record-keeping unit. A site is a collection of features and artifacts that I have chosen to record together. Most often, sites were determined by the area that could most effectively be mapped. If a large patch of thorns made it difficult to map two sections of what appeared to be a single concentration, I created two separate sites. At other times, a feature very close to a site was missed during the initial documentation. Later these features were recorded as independent sites. It was only later, during the analysis phase of the project, that I grouped sites based upon a presumed affiliation as places. For example, five sites (NEAMS 101, 102, 122, 123, and 134) recorded in the field were shown later to be part of a single, continuous, ceramic scatter. Through analyses of the location of the scatter and characteristics of the ceramics it contained, I labeled these five sites as one place—a 3-hectare, non-monastic settlement. In this way, the term "site" has two meanings. The first is a heuristic category used to group archaeological materials recorded during survey. The second meaning is a socially meaningful place within a landscape.

Summary

The preceding discussion was intended to highlight some of the difficulties and biases inherent in systematic survey. Throughout the discussion, I have stressed the importance of considering the specific research questions in devising an appropriate field methodology. No single methodology can accommodate the variety of possible research questions, field conditions, and project resources. While it is important for methodologies to be explicitly conceived and documented, it is also important to remain flexible in their application. In subsequent portions of this chapter, I will detail the methodologies used in my own survey. First, however, I will review other surveys conducted in South Asia.

Archaeological Survey in South Asia

Exploration and reconnaissance have been major parts of South Asian archaeology for at least a century and continue to be the primary method for finding archaeological sites to this day. In the last twenty years, several systematic surveys have been conducted throughout South Asia. Several surveys focusing on Harappan sites have been completed or are currently in progress (Possehl 1980; Mughal 1982; see also Khan, Knox, and Thomas 2000 for a recent survey in northwest Pakistan). In the Gangetic Plain, surveys have focused on Early Historic Period settlements (Lal 1984; Erdosy 1988; Chakrabarti 2001a). The most intensive survey to date in India was conducted at the city of Vijayanagara (14th–16th century) in southern India (Sinopoli and Morrison 1992 and in prep.; Morrison 1995a). More recently, Shaw (1999, 2000, 2002; Shaw and Sutcliffe 2001) completed a survey at the Buddhist pilgrimage site of Sanchi. While the methodologies of these surveys differ, with widely varied intensities, all have aided in developing regional archaeological syntheses. Given the similarities to my own research, Shaw's field methodologies warrant further discussion.

Shaw's "village-to-village" survey focused upon 750 square kilometers surrounding the Early Historic Period Buddhist monastery and *stupa* at Sanchi in central India (Shaw 2002). In this area she found the remains of Buddhist monasteries, Buddhist sculptural elements, settlements, and reservoirs, as well other archaeological sites ranging from the Chalcolithic to the Late Medieval (Shaw 2000). The questions orienting her research, like mine, concerned the broader social relationships that existed between the monastic and non-monastic communities in the Early Historic Period. In the course of her survey, Shaw identified several large reservoirs at the bases of hills where Buddhist monasteries are found (Shaw and Sutcliffe 2001). Based upon analyses of these reservoirs, she has argued that, in contrast to the modern emphasis on wheat in the area, the reservoirs she identified were intended to irrigate rice.

The Northeast Andhra Monastic Survey: Field Methods

The field methods of my project were heavily influenced by the Vijayanagara Metropolitan Survey directed by Carla M. Sinopoli and Kathleen D. Morrison (Sinopoli and Morrison 1992 and in prep.; Morrison 1995a). This methodology is intensive, with 20-meter intervals between surveyors and the careful documentation of small sites (what many would label non-sites). The primary difference was my decision to conduct a "full coverage" survey (Fish and Kowalewski 1990; Cowgill 1990). The decision was based upon the goals of my research, where spatial patterning between sites was among the central concerns (Kintigh 1990).

Systematic survey was conducted on the hill on which Thotlakonda is found and on floodplains to the north and south. In addition, two adjacent hills were explored unsystematically. The purpose of the explorations was to gain a quick understanding of the archaeological potential of each. Most sites were left unrecorded. While some patterns noticed during the exploration have proven useful to understanding the distribution of sites in the survey area, time did not permit more intensive survey of them.

Survey Methodology

Throughout most of the survey area, I employed a 20-meter spacing between surveyors. This spacing was chosen to allow for the identification of a high proportion of small sites (with a 20-meter interval, 50 percent of sites visible at 5 meters would be identified). In some areas of denser vegetation, this strict spacing had to be abandoned (see figure 6.2). In these cases, a looser 20-meter spacing was attempted, with surveyors doing the best they could, given their situation. The areas where this occurred were carefully recorded on field maps. It should be expected that a higher percentage of archaeological materials were missed in these areas. This is in part

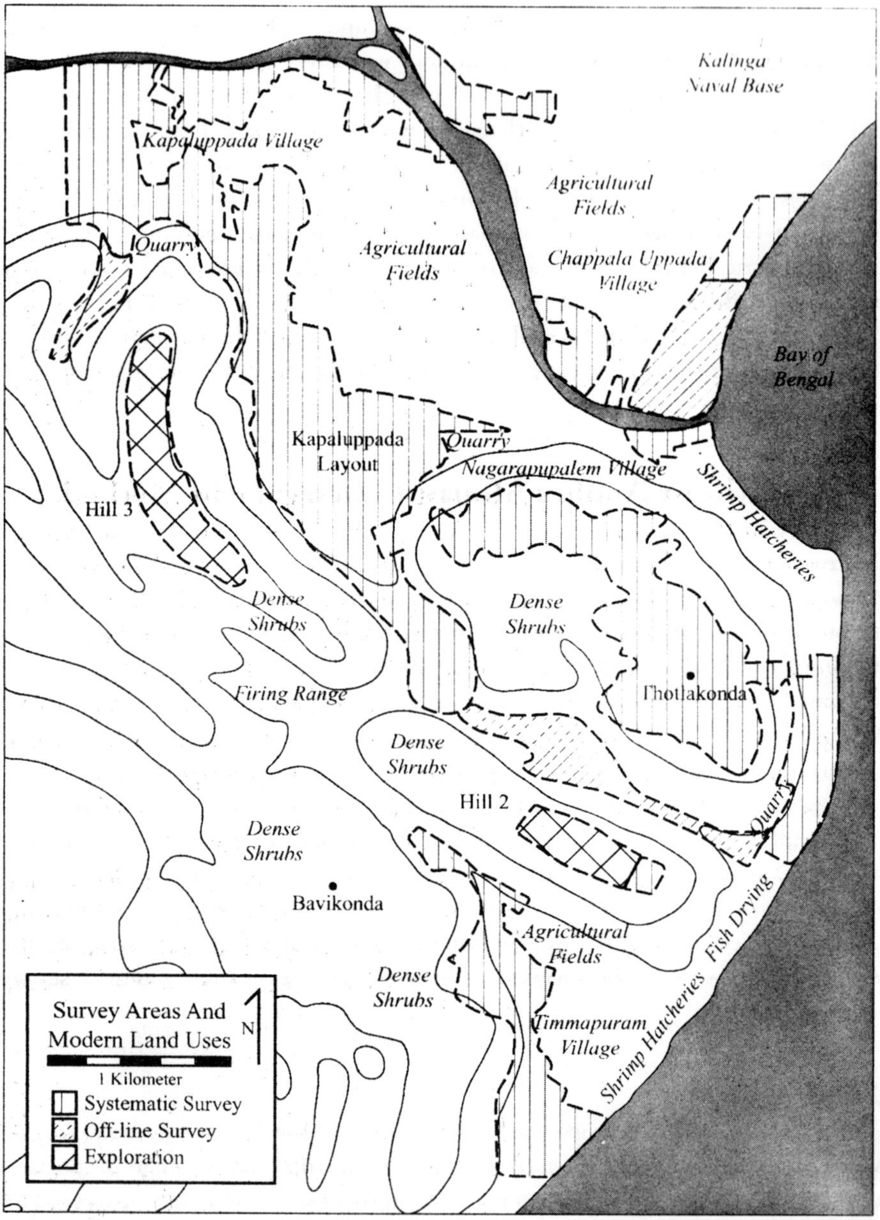

Figure 6.2. Areas surveyed and modern land uses in the region surrounding Thotlakonda Monastery.

due to the irregular spacing between surveyors, as well as the dense vegetation that almost certainly concealed some features. Other portions of the research area were not surveyed due to the presence of thick vegetation, modern villages, steep hill slopes, active agricultural fields, or other modern constructions (see figure 6.2).

The number of people surveying at any one time ranged between one and five. For most of the survey, I had one full-time assistant. At other times, graduate students in history and archaeology from Jawaharlal Nehru University and Deccan College worked with me. Each new crew member received two days of training in the use of a compass and site identification prior to starting survey.

As sites were found, the entire survey team would gather to document the site and make artifact collections. Each site was numbered sequentially according to the order in which it was recorded (e.g., NEAMS 1, NEAMS 2, etc.). Field forms were employed to maintain consistency in the documentation between sites. For each site, the location, environmental setting, and modern features were recorded. Portions of the site form also detailed potential disruptions to the site through erosion or modern disturbance. A section of the site form recorded the nature of the artifact scatter and the methods used in its collection. The most important portion of the site form was a prose description of all of the archaeological features present and preliminary thoughts on their significance. This section was also used to expand on information from other portions of the site form and for observations that did not fit neatly into any of the existing categories.

The latitude and longitude of each site was recorded using a handheld Garmin eTrex GPS unit. The accuracy reported by the unit was typically +/− 7 to 8 meters. The GPS unit was also used to record the boundaries of the survey area. Field maps were drawn of more complex sites. These were done with a compass and pacing from a site datum, recorded with the GPS. The accuracy of a pacing varies by distance but, for the average site, was likely to have been roughly 50 centimeters to one meter. This means that the mapping accuracy within sites is higher than between them.

Artifact Collections

A flexible strategy was employed for the collection of artifacts. For the most part, collections were made in 2 × 2 m collection units laid in a grid across an artifact scatter. The interval between collection units varied depending upon artifact density and site size. Collection units were extended slightly beyond the point where visible artifact densities began to dwindle. All ceramic scatters with a density of more than five sherds per square meter were collected. Scatters of lower density were collected if the concentration was higher than the surrounding area. For example, in areas otherwise devoid of artifacts, scatters with only a few sherds per square meter were collected. In many instances, the grid laid across the site failed to place a collection unit on particularly dense areas of sherds. In these situations, additional units (judgment units) were opportunistically placed in specific locations. This allowed for collection of these units separately from the systematic units. Collections were completed by gathering diagnostic sherds (e.g., decorated sherds, rims, bases, and other interesting artifacts) from across the site. These were collected to maximize the assemblage of dateable material.

At several sites, dense vegetation or other difficulties prevented the use of a collection grid. In these situations, judgment units were placed opportunistically where possible. An attempt was made to sample the entire scatter, but I recognize the limitations of these collection units in terms of statistical analysis. At sites with only a few artifacts (typically far less than one artifact per square meter), a 100 percent sweep was performed. Here, the area within five meters of all archaeological features was searched, and all artifacts collected.

The Survey Area

Permits allowed for survey up to five kilometers from Thotlakonda Monastery. With the exception of the northwestern corner of the survey area, at no point did the survey area extend this far (see figure 6.2). The survey area was defined by a combination of geographic features and modern constructions. The northern periphery of the survey was determined by an Indian naval base. Survey within or even close to the base was not possible. On the east, the survey area was defined by the Bay of Bengal. The southern extent of the survey area was defined by a low hill running from the Buddhist site of Bavikonda to the ocean. To the west, survey was bounded by another hill. The area encompassed has a large degree of variation in environment, topography, and modern land use. All had profound impacts on the locations in which survey was conducted. Within this area, a total of 7.3 square kilometers was intensively surveyed and a further 0.6 square kilometer was explored unsystematically.

With the exception of the two hilltops that were explored unsystematically, all of the terrain that could be systematically surveyed, was. The areas remaining were inaccessible for a variety of reasons. Several modern villages were located within the survey area. Along the coast were several aquaculture farms, with very large pools for raising shrimp. In addition, large portions of the survey area were under rice cultivation or other crops. While fallow agricultural fields were examined, those that were intensively irrigated or recently planted were not. In addition to these modern land uses, there were also tracts that were inaccessible for other reasons. Large areas were covered in dense thorny shrubs. While attempts were made to investigate them as far as possible, in many areas the thorns were too thick to allow movement, let alone the identification of archaeological remains. Steep hillsides were also, for the most part, omitted from survey; dense vegetation, steep slopes, and the presence of numerous loose boulders made survey in these areas hazardous. In some locations, hillsides were less systematically explored, but no sites were found.

Within the areas systematically surveyed were a variety of environmental conditions and modern land uses. Each of these had an impact on the ability to survey and identify archaeological remains. In general, the hilltop on which Thotlakonda is found is covered in grasses with patches of thorny shrubs. Some of the denser patches could easily have concealed additional small sites. Another difficulty was the presence of large fields of loose boulders. These boulder fields made the identification of sites problematic. Given that most of the archaeological remains were constructed of unmodified boulders, the high density of naturally occurring boulders created numerous stone alignments and piles of boulders that could easily be misidentified as walls or cairns. On the hilltops the primary difficulty was establishing which of these concentrations or alignments were natural versus those that were modified through human action.

All of the hills in the Thotlakonda area had extensive evidence of erosion and soil deflation. The area immediately surrounding Thotlakonda also had been heavily disturbed by modern construction as part of the Andhra Pradesh Department of Tourism's development of Thotlakonda into a historic monument. Several roads, parking areas, and a drink kiosk were erected around the monastery. During their construction, it can be assumed that significant numbers of sites were destroyed. Finally, the main reservoir at Thotlakonda was refurbished by the Department of Tourism, significantly damaging and concealing the original reservoir.

Survey below Thotlakonda Hill had a different set of problems. Most of the surveyable area was regularly plowed. It can be expected that architectural remains were destroyed and artifact scatters were altered by plowing. One large area to the west of Thotlakonda Hill had recently been developed for a new housing community. The Kapulauppada Layout is divided into discrete housing plots by asphalt roads. In the process of building these roads, the entire area was cleared of vegetation and bulldozed. The result was heavy disturbance to the ground surface, but the construction work also revealed a large area that would most likely have been unsurveyable because of thick vegetation. While damaging archaeological sites, the construction was more a benefit than a hindrance in terms of survey.

With the exception of a single ceramic scatter (NEAMS 132) in the floodplain, all of the sites found during survey were located either on top of hills or at their bases. There are two possible explanations for this. The first is that this is a genuine archaeological pattern—that sites were rarely located in the floodplains of the region. Perhaps floodplains were reserved, as they are today, for agricultural fields. The second possibility is that archaeological remains have been buried by years of silt deposition and are no longer visible on the surface. The single site found on the floodplain was located near a modern well, suggesting that older material may have been redistributed on the modern ground surface during its construction. Without a systematic, subsurface survey of the floodplain, this question cannot be answered at this time.

Summary

Throughout the survey area there were varied environmental and modern land-use conditions. Survey and site documentation were adjusted to accommodate this diversity throughout the course of the survey. The methodologies employed were designed to address my research questions within the specific contexts of the local area surrounding Thotlakonda Monastery. The consistent goal was to isolate archaeological remains from modern and natural features. There are no blanket rules that apply to all types of sites to reliably identify those that are archaeologically significant. Different types of remains required different criteria to identify them. In the remainder of this chapter, I will summarize the archaeological features found by the Northeast Andhra Monastic Survey and the criteria used to identify them. In most cases, identification was made in the field, based upon a fixed set of criteria. In some cases, subsequent analysis has called into question these identifications. In general, I rely upon my field judgments, when I had the feature in front of me and could balance all of the criteria most effectively. I have only reversed my field identifications in those situations where it is clear that a mistake was made in the initial documentation.

Survey Results

Altogether, 134 archaeological sites containing 328 individual archaeological features were identified in the Northeast Andhra Monastic Survey (see figure 6.3). The most common archaeological remains encountered, by far, were small cairns constructed of unmodified boulders (see figure 6.4). It is likely that these cairns were erected as funerary memorials for local monks and laity. Other sites recorded include walls, reservoirs, cisterns, mortars, postholes in flat sheetrock, a few potential structures, stone columns, ceramic scatters, and a *stupa*. Each of these will be addressed below.

Cairns

A total of 231 cairns were identified in the course of the Northeast Andhra Monastic Survey. Cairns consisted of small piles of unmodified stones, ranging between 50 centimeters and 12 meters in diameter. The highest were several meters, with the most heavily eroded only 15–20 centimeters. Identification of the cairns was made difficult by the presence of numerous recent stone piles and natural concentrations of loose boulders. Early in the survey it became apparent that, as in the Leskernick Hill project (Tilley et al. 2000, see chapter 4), specific criteria

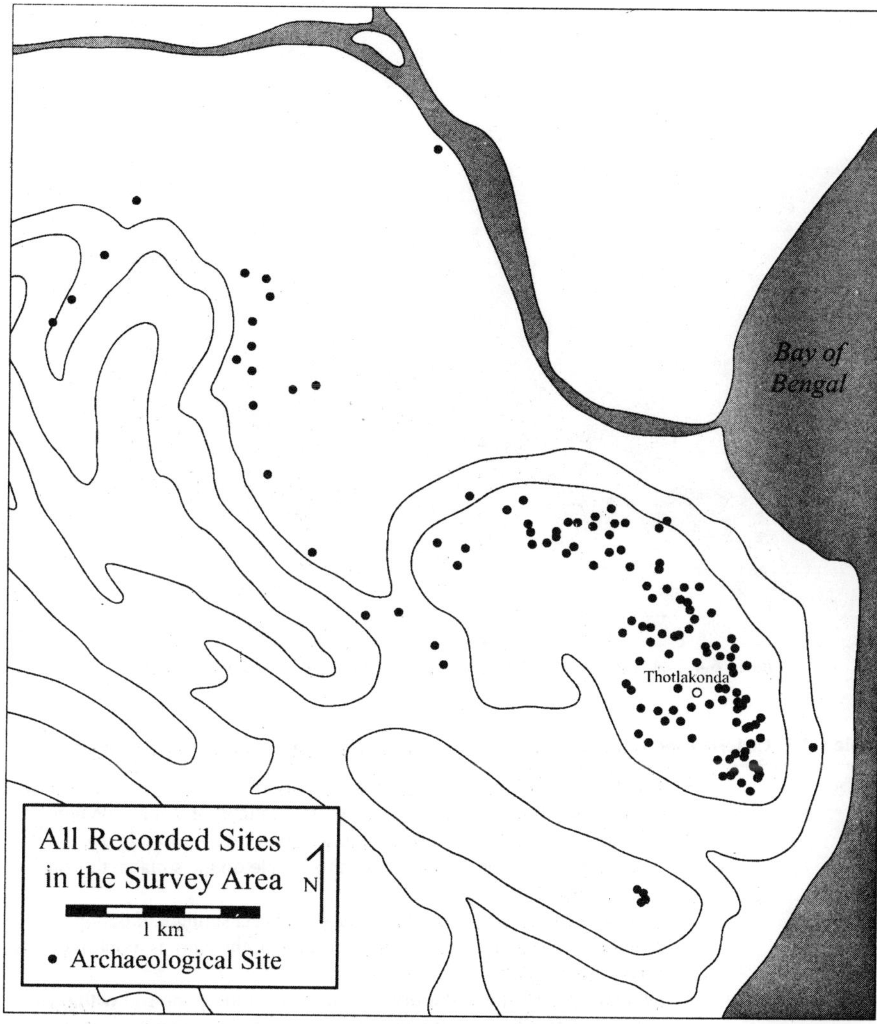

Figure 6.3. All archaeological sites recorded during the Northeast Andhra Monastic Survey.

were needed to differentiate modern, natural, and archaeological cairns (see also Schiffer 1983). I present these criteria in table 6.1.

The main goal of the criteria was to prevent misidentification of recent cairns as old. In the last twenty years, Thotlakonda's excavation and development as a historic site has created many piles of debris that appear similar to cairns. Otherwise, it does not appear that significant occupation or disturbance has occurred on Thotlakonda Hill since the monastery was abandoned. By eliminating the cairns constructed in the last twenty years, it should be possible to record only those constructed in the Early Historic Period. Table 6.1 lists the criteria used to identify cairns during

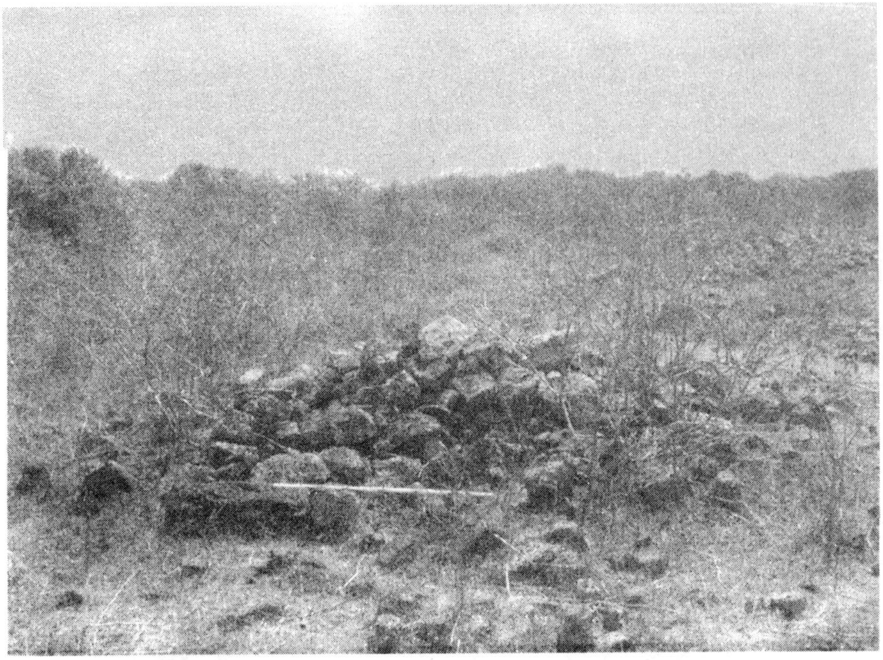

Figure 6.4. A well-preserved cairn (scale-bar in photograph is 1 meter).

Table 6.1. Criteria used to identify cairns during the Northeast Andhra Monastic Survey

Color	The local stone changes from red to dark black/gray over time. Those faces that have not been exposed to sunlight remain red. When identifying a cairn, all of the stones should be uniformly dark on exposed surfaces. If red stones are visible on the surface, the cairn is modern or disturbed.
Lichen	Lichen is found on surfaces exposed to direct sunlight. If lichen is facing downward or away from the light, the cairn is modern or has been disturbed.
Soil development	Old cairns trap dirt and debris. Thus, if a cairn has no soil within its cracks, it is likely to have been constructed recently. Exceptions are cairns found on sloping sheetrock. The flow of water through the base of the cairns, in some cases, may have served to continually cleanse the cairn of accumulated debris.
Plant growth	With soil come plants. The more vegetation a cairn has, particularly slow-growing shrubs, the more likely it is more than ten or twenty years old.
Stacked stones	There are many areas of increased stone density in the survey area. For these to be considered cairns, they should be reasonably discrete and, most importantly, have stones stacked upon each other. Stone densities can be natural, but stones do not stack themselves. However, a few stacked stones are not sufficient to identify a cairn. Cairns consist of piles of eight or more stones.

survey. The first four criteria were used to determine if a cairn was archaeological or recent, with the last used to determine if it was a natural concentration of stones.

The single most important gauge for the age of cairns is the color of the boulders used to construct them. The stone on Thotlakonda Hill changes from red to dark black/gray with exposure to sunlight. On the northern side of Thotlakonda lies a Survey of India marker. As shown in a 1936 map of the area, this marker was erected in the 1920s or early 1930s by British survey teams while mapping the east coast of India. The marker consists of a small cement obelisk erected atop a large cairn. The stones of this cairn have significantly darkened, but they still retain a slight reddish color. This demonstrates that it takes roughly a century for the local stone to darken once a fresh face has been exposed to sunlight. Thus, any cairn with red stones was either constructed or disturbed in the last century. With the exception of color, none of the other criteria are sufficient by themselves to identify a cairn as modern. In practice, identification was based on a judgment using all of the criteria, with deficiencies in one or more not necessarily indicating the cairn was constructed in the last twenty years.

Of the 231 cairns identified using these criteria, 197 were located on Thotlakonda Hill (see figure 6.5). The surrounding hills were also dotted with numerous cairns, with twenty-three recorded on Hill 2 and four on Hill 3. Both hills have significantly more cairns than were recorded. Below Thotlakonda Hill were seven more cairns, five in the Kapulauppada Layout and two in a small valley on the north of Hill 3. Cairns ranged between 50 centimeters and 12 meters in diameter, with an average diameter of 2.5 meters. Seventy-five percent of the 197 cairns found on Thotlakonda Hill were located in positions with a view of the monastery. In contrast, unsystematic exploration of Hills 2 and 3 demonstrated that almost all of the cairns on these hills were located in positions where the monastery could be seen. This pattern was most clear on Hill 3. On the side of the hill facing the monastery, approximately seventy-five cairns were found during unsystematic exploration. On the side facing away from Thotlakonda, not a single cairn was found. Together, these cairns comprise a large mortuary landscape. The patterns of association and visibility of cairns will be explored at greater length in chapter 8.

Walls and Terraces

After cairns, the most common features recorded during field research were walls. Thirty-three walls and terraces were recorded in the course of the survey. Perhaps more so than in any of the other features discussed here, there was a great deal of variation in the forms of the different walls recorded. Many were single or double-coursed lines of unmodified boulders. Walls of this sort were used in structures and for small terraces. In other cases the walls were long lines of rubble, with

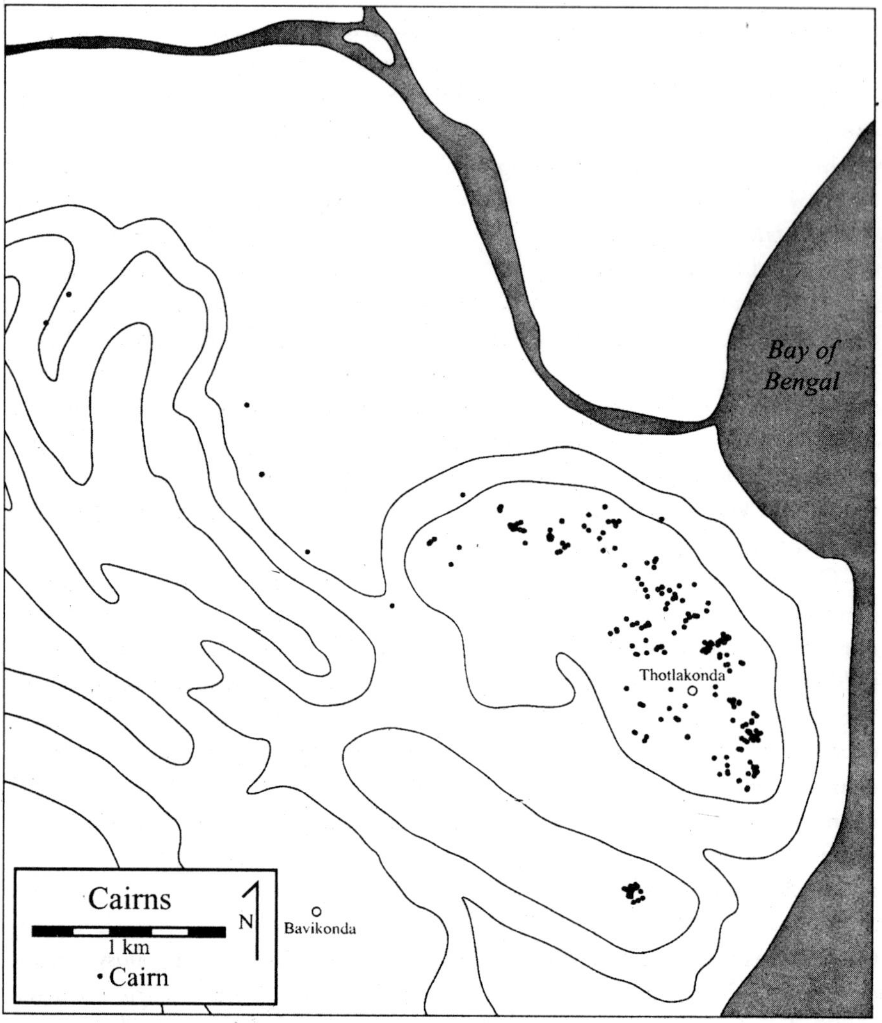

Figure 6.5. Map of cairns found during the Northeast Andhra Monastic Survey.

no clear coursing. Throughout the survey area, numerous walls ran perpendicular to the slopes of hills. Some retained sediments creating terraces; others did not. It is difficult to discuss walls in isolation from the other archaeological features found during survey. Rather than discuss them here, I will incorporate them into discussions of other archaeological features as they apply.

The identification of walls had many of the same difficulties as cairns. In the case of rubble walls, all of the criteria used for cairns were applied. For walls with coursing, these criteria were used in conjunction with an analysis of the number of stones in alignment. In many archaeological projects a wall is defined as an alignment of three or four stones. As stated earlier, Thotlakonda Hill is covered in dense boulder fields. Within these fields, alignments of three or four stones are common and natural. In these contexts only alignments of seven or eight stones were recorded. Where the boulder density was lighter, fewer stones could reliably indicate a wall. Thus, the criteria used for the identification of walls were flexible, accommodating the environmental context of the area in which a wall was found. The goal was to limit the misidentification of naturally occurring stone alignments. However, given these criteria, it is likely that more heavily eroded or fragmentary walls were missed.

Stupa

On the northern rim of Thotlakonda Hill I found a single *stupa* (NEAMS 110). As discussed in the introduction, cairns and *stupas* are differentiated by the presence of circumambulatory paths and/or a *chhatra.* This site had evidence for both. It is possible that several of the largest cairns (those larger than 10 meters in diameter) identified during survey were *stupas* as well. However, none of those larger cairns were associated with either a path or *chhatra.* The remains of the *stupa* consisted of a large pile of unmodified boulders surrounded by two circular walls (see figure 6.6).

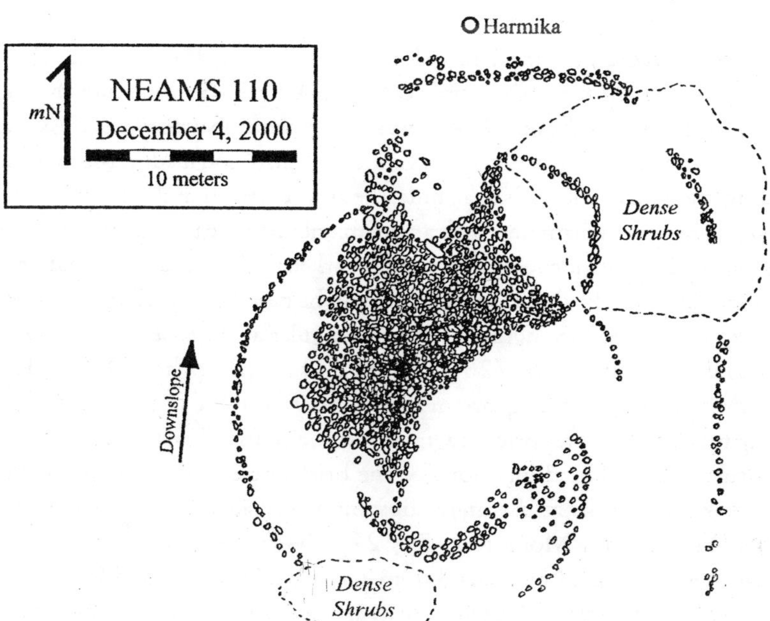

Figure 6.6. Plan of NEAMS 110, a stupa *on the northern rim of Thotlakonda Hill.*

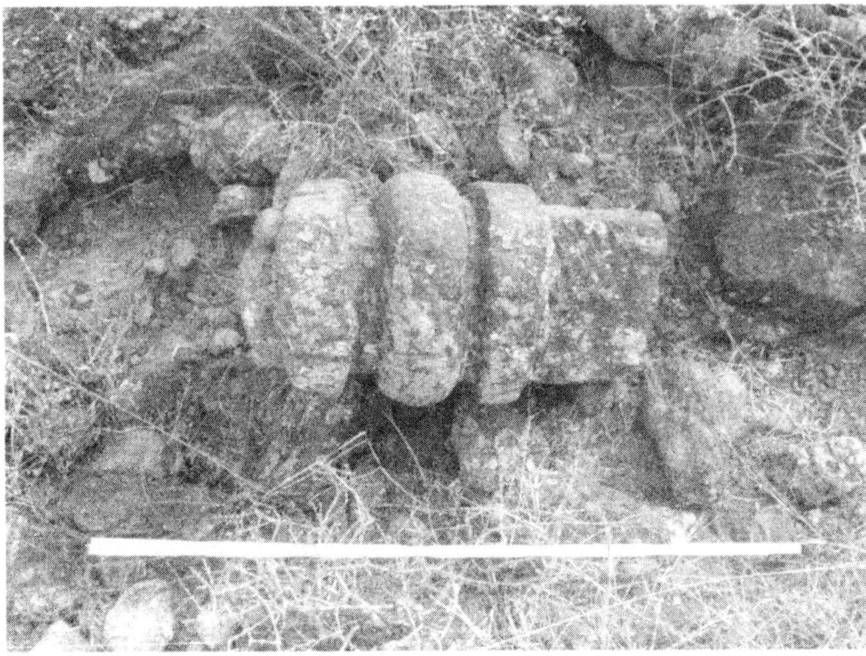

Figure 6.7. The chhatra *found at NEAMS 110 (scale-bar in photograph is one meter).*

The site was located on a moderate slope and is eroding down the hill. The *chhatra* was found several meters below the central rubble pile. Surrounding the *stupa* are two concentric walls that may have defined a circumambulatory path. As with the rubble pile, they were constructed of unmodified small and medium-sized boulders.

Using the concentric walls as a guide, the *anda* (central tumuli) might have been as much as 18 meters in diameter, with a circumambulatory path four meters wide. It is also possible that the inner concentric wall marked the base of a drum that originally held a smaller *anda*. In this case, the *anda* might have been, perhaps, 15 meters in diameter. The *chhatra* (see figure 6.7) is rectangular at the base (45 × 28 cm) and tapers to a square at the top (26 × 26 cm). The total height is 60 cm. The base of the *chhatra* consists of a square molding. Above this are two rounded moldings creating the comb. Several brick fragments were also found on the southeastern side of the rubble pile. The dimensions of the bricks were 7 × 10 × >20 cm. This would make the bricks at this *stupa* substantially smaller than the bricks typically found at Thotlakonda Monastery (7 × 27 × 54 cm and 6 × 26 × 50 cm).

This *stupa* is located over one kilometer from Thotlakonda Monastery, overlooking a non-monastic settlement (see figure 6.8). The *stupa* is also close to a cluster of cisterns, columns, and cairns. It is possible that this *stupa* is part of a subsidiary

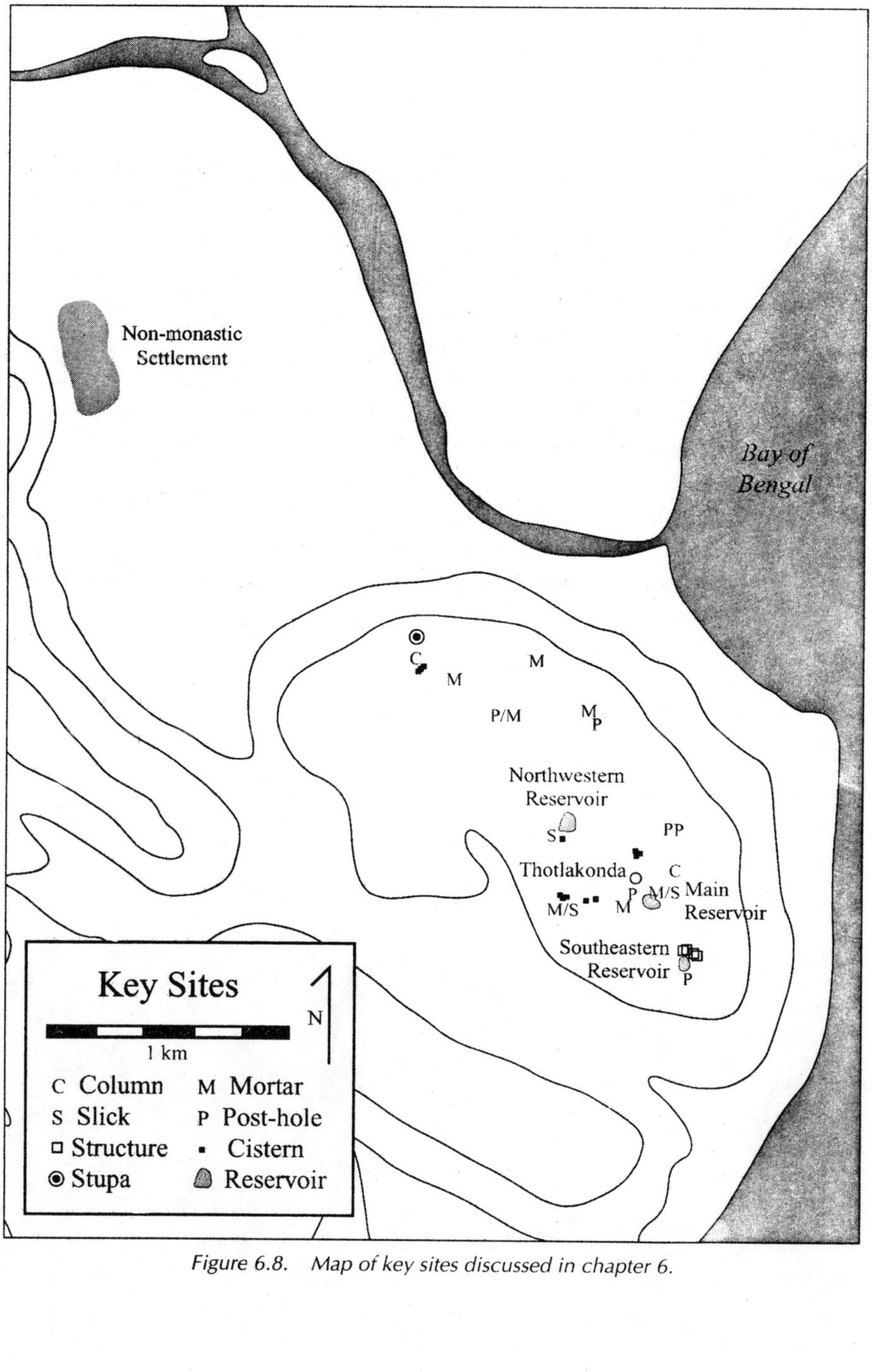

Figure 6.8. Map of key sites discussed in chapter 6.

ritual space separate from the monastery. This possibility will be addressed in greater detail in chapters 7 and 8.

Columns

Four simple, undecorated columns were found at two sites on Thotlakonda Hill (see figure 6.8). Three standing columns were found near the monastery at NEAMS 133. One column was also found at NEAMS 116 in association with several cisterns and cairns. The column was also located close to the *stupa* discussed above. The three columns at NEAMS 133 were found standing in a line roughly one hundred meters east of Thotlakonda Monastery (see figure 6.9). It is possible these are the remains of a *mandapa* (columned hall), but no other columns were found in the area despite good visibility. All of the columns were broken at the top, with the tallest 1.4 meters. All were roughly square (35 × 35 cm, 45 × 45 cm, and 50 × 45 cm).

The single column at NEAMS 116 is mostly square (40 × 50 × 222 cm) and broken at one end. Its unfinished surfaces suggest that it may not have been completed. However, the column does not appear to have been abandoned at some

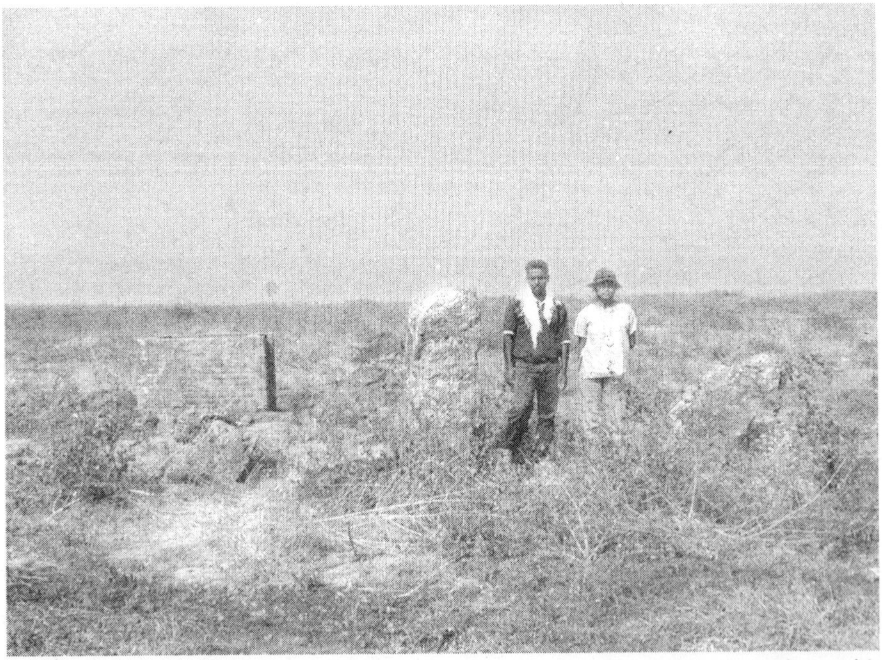

Figure 6.9. The standing columns at NEAMS 133. (The brick structure in the background is modern).

random midpoint. The entire surface received the same treatment, with no portions appearing more finished than any other. It is possible that the column was left with a rough finish in order to be plastered. This column is found close to several cisterns, cairns, walls, and the *stupa* discussed above. The unfinished character of the column suggests that the cisterns identified at this site may have been quarries. This point will be addressed at greater length below.

Structures

In addition to the line of columns (NEAMS 133) discussed above, I identified three or four other potential structures. All were located on a terrace north of the southeastern reservoir. NEAMS 28 had the remains of two semicircular walls (see figure 6.10). One of the semicircular walls had two discernible courses of stone, while only a single course remained of the other. It seems that these walls were either small terraces or, more likely, small structures. Given their size, they would be roughly similar in ground plan to the modern thatch huts found today in the villages below Thotlakonda Hill.

West of NEAMS 28 were the remains of one or two rectangular structures, recorded as NEAMS 29. The better preserved of the two structures consists of a rectangular (4.7 × 3.4 m) wall of unmodified boulders. The southwestern wall is poorly preserved, with only a few stones in rough alignment, but the other walls consist of a clear single course of stones. The rectangular wall may be the foundation

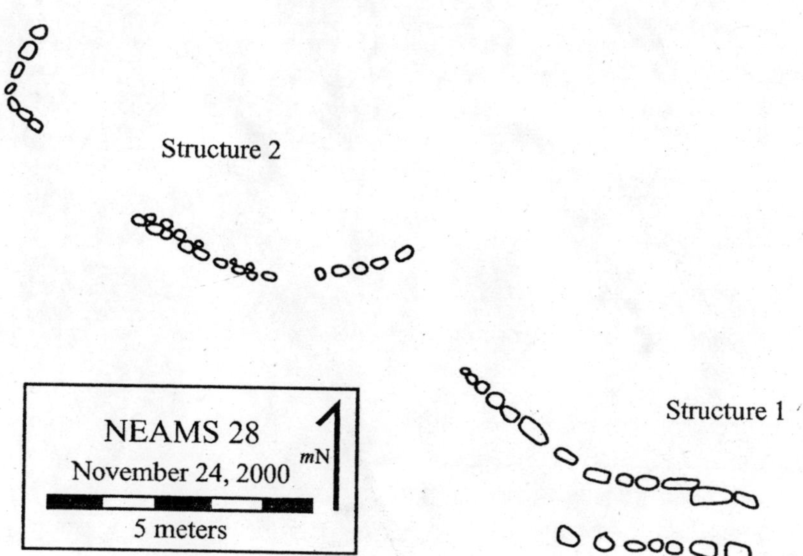

Figure 6.10. Plan of structures at NEAMS 28.

for a thatch structure or the walls of a small enclosure. Considering the size, the former is more likely. Additional walls, poorly preserved, may indicate that a second structure was located to the northeast. Unfortunately, few artifacts were found in association with the structures.

Mortars, Sheetrock Postholes, and Slicks

Three closely related features found in many locations on Thotlakonda Hill are mortars, slicks, and sheetrock postholes (see figure 6.8). All are found on portions of exposed sheetrock, in the case of mortars and slicks, often in close association with cisterns or reservoirs. Mortars are small circular depressions created by grinding foods, pigments, or other substances into powder (see figure 6.11). The twelve mortars found during survey range between 9 and 23 centimeters in diameter, and 9 and 23 centimeters deep. The bottoms of the mortars are rounded by repeated grinding of material with a pestle.

At first glance, sheetrock postholes appear similar to mortars. The differences are that the postholes are deeper and have flat bottoms. The eight sheetrock postholes range between 11 and 16 centimeters in diameter. Those postholes not filled with packed dirt ranged between 18 and 42 centimeters deep. With the exception of

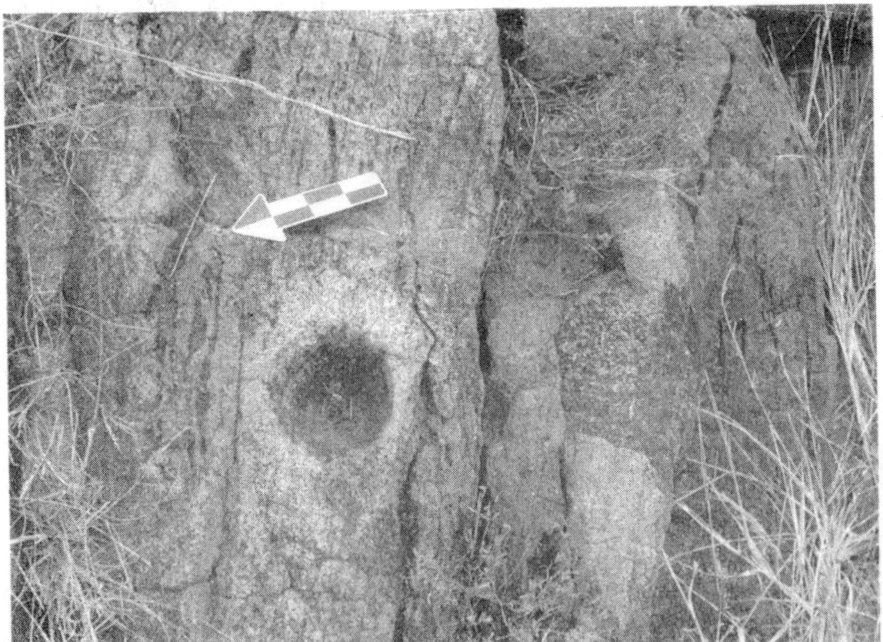

Figure 6.11. A mortar and slick (scale-bar in photograph is 25 centimeters).

NEAMS 82, where two were found, postholes were always found individually. Given their shape and position distant from cisterns or reservoirs, it is unlikely they were used as mortars. Rather, as I will argue in chapter 8, these features may have been used to hold flags that marked paths leading to the monastery.

Slicks are smoothed areas of sheetrock found adjacent to cisterns and reservoirs. As with mortars, they were used for grinding. Most are small, roughly 15 centimeters wide by 20–30 centimeters long. In a few cases, large (1 m × 50 cm) slicks were found. These may have been used for washing clothes. The age of slicks is almost impossible to determine independently. Rather, they must be dated contextually in relation to other archaeological remains. All of the slicks found were adjacent to reservoirs or cisterns that were contemporary with Thotlakonda Monastery, suggesting the slicks are also contemporary. The single indicator used to assess the age of mortars and sheetrock postholes was the color of the stone on the interior. If the interior of a mortar or posthole was red, it had either been created recently or was an older feature that had been reused recently. Several mortars and postholes were rejected for this reason.

Cisterns

Nine cisterns were found beyond Thotlakonda Monastery on Thotlakonda Hill (see figure 6.8). These cisterns are in addition to the three cisterns located within the monastery, discussed in chapter 5. Six of the cisterns I recorded had already been excavated by the Andhra Pradesh Department of Archaeology and Museums (Sastry, Subrahmanyam, and Rao 1992). All six were found close to the monastery. During the course of survey I identified three more cisterns on the northwestern portion of Thotlakonda Hill. While the size and elaboration of the cisterns varied, all were carved into large exposures of sheetrock.

The largest and most elaborate cisterns recorded lie to the southwest of the monastery (NEAMS 66). Three cisterns are located on a large patch of sheetrock adjacent to two large cairns. Numerous slicks and mortars were found on the steps leading into the cisterns. A channel between the cisterns served to direct overflow from the highest cistern to the lowest. The sheetrock surrounding the cisterns had been smoothed and channels created to direct rainwater into them. At the time the site was surveyed (February 2001), the two easternmost cisterns still contained water.

Three smaller cisterns were found to the south and northwest of the monastery. The two to the south are located only a hundred meters from the *viharas* of the monastery. The lack of mortars and slicks suggests that these cisterns may have been used for drinking water or bathing by the monks. To the northwest of the monastery was one cistern, located on a low hill above a former reservoir. This cistern had evidence for numerous slicks and a mortar. All three of these cisterns were irregular in shape, carved to fit neatly into the patches of sheetrock on which they were found.

On the northwestern portion of Thotlakonda Hill, I found an additional three, previously unknown, cisterns (see figure 6.12). All three were partially buried, so their exact dimensions were difficult to determine. The clearest (cistern 1) is at least 2 × 4 meters, but potentially larger. A single, squarish mortar lies adjacent to it. To the east of this cistern is another. Cistern 2 is one of the odder features recorded during the course of the survey. It consists of a stone pedestal surrounded by a carved trough (see figure 6.13). On the southeastern side of the pedestal, the trough appears to open up into a larger cistern, now covered in sand. Only a small portion of this cistern is visible. It is unclear what its dimensions are. As for the pedestal, it is roughly one meter square, with the trough 40–50 centimeters wide on all sides. The trough is at least 20 centimeters deep, but the bottom is covered in dirt. It is unclear how much farther down the soil goes. Chisel marks are found on the edges of the trough.

One possible explanation for this feature is that it is part of a quarry, with the pedestal being the top of a column that was only partially removed from the sheetrock. This interpretation is reinforced by the presence of an incomplete column near cistern 1 (discussed above). It is possible that these cisterns were the product of quarrying for the construction of the monastery or some other feature. This interpretation does not contradict the subsequent use of these features as cisterns. Rather, it suggests that the cisterns found throughout the hill may have also served as quarries for the production of the columns used at the monastery. The resulting cisterns were an added benefit.

The third cistern at the site is buried in sand. Only a small, oval depression (5 × 2.5 m) is visible. All three of these cisterns are located close to the *stupa* (NEAMS 110) discussed earlier. The area also has numerous cairns, walls, and a sheetrock posthole. Taken together this may indicate that this was a subsidiary ritual space to Thotlakonda Monastery, located more than one kilometer to the southeast. This issue will be investigated in greater detail in chapters 7 and 8.

Reservoirs

In the course of excavation, the APDAM recorded a large reservoir adjacent to Thotlakonda Monastery on the southeast (Sastry, Subrahmanyam, and Rao 1992). In the course of survey, I identified two more reservoirs. One was located farther to the southeast and another to the northwest of the monastery. Reservoirs were identified through the combination of many different features, including dams, mortars, slicks, and terraces. All three reservoirs (see figure 6.8) were located in

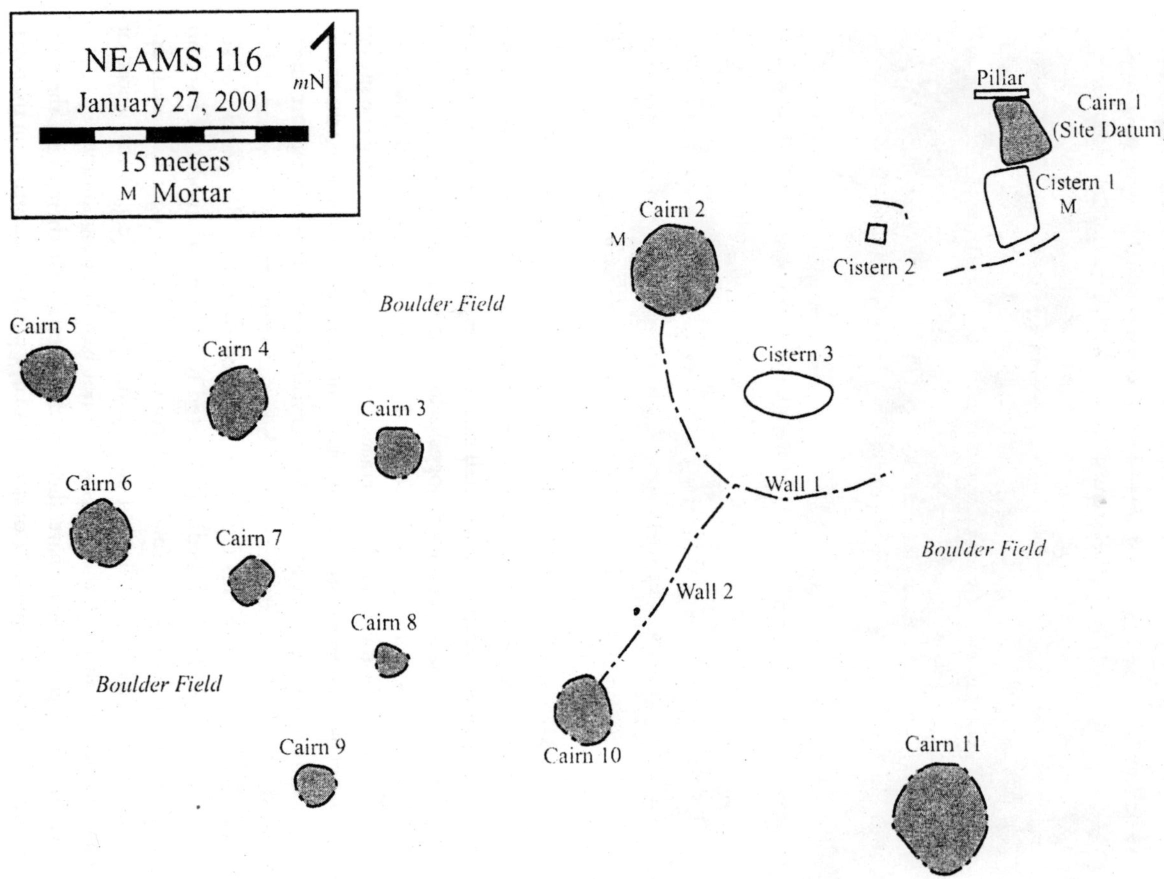

Figure 6.12. Plan of NEAMS 116.

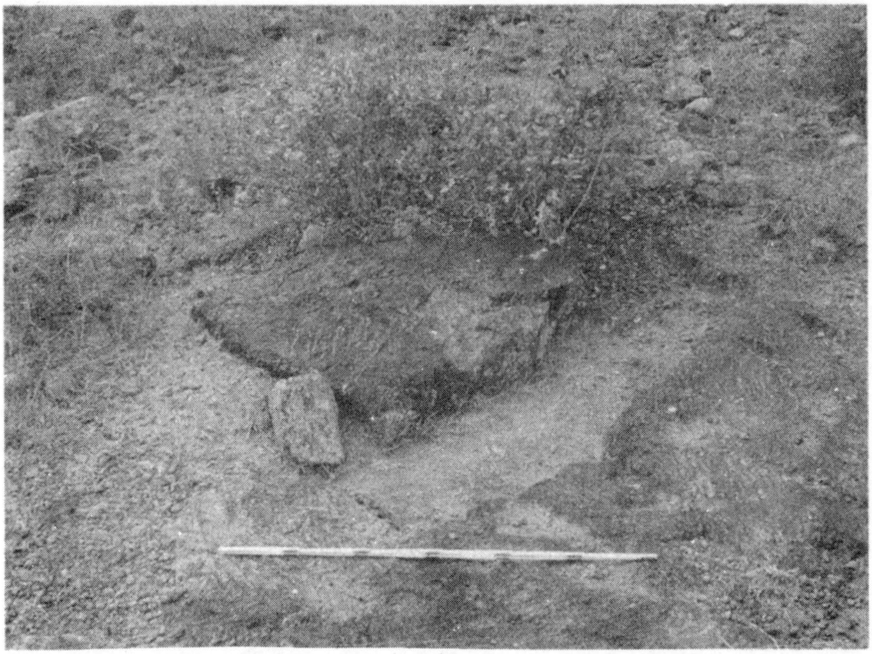

Figure 6.13. The stone pedestal in cistern 2 at NEAMS 116 (scale-bar in photograph is 1 meter).

positions where a relatively small dam could retain a large amount of water. All were rain-fed, collecting water during the monsoon for use in the dry season. All emptied at the side of the hill down small ravines. Despite searches, no agricultural or other terracing was found on the slopes below the reservoirs.

The main reservoir was reconstructed as part of the development of Thotlakonda as a historic site. Any terraces that may have surrounded the site are now covered by a modern embankment wall. The terracing surrounding the northwestern and southeastern (see figure 8.4) reservoirs are still, for the most part, intact. Morrison (1995a), in her studies of reservoirs and agriculture at Vijayanagara, has suggested that terraces of this type were intended to reduce the quantity of silt that flowed into the reservoir beds. This acted to reduce the amount of reservoir maintenance each year. These small "silt control" terraces might have been opportunistically employed for limited agricultural purposes (e.g., herbs, spices, or medicinal plants), although the yields would not have been significant.

While all three reservoirs have slicks and mortars near their edges, the main reservoir has the largest number. Located on a large patch of sheetrock on the north of the main reservoir are traces of at least two mortars and ten to twenty slicks. Given the proximity of the refectory to this portion of the main reservoir, it is not surprising that a high concentration of grinding features would be present.

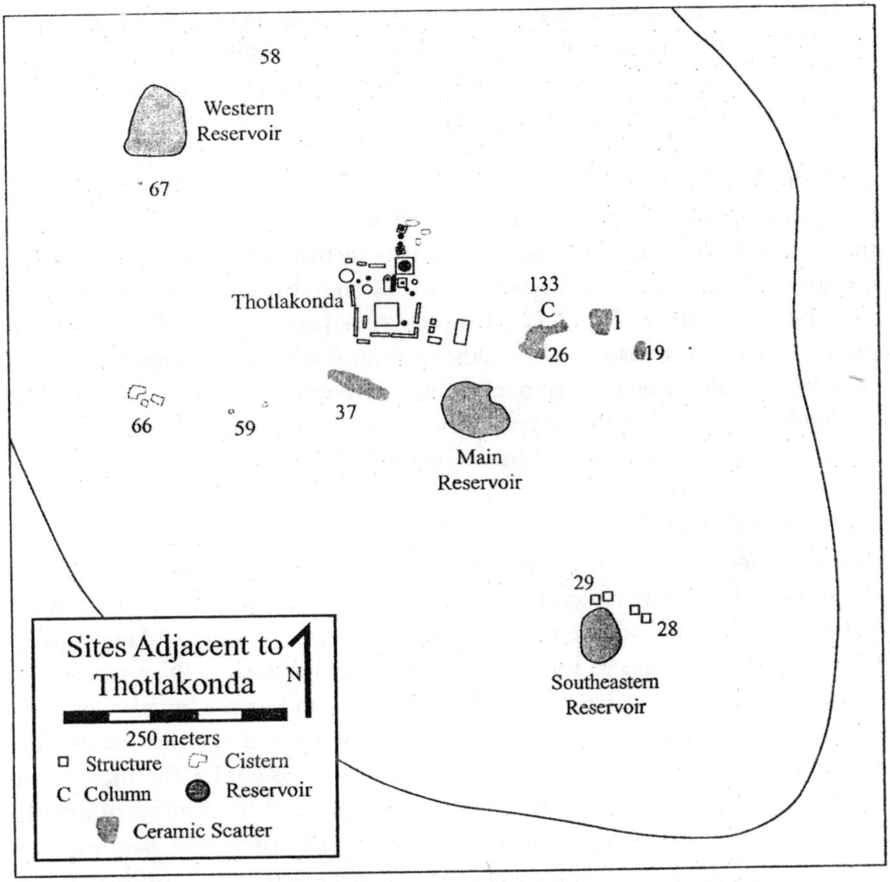

Figure 6.14. Thotlakonda Monastery and adjacent archaeological sites.

The southeastern reservoir has several interesting features (see figure 6.14). First, all of the structures discussed previously lie on a terrace marking the northern edge of the reservoir. On the southern end lies an outcrop with several slicks, as well as a sheetrock posthole. Further south lies an area of dense cairns. The smallest of the three reservoirs, it is the best preserved.

The dimensions of the northwestern reservoir are less clear (see figure 6.14). The southern and western boundaries are marked by terraces, but to the east and north lies a large, relatively flat field. The field slopes gently to the southwest. It seems that water would have filled some portion of it when the reservoir was in use. To the south, on a low hill above the reservoir, lies a cistern.

Taken together, the cisterns and reservoirs would have allowed for significant quantities of water to be collected during the monsoon for use in the monastery during the dry season. However, this functional explanation may be only part of the story. Most of the cisterns and reservoirs, both within and beyond the monastery, have large cairns or *stupas* associated with them. This suggests that water may have had an important role in mortuary ritual.

Ceramic Scatters

Forty-two of the 134 sites recorded during the survey had ceramics visible on the surface. While many had just one or two sherds, twenty sites had sufficient quantities to gather using collection units. The largest scatter consisted of several sites (NEAMS 101, 102, 122, 123, 134) at the northern base of Hill 3, marking the presence of a non-monastic village. Other ceramic scatters also comprised multiple sites. Before addressing these scatters in detail, it is necessary to review the methods and underlying goals of the analyses performed on the pottery sherds collected at Thotlakonda and the sites identified during survey.

Ceramic Analysis

The ceramics collected at the monastery and during survey were all found on the surface. They were typically small, fragmentary, and eroded (see figure 6.15). Without the aid of stratigraphic excavation, the precise chronological relationships between different wares and forms were not easily investigated. Nevertheless, the ceramics provided several important clues to understanding the broader social role of Thotlakonda. First, a low frequency of exotic wares and evidence for extensive local ceramic production suggests that the monastery was not heavily engaged with long-distance trade. Second, similarities in the types and frequencies of different ceramics from different sites demonstrate that the monastery may have employed non-monastic labor for cooking and other mundane activities. Finally, I was able to broadly characterize the ceramics from Thotlakonda and determine that all sites with ceramics in the survey area but one (NEAMS 132) were contemporary with the monastery.

In the following discussion I will focus on only three of the forty-two ceramic scatters that were identified during survey. These scatters were found in the monastery, in a line east of the monastery, and in the floodplain three kilometers northwest of the monastery (see figures 6.8 and 6.14). Before moving on to discussions of these three scatters, I discuss the methods used in the ceramic analysis, and some general results concerning the ceramics as a whole. The goal of this presentation is only to review that information critical to arguments proposed in subsequent chapters. A more complete discussion of the ceramics collected during survey can be found in Fogelin (2003c).

The ceramic analysis followed a straightforward plan. First, the APDAM graciously allowed me to reexamine the ceramics excavated by them at Thotlakonda.

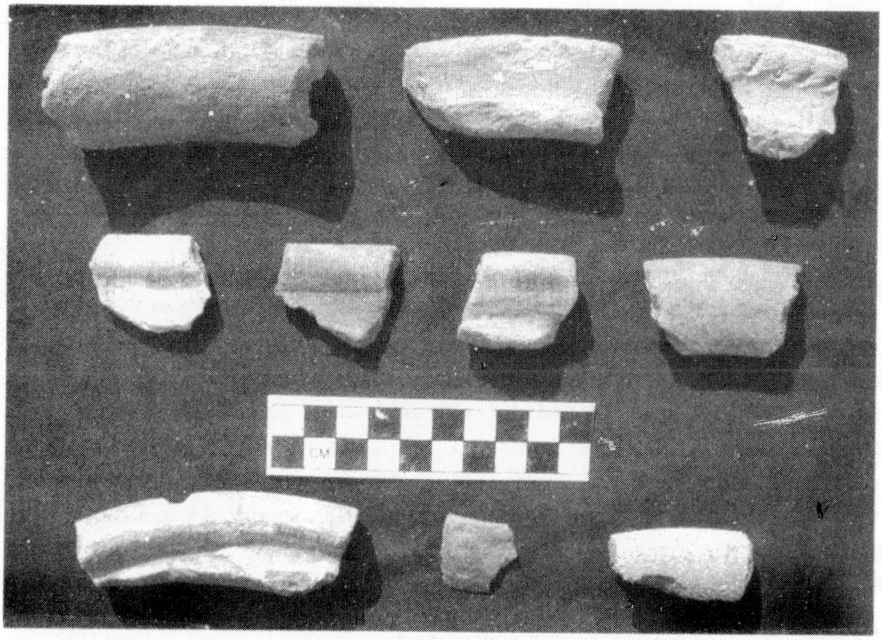

Figure 6.15. Examples of pottery collected in and around Thotlakonda Monastery.

Next, I made additional collections at the monastery. I then compared the ceramics from Thotlakonda with ceramics collected during survey. As discussed in chapter 2, the existing ceramic typologies in South Asia focus on exotic wares with broad geographic and temporal distributions. These typologies do not provide sufficient resolution to determine if sites found during survey were contemporary with Thotlakonda Monastery. With this in mind, the methods employed in examining the ceramics from the survey area were intended to allow for the construction of a more precise understanding of local ceramics from north coastal Andhra Pradesh. This necessitated a careful recording of a large number of variables in the hope of finding some that were particularly discriminating. For diagnostic ceramics, as many as thirty-seven variables were recorded per sherd. Eleven variables were recorded on body sherds. While providing a large amount of detailed information on each sherd, the time spent recording these variables significantly reduced the total number of sherds analyzed.

Color and Ware

The existing ceramic typologies for peninsular India are based primarily upon the surface features of pottery—color and type of surface finish (e.g., Northern Black

Polished Ware). For this reason and others, color and finish were recorded for the interior and exterior of each sherd. The types of surface treatment (e.g., slip, burnishing, polishing, etc.) were recorded on both surfaces as well. It should be noted that many sherds were significantly eroded, limiting the ability to recognize different treatments. Together, the data on color and treatment allowed the ceramics to be classified by the existing South Asian ware typology.

Vessel and Rim Form

The most successful portion of the ceramic analysis was based upon analyses of the vessel and lip forms. As I began my study, I examined a large sample of the ceramics, creating a preliminary classification of the different rim forms by eye (see figure 6.16). Over the course of the analysis, I added several other rim forms to the classification when I found rims that did not fit my original categories. At the completion of the analysis, I compared my *ad hoc* classification with several metric variables (see figure 6.17) to determine if the classification had statistical validity. At least two rim forms ("simple round" and "simple angular") appear to have statistically significant variation in their metric measurements and show interesting patterns of variation both within the monastery and between the monastery and sites found during the survey. As for the other lip forms, in most cases the sample sizes were too small to allow for robust statistical analysis.

Bowls and Jars

In addition to lip form, I also recorded whether sherds were likely to be bowls or jars. Jars are vessels with openings smaller than the maximum diameter of the vessel. Bowls are vessels with openings roughly equal to the maximum diameter of the vessel. An analysis of bowls versus jars, when combined with size and other criteria, can inform upon aspects of food preparation, serving, and eating (see Sinopoli 1991; van der Leeuw 1977; Arnold 1985). For example, small bowls are often used for serving food, while larger jars are often used for storage. Large bowls are often used for cooking. Thus, the relative frequencies and sizes of bowls and jars can serve to identify cooking, eating, and storage spaces. Combined with other data, the frequencies of bowls and jars can also demonstrate if cooking was done individually, at the family level, or communally.

Bowls also have particular significance in monastic contexts. In the *vinaya* literature bowls are listed as one of the basic accoutrements, along with robes, that every monk or nun must posses (see chapter 3). These texts state that monks were to beg daily for their food, eating anything placed in their bowls. As Schopen (1997) has argued, the centrality of the bowl allowed for its eventual use as a catchall term for a monk's often extensive personal possessions. Thus, a monk's bowl was

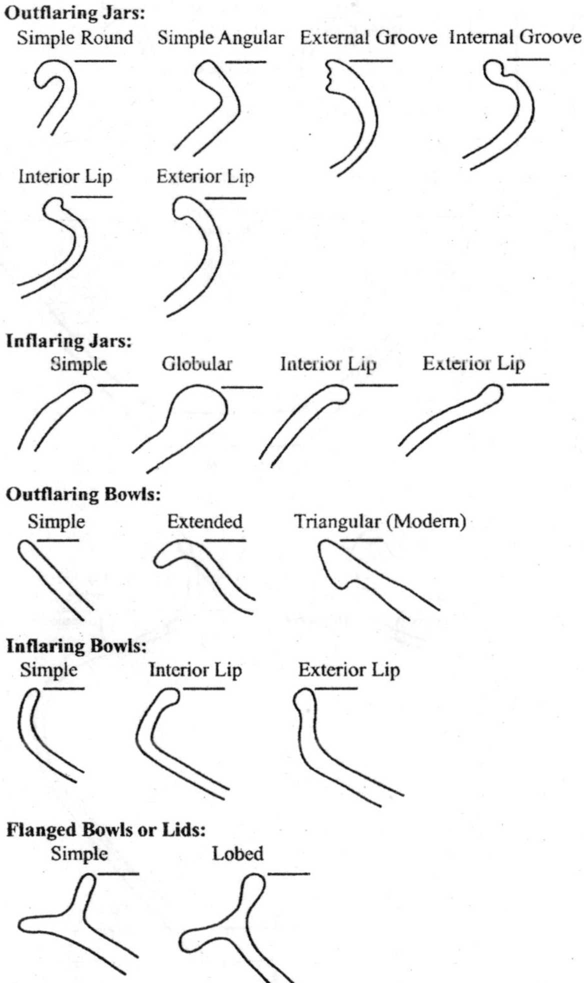

Figure 6.16. Lip forms identified at Thotlakonda and archaeological sites found in the Northeast Andhra Monastic Survey.

a highly symbolic and important material possession. Given the monastic focus of this research, an examination of the relative frequency of bowls might provide insight into the lives of Buddhist monks.

Paste and Non-plastic Inclusions

The pastes (the clay fabric as seen in a cross-section) of all sherds were examined with a 7x hand lens for their general consistency (e.g., fine, medium, and coarse)

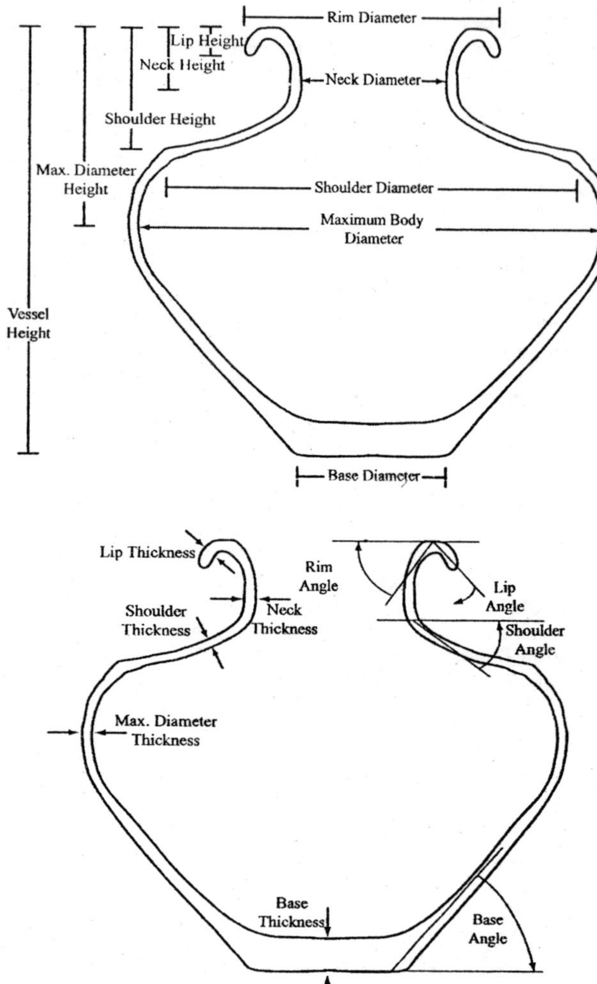

Figure 6.17. Metric measurements used in the ceramic analysis. (Note: All diameters are measured to the exterior of the vessel).

and the types and quantities of non-plastic inclusions (the non-clay components of ceramics). The frequencies of non-plastic inclusions were judged in comparison to representative charts provided in the Munsell Color System (2000, 9–10). The goal of these analyses was to better characterize the ceramics by documenting sources of variability that could be related to raw material selection and production techniques. As the existing ceramic chronology is based upon surface color and finish, I hoped that the addition of an analysis of the paste might allow for the identification of sub-periods or sub-types within the existing wares. In the end, the ceramics from Thotlakonda and nearby sites showed remarkable consistency in the frequencies and types of non-plastic inclusions. While this prevents the identification of sub-periods or sub-types, it has important implications regarding ceramic production.

Typically, most naturally occurring clays contain 20 percent to 50 percent of non-plastic inclusions (Rye 1981, 39). In simple forms of ceramic production, little is done to alter the natural frequency except the removal of larger rocks or pieces of organic matter. With more elaborate production, the percentages of non-plastic inclusions may be altered significantly. Clay may be sieved to remove larger particles, or clay may be suspended in a liquid, with larger particles sinking to the bottom. In addition to removing undesirable non-plastic inclusions, ceramic production can also involve adding them. Non-plastic material added to pottery is labeled "temper." Many types of non-plastic inclusions have desirable effects on the functional attributes of finished pottery. For example, the addition of organic material (e.g., seeds or chaff) to pottery reduces the chance that a pot will crack when placed in a fire (see Sinopoli 1991, 14). Thus, the presence of organic tempers can support the identification of cooking pots. The final percentage of non-plastic inclusions within a piece of pottery is the result of their natural frequency in the source clay, combined with the production techniques that alter them. Thus, similarities in the frequencies and types of non-plastic inclusions suggest similarities in clay sources and/or production techniques.

My analysis demonstrates that non-plastic inclusions are remarkably homogenous across all of the wares within my sample, whether natural or deliberately added as temper. In general, most sherds contained just over 10 percent sand, with no clear patterns of difference associated with different vessel forms. As will be discussed in greater length below, this homogeneity is itself interesting—suggesting that most of the ceramics I analyzed were locally produced. Further analysis with larger numbers of sherds or the use of more precise laboratory techniques may identify patterns that were not visible in the existing sample. At this time, however, non-plastic inclusions do not appear to be an effective marker for chronological or functional types in the area surrounding Thotlakonda.

General Characteristics of the Ceramics

The ceramics collected at Thotlakonda Monastery and the sites recorded during survey are similar to those described by the APDAM (Sastry, Subrahmanyam, and Rao 1992), with undecorated Red Wares making up the majority of the assemblage (see figure 6.18). Other wares included Black-and-Red Ware, Red-and-Gray Ware, Black Ware, Black-and-Gray Ware, Gray Ware, and Red-and-Tan Ware. Sherds

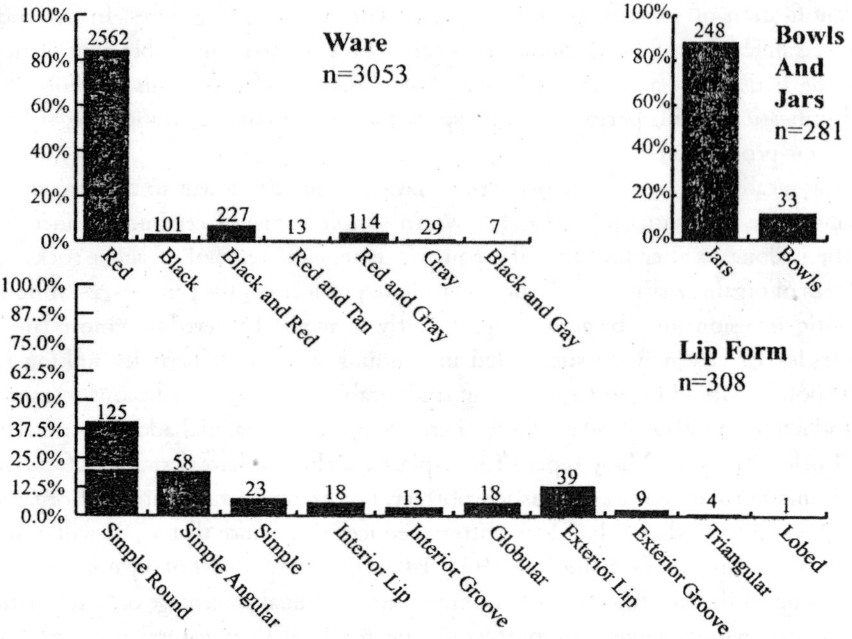

Figure 6.18. A summary of all of the analyzed ceramics from the Northeast Andhra Monastic Survey.

typically had a medium to coarse paste, with fine pastes occurring rarely. All of the bases collected during survey (n = 25) had marks indicative of removal from a wheel with a string. Given this, it seems that large portions of the assemblage were wheel-made, but there is also the possibility for hand-made vessels as well. It is also likely that individual vessels would have combined both techniques, beginning a vessel on a wheel and completing it by hand (see Sinopoli 1991; Rye 1981; and Kramer 1997). In total, 578 diagnostic sherds (rims, bases, and decorated body sherds) and 2,479 undecorated body sherds were collected and analyzed during research in and around Thotlakonda Monastery.

Non-plastic Inclusions

As shown in table 6.2, the mean frequencies of visible non-plastic inclusions in the ceramics range from 8.28 percent to 15 percent by ware. More specifically, three wares (Red Ware, Black-and-Red Ware, and Red-and-Gray Ware) range between 11.46 percent and 11.88 percent. As discussed above, the final frequencies of non-plastic inclusions are the product of their natural frequency in clay deposits in combination with production techniques that can either add them (as temper) or remove them (through sieving or suspension). The similarity in the frequencies of non-plastic inclusions among the Red Ware, Black-and-Red Ware, and

Table 6.2. The mean percentage of non-plastic inclusions by different ceramic wares of all sherds collected during the Northeast Andhra Monastic Survey

Ware	*n*	*Mean*	*Standard Deviation*
Black	101	10.15%	4.62%
Black-and-Gray	7	8.28%	6.34%
Grey	28	8.96%	4.05%
Red	2548	11.88%	4.72%
Black-and-Red	224	11.46%	4.66%
Red-and-Gray	114	11.72%	4.76%
Red-and-Tan	13	15.00%	6.12%

Red-and-Gray Ware suggests that they were all constructed with clay from the same source, and/or with the same production techniques. It is likely that the most common ware in the assemblage, Red Ware, was produced locally. Thus, it is also likely that the Black-and-Red Ware was locally produced. Significantly, this demonstrates that the widespread distribution of Black-and-Red Ware is a result of its widespread production, not trade from a restricted source.

Table 6.3 lists the mean frequencies of non-plastic inclusions by different lip forms. Because of the tight range in mean frequencies of non-plastic inclusions (11.56 percent–15 percent), none of the differences in means are significant (prob. <.05) using the Students t-test or an Analysis of Variance (f = 0.37). This result is partially due to the smaller sample sizes of these sherds in comparison with the tests discussed above. However, the similarity in the frequencies of non-plastic inclusions supports the argument that most of the ceramic assemblage at Thotlakonda and sites found during survey were locally produced.

The remainder of this ceramic analysis focuses upon assemblages from a few specific sites. This general discussion has been intended to demonstrate one important point—the ceramics from Thotlakonda and the sites I recorded were, in general, locally produced. Rather than ceramics providing evidence for monastic

Table 6.3. The mean percentage of non-plastic inclusions by different lip types of all sherds collected during the Northeast Andhra Monastic Survey

Lip Form	*n*	*Mean*	*Standard Deviation*
Ext. Groove	9	13.3%	5.59%
Ext. Lip	39	11.56%	5.07%
Globular	18	13.3%	4.20%
Int. Groove	13	12.31%	4.84%
Int. Lip	16	13.75%	4.28%
Lobed	1	15%	–
Simple	21	11.24%	4.82%
Simple Angular	58	13.75%	4.50%
Simple Round	125	12.50%	3.87%

involvement in long-distance trade, they demonstrate that the monastery was interacting with local populations to acquire ceramics—and the goods they contained.

Ceramics from Thotlakonda Monastery

During excavation at Thotlakonda the APDAM saved about one hundred sherds as a type collection of ceramics from the site. Prior to the start of my survey, I spent a month in the APDAM offices in Hyderabad familiarizing myself with their collections from Thotlakonda and other archaeological sites in north coastal Andhra Pradesh. Upon arriving in Visakhapatnam, I made additional collections of diagnostic sherds from the backdirt of the APDAM excavations at Thotlakonda. The vast majority of sherds were found adjacent to the refectory on the southeastern side of the monastery. The 161 diagnostic sherds I collected at Thotlakonda served as the foundation for this analysis. Most were rims, with a few bases and decorated body sherds.

Ware

Of the 161 sherds I collected at the monastery, 152 (94.5 percent) were simple Red Ware (see figure 6.19). Of the remainder, four sherds (2.5 percent) were Black Ware

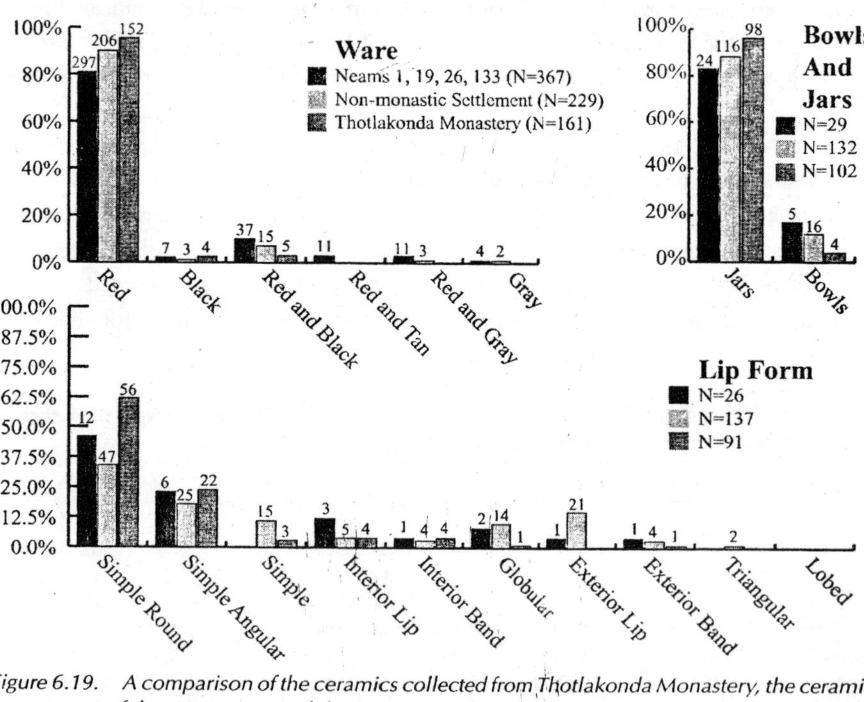

Figure 6.19. A comparison of the ceramics collected from Thotlakonda Monastery, the ceramic scatters east of the monastery, and the non-monastic settlement.

and five sherds (3 percent) were Black-and-Red Ware. The pastes of all wares were generally medium to coarse, with sand the most common non-plastic inclusion. For the most part, the sherds were undecorated, but six sherds were slipped (a thin application of colored clay), one was burnished (polished), and three were both slipped and burnished. Six sherds were decorated with simple incised grooves, four on the interior lip of the vessels, two on the exterior of the lip. One fragment of a large storage vessel with a thumb-impressed, appliqué band below the rim was also found. A similar sherd was also found at the non-monastic settlement (see figure 6.21). These sherds will be discussed in conjunction with my analysis of that site.

Bowls and Jars

Of the 161 diagnostic sherds collected at Thotlakonda, 102 could be identified as either bowls or jars (see figure 6.19). Of these, four (4 percent) were bowls and 98 (96 percent) were jars. In contrast, the non-monastic settlement had 5 bowls (12 percent) and 24 jars (88 percent). Despite the heightened symbolic value of monks' bowls, these numbers suggest that they are relatively scarce within the ceramic assemblage of Thotlakonda.

There are several potential explanations for this low frequency. First, given bowls' symbolic importance, the monks might have been exceptionally careful not to break them, reducing their frequency in the archaeological record. Second, monks may have used bowls made of more precious materials, such as gold, silver, or copper, that were less likely to be broken. Third, given the symbolic importance of monks' bowls, they may have been deposited in archaeological contexts (e.g., graves) different from those of regular vessels. Fourth, it is common in South India today for large group meals to be served on banana leaves. Given that the monks at Thotlakonda ate communally, it is possible that banana leaves were an expedient and acceptable alternative to ceramic bowls. Finally, the bowls might have been made from coconuts or wood—materials, like banana leaves, that would not have been preserved. Given the available information, it is not possible to determine which of these potential explanations is best.

Ceramics from Sites Found during Survey

In addition to the monastery, ceramics were collected from forty sites identified during survey. In many cases, only a few sherds were found. In others, systematic collections were made using collection units as discussed earlier. For purposes of analysis, ceramics from sites in close physical proximity were grouped together. For example, five sites (NEAMS 101, 102, 122, 123, and 134) have been grouped as a single site, the non-monastic settlement.

Refectory Ceramic Scatter

NEAMS 1, 19, 26, and 133 all lie to the east of the monastery in a line from the refectory toward an erosion gully leading off the eastern side of Thotlakonda Hill (see figure 6.14). All four of these ceramic scatters may be the product of erosion from the monastery. Alternatively, they may be the remains of activities performed outside the monastery. This latter interpretation is strengthened by the presence of three undecorated standing columns at NEAMS 133. These columns may be the remains of a structure, perhaps resembling a *mandapa* (a columned hall). Given the close proximity of these four sites, I analyzed their ceramics as a single group.

As shown in figure 6.19, the sherds found at NEAMS 1, 19, 26, and 133 are broadly similar to those at the monastery. While a few modern Red-and-Gray Ware and Gray Ware sherds are present, they are easily explained by the modern use of the area for picnics and parties. Once excluded, the remaining wares are similar in type and frequency to the monastery. The assemblage of lip forms is also similar. The one notable difference in the assemblages is the higher proportion of bowls. While the assemblage at the monastery contains only 4 percent bowls, the sites east of the refectory have 17 percent bowls. However, using a chi-square test, this difference is not statistically significant (prob. = .086).

Ceramics from the Non-monastic Settlement

The non-monastic settlement lies three kilometers northwest of Thotlakonda Monastery at the base of an adjacent hill (see figure 6.8). The settlement was identified through the presence of a large, often dense, scatter of pottery similar in style to the ceramics found at the monastery. No architectural or other features were found. The settlement is composed of NEAMS 101, 102, 122, 123, and 134. The use of separate site numbers in no way implies that the site was disarticulated. The scatter is continuous between the separate collection areas. For this reason, the five sites have been grouped for analysis. Circling the settlement are five additional ceramic scatters. These sites demonstrate that the boundaries of the settlement were indistinct and permeable.

Ceramic Scatter Description

Today, the settlement is found in the midst of agricultural fields and cashew orchards (see figure 6.20). While many of the fields were fallow at the time collections were made, several others were planted in rice, chilies, bananas, and other crops. Particularly in the case of the rice paddies, collections could not be made in the agricultural fields. In contrast, the cashew orchards were easily investigated. A large number of sherds were collected at the settlement (8,279 sherds). Only a sample

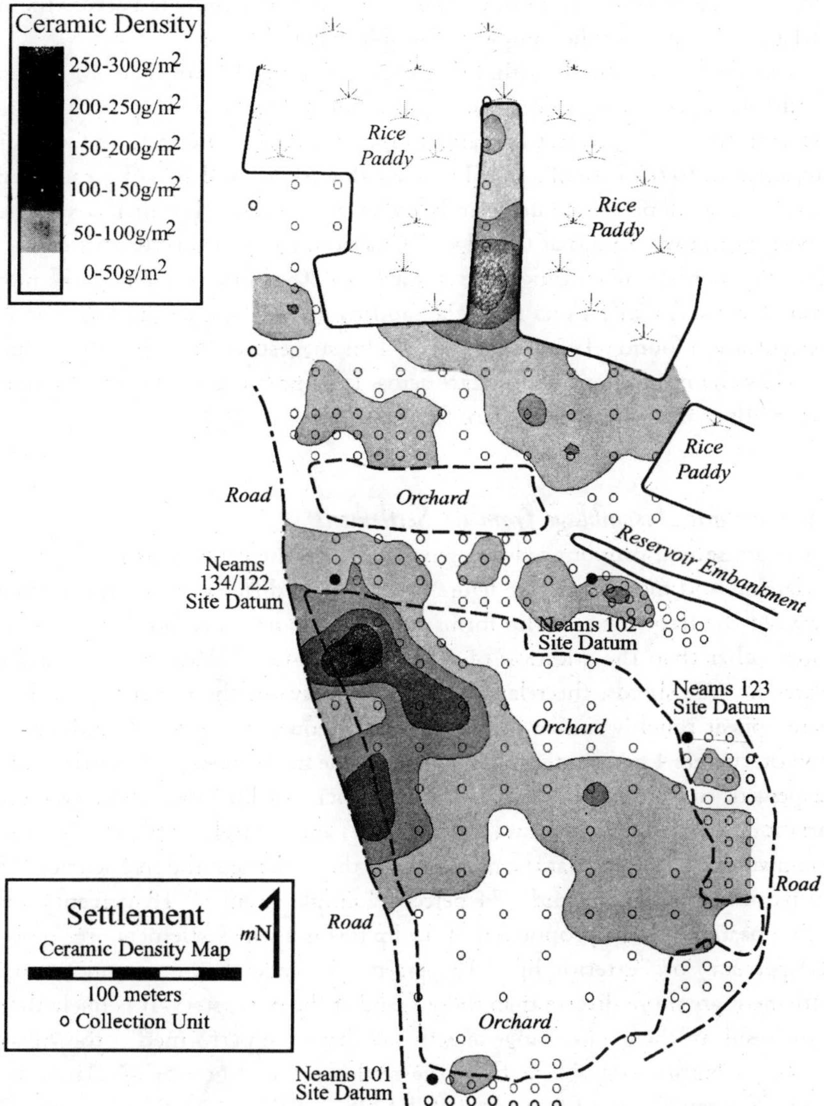

Figure 6.20. Map of the non-monastic settlement with ceramic density contours.

could be measured and drawn in the available time. For the most part, I focused my attention on 137 diagnostic sherds, though I also examined 846 undecorated body sherds. The settlement was originally found in February 2001, with large portions of the scatter systematically collected. Additional systematic collections were made in February 2002 in a cashew orchard to the south of the original investigations. In addition, targeted collections of diagnostic sherds were conducted across the entire settlement to increase the sample of dateable material.

The density of sherds within the settlement ranged from 0 to 300 grams of sherds per square meter (see figure 6.20). The scatter had three areas of higher concentration. The greatest concentration of sherds was found to the west of the site, adjacent to the base of a hill. To the north was a second area of greater density, found on a small parcel of fallow land between rice paddies. The final area of greater concentration was found at the edge of a modern reservoir on the east of the site. Here the sherds were eroding from strata 20 to 30 centimeters below the modern ground surface. Collections from the modern ground surface directly above this concentration found relatively few sherds. This suggests ceramic-bearing strata may lie below the modern ground surface across large portions of the site, with only a few sherds making it to the surface for collection.

The Ceramic Assemblage from the Settlement

There are several pronounced differences between the ceramic assemblages of the settlement and monastery (see figure 6.19). These differences are most visible in terms of the frequencies of lip forms and the proportion of bowls to jars. As for wares, other than the addition of a few Red-and-Gray Ware (n = 3) and Gray Ware (n = 2) sherds, the relative frequencies between the monastery and settlement appear roughly similar. In contrast, the frequencies of bowls and jars at the monastery were 4 percent to 96 percent, while the frequencies at the settlement were 12 percent to 88 percent. The relative frequencies of lip forms show even greater variation. While "simple round" (62 percent) and "simple angular" (24 percent) dominate the assemblage at the monastery, at the settlement the frequencies of both are reduced ("simple round," 34 percent; "simple angular," 18 percent). Unlike the monastery, a large proportion of the lip forms at the settlement are "globular" (10 percent) or "exterior lip" (15 percent). In general, the ceramics from the settlement are more diverse than those found at the monastery. It is likely that this is the result of the greater range of activities that were performed at the village.

The ceramic assemblage from the settlement has greater similarity to the grouped assemblages of four sites (NEAMS 1, 19, 26, and 133) immediately east of the refectory at Thotlakonda (see figure 6.19). The similarities between the two are most prominent in the frequencies of bowls and jars and in the reduced frequency of "simple round" and "simple angular" lip forms. The similarities in the ceramic assemblages between the settlement and sites east of the refectory may be the traces of non-monastic laborers who worked for the monks. The similar diversity in the ceramics suggests that, like the settlement, a greater range of activities occurred in this area than in the adjacent monastery. This issue will be addressed at greater length in subsequent chapters.

Storage Jars

One final similarity between the monastery and settlement occurred in a relatively rare vessel form, very large jars with "globular" lips and appliqué chain motifs. Fourteen sherds of this type were found by the APDAM at Thotlakonda (Sastry, Subrahmanyam, and Rao 1992, figures 22–24). In addition, I found two sherds of this type at the monastery, one in the sites east of the refectory, and one in the settlement (see figure 6.21). The rim diameters of the two globular storage jars I found at the monastery were 46 and 45 centimeters. The single example from the settlement had a rim diameter of 51 centimeters. The sherds collected by the APDAM are similarly large. As no whole vessels were found, it is not possible to estimate their capacity. However, the large size of their rims suggests they were very large vessels. Given this, these jars were almost certainly used for storage. Further, as discussed above, the frequency and types of non-plastic inclusions in the pastes of these storage jars are consistent with all other sherds found in the survey, suggesting they were produced locally.

The occurrence of these vessels allows several statements to be made concerning the relationship between the monastery and settlement. First, the similarity in design, size, and frequency of non-plastic inclusions demonstrates the two sites are contemporary. Second, given that jars this large were likely used for storage,

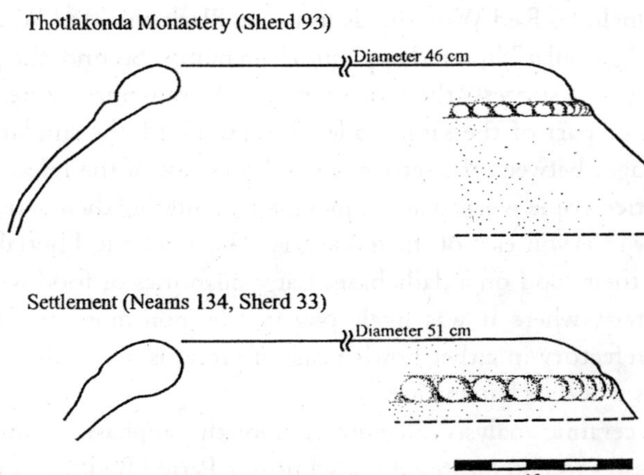

Figure 6.21. A comparison of large, "globular" lipped, storage jars from Thotlakonda Monastery and the settlement.

these sherds show that the monastery and settlement were trading with each other, or with the same third party. The local production of the vessels suggests that the goods they contained were similarly locally produced. It seems likely that the movement of these jars, and the goods they contained, went from the settlement to the monastery. At the minimum, these sherds show that the settlement and monastery were part of the same trade network. Although much of the Buddhist literature emphasizes donation through daily almsgiving, these large storage vessels demonstrate donation and/or trade on a much larger scale.

Conclusion

Though based upon surface material, this analysis of ceramics from the monastery and adjacent sites has several implications for the broader understanding of the social role of Thotlakonda Monastery in its local context. Without the aid of stratigraphic excavations, I was not able to divide the four centuries of occupation at Thotlakonda into sub-periods using ceramics. However, I was able to characterize the ceramics from the monastery and identify sites in the survey as roughly contemporary with the monastery. With the exception of NEAMS 132, all of the sites with ceramics are contemporary with Thotlakonda Monastery. That does not mean the sites were present for the entire four centuries Thotlakonda was occupied; it means only that they were occupied for some undetermined amount of time between the second century B.C. and the second century A.D.

Other patterns in the ceramics suggest economic and social ties between the monastery and the local populations. First, the majority of ceramics were locally produced. This includes Red Ware sherds, as well as Black-and-Red Ware and large storage jars with "globular" lips and appliqué chain motifs. Second, the presence of these large storage jars suggests the monastery and the settlement were interacting with each other, or part of the same trade network. Third, the similarities in the ceramic assemblages between the settlement and sites east of the refectory suggest that non-monastic people worked at the monastery, centering their activities in the refectory and the reservoir east of the monastery. The monks at Thotlakonda were not begging for their food on a daily basis. Large quantities of food were brought into the monastery, where it was likely prepared by non-monastic labor. Food was served in a refectory in either bowls made of precious materials or perishable materials such as wood or banana leaves.

Overall, this ceramic analysis calls into question the emphasis on long-distance trade that permeates the literature on Early Historic Period Buddhist monasticism (see Thapar 1966, 2002; Ray 1986, 1989; Lahiri 1992). At least at Thotlakonda, the vast bulk of the evidence suggests local trade and interaction. A few sherds of Rouletted Ware and five Roman coins show the monastery was engaged in long-distance trade, but the meager numbers suggest that this role was not central. That said, the general similarities in ceramic forms at many sites demonstrate that both monks and local residents of north coastal Andhra Pradesh were part of the larger social networks that spanned the east coast of India.

The ceramic analysis and survey were designed to investigate the local relations between a single Early Historic Period Buddhist monastery and its immediate local context. Despite the narrow geographic focus, 328 archaeological features were identified, ranging from simple cairns of unmodified boulders to large ceramic scatters. Together, these archaeological features allow investigation of the ritual and economic ties between the monks at Thotlakonda and the local populations on the floodplains below. These issues will be addressed in detail in chapters 7 and 8. Together, site data and ceramic data serve as the foundation of all subsequent analyses.

The Architectural Layout and Organization of Thotlakonda Monastery

7

THE ARCHITECTURAL LAYOUT of Thotlakonda informs upon several underlying tensions concerning its broader social role. The monastery is divided into three different areas, with architectural boundaries created to maintain separation between them (see figure 7.1). Each section was oriented, in the main, toward different activities. At the center of Thotlakonda was an inwardly focused cloister where the monks could live in isolation from outside concerns. To the east was a refectory, an area where non-monastic labor prepared food and performed other support activities (e.g., cleaning, water carrying, etc.). To the north of the cloister was an area for public worship. Here the monks shared ritual space with non-monastic populations. As discussed in chapter 3, existing interpretations of the broader social role of Early Historic Period Buddhist monasteries have emphasized either their religious isolation (e.g., Brown 1965; Cunningham [1854] 1997; Basham 1967; Lamotte 1988) or economic engagement in long-distance trade (e.g., Thapar 1966, 1997, 2002; Ray 1986, 1989; Lahiri 1992). The architectural isolation of the cloister shows an attempt by the monks to segregate themselves from broader society. While the refectory focused on the wider economic role of the monastery, it appears that trade and interaction were more locally oriented. The third area, devoted to public worship, demonstrates another monastic role—engagement with a broadly based *stupa* cult involving both the monks and local laity.

In this chapter I examine the architectural layout of Thotlakonda Monastery and archaeological remains immediately adjacent to it in order to identify underlying tensions in the social role of the monastery and the architectural methods used to overcome these tensions. I first examine the historical development of the monastery, particularly in relation to the nearby monastery of Bavikonda (see figure 5.8). Next, I address each of the architecturally defined spaces within the monastery, examining specific structures with the aim of further deciphering the social implications of the broader space in which they are found. I conclude with a discussion of

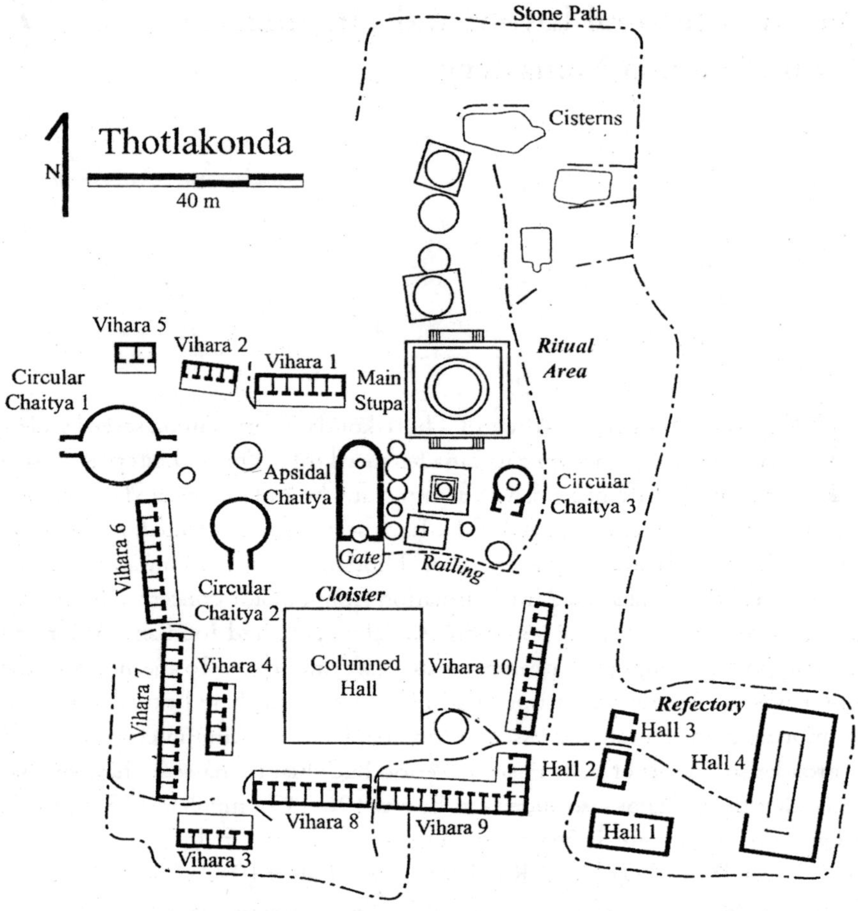

Figure 7.1. Plan of Thotlakonda Monastery.

what the spatial divisions of the monastery imply regarding the interpretation of Thotlakonda's greater social role.

Architectural Development of Thotlakonda Monastery

As discussed in chapter 5, the chronological sequence of construction at Thotlakonda is somewhat sketchy (c. second century B.C. through the second century A.D.). However, earlier structures at Thotlakonda were made of larger bricks, with later construction made of smaller bricks. When combined with other evidence, the excavators (Sastry, Subrahmanyam, and Rao 1992) have developed a three-stage sequence of construction. During the earliest phase, the monastery consisted of a few *viharas*, two *chaityas*, and several small votive *stupas* (see figure 7.2).

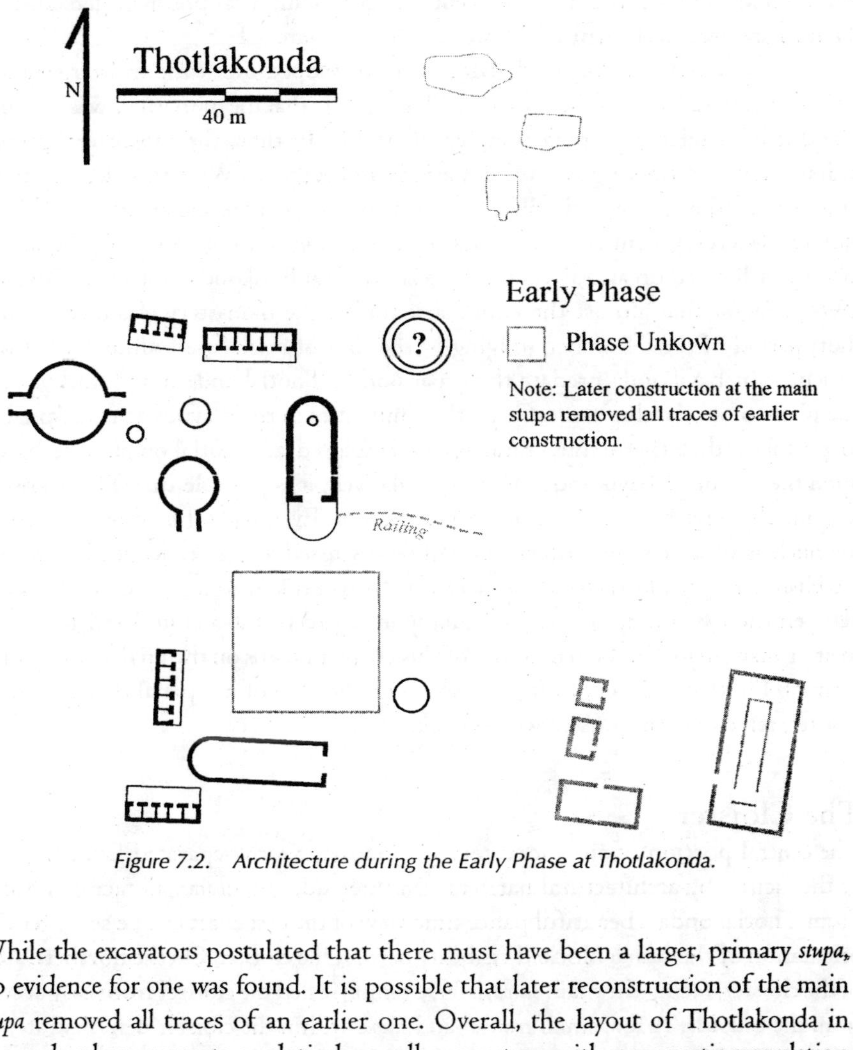

Figure 7.2. Architecture during the Early Phase at Thotlakonda.

While the excavators postulated that there must have been a larger, primary *stupa*, no evidence for one was found. It is possible that later reconstruction of the main *stupa* removed all traces of an earlier one. Overall, the layout of Thotlakonda in the early phase suggests a relatively small monastery with a monastic population of ten to fifteen individuals. In contrast to the later phases, the original monastery lacked a clear cloister, showing an open format, with *viharas*, *chaityas*, and votive *stupas* intermixed.

In the middle and late phases, the monastery developed a more formal layout, creating the separate architectural spaces (cloister, refectory, and public ritual space) discussed in depth below. A marked increase in the number of monastic cells testifies to an increase in the resident monastic population to about sixty-five individuals. At this time the existing main *stupa* was erected, an earlier *chaitya*, located in what would become the cloister, was converted into a *vihara*, and numerous votive *stupas* were erected. Each of these developments has critical implications in understanding the final architectural form of Thotlakonda (see figure 7.1).

Broadly stated, Thotlakonda Monastery developed over time from a smaller, open format to a larger, closed format. This suggests that the monastery was initially founded by a relatively small number of people. In time, the monastery gained in importance, attracting greater donations and support. With this development came a marked increase in the size and formality of the monastic architecture. This pattern of development stands in contrast to Bavikonda, a contemporary Buddhist monastery located on an adjacent hill. Excavations at Bavikonda monastery (Prasad 1994) suggest that almost the entire structure of the monastery was erected in a short period of time. Further, judging by the sizes of bricks used, almost all of the structures at Bavikonda predate the expansion of Thotlakonda in the middle and late phase of its development. Given the similarities in their layout, it is reasonable to postulate that the architectural forms employed at Thotlakonda were based upon the layout of Bavikonda. More speculatively, it is possible that Thotlakonda was initially a retreat for the monks at Bavikonda. Eventually this retreat served as the nucleus of a new monastery. As will be discussed at greater length below, the establishment of Thotlakonda as a retreat helps explain some of the differences between the two monasteries, particularly in regard to the architectural forms of their primary *stupas*. In the remainder of this chapter I focus on the final architectural form of Thotlakonda, exploring the social implication of its spatial divisions into cloister, refectory, and public worship space.

The Cloister

The central portion of the monastery is a cloister, clearly separated from the rest of the facility by architectural barriers. On three sides lie *viharas*, all facing inward. From Thotlakonda a beautiful panoramic view of the east coast can be seen, yet the orientation of the *viharas* blocked visibility beyond the cloister. On the northern side of the cloister, facing the main *stupa*, a large railing sealed the cloister from easy access from the outside. A few small *chaityas* and *stupas* within the cloister demonstrate, as Schopen (1997) argues, that the monks at Thotlakonda were engaging in ritual focusing on the *stupas*. A large pillared hall in the center of the courtyard was likely used as a location for religious teaching and worship.

The architectural layout of the cloister provides one avenue for understanding the role it served in the monastery. The cloister was designed to isolate the monks from the broader world in which they lived. Together, the *viharas* and railing served as visual and physical barriers separating the cloister from the rest of the monastery and the broader landscape. All of the *viharas* faced the columned hall in the center of the cloister. As discussed in the APDAM report (Sastry, Subrahmanyam, and Rao 1992, 38–47), the roofs of the *viharas* were angled downward, toward the exterior.

Thus, the highest point on the roofs pointed inward toward the cloister. The overall effect for an individual standing within the cloister would have been a surrounding wall, almost completely obscuring any views beyond the monastery itself.

As will be discussed later, several passages led beyond the cloister. Of these passages, one led to the refectory, another to the public worship space, and a third beyond the monastic walls via a *chaitya*. In addition to these primary passages, there are also numerous small, stone paths leading behind the *viharas*. Sastry, Subrahmanyam, and Rao (1992, 59) suggest that these paths may have led to washing areas and toilets. They demonstrate that, while isolation was critical to the function of the cloister, the segregation of the cloister was not absolute. When necessary, the monks could move beyond it.

Columned Hall

The columned hall was the centerpiece of the cloister, providing the only large meeting area within the monastery. It is likely that this space was used for religious instruction and other religious gatherings (see chapter 3). At the center of the hall was a raised, brick platform (2.4 × 2.0 m). Steps, with a moonstone threshold, ascended one side of the platform. Throughout Thotlakonda, moonstones were laid before stairs ascending into monastic cells and other buildings. The stairs and moonstone indicate that the platform was intended for religious instruction by a leading monk, rather than as a platform for holding ritual objects (Sastry, Subrahmanyam, and Rao 1992, 48). This, in turn, has implications for the presumed form of monastic hierarchy that existed among the monks within the monastery.

The presence of the platform in the center of the hall suggests that some members of the community were elevated, physically and metaphorically, over other monks. The arrangement of the platform is also interesting, given its similarities with the spatial plan of pilgrimage *stupas* (see chapter 4). In previous research (Fogelin 2003a) I suggested that ritual spaces in which an audience surrounds an object or action fostered egalitarian ritual. In this case, however, the elevation would have focused on an individual, most likely the abbot. The abbot would have, in effect, taken the place of the typical focus of worship, the *stupa*. The placement of a *stupa* upon a square platform was common throughout South Asia at this time and is also the arrangement found at the main *stupa* at Thotlakonda. It is difficult to think of a more direct means of routinizing the charisma of the Buddha than an abbot or other teacher occupying, symbolically, the location normally reserved for the relics of the Buddha or another prominent disciple.

The final point concerning this platform considers the positioning of those who would have listened to the sermons or teaching. Given that the platform lies at the center of the columned hall, the audience would have been arranged in an arena format around the abbot or teacher. Following from my previous interpretations of Buddhist religious architecture (Fogelin 2003a), this arrangement would have fostered an egalitarian relationship between audience members by promoting interaction between them. In sum, the implication of the platform is that while there was a small number of individuals at the monastery with higher status, the remainder of the monastic population was roughly equal in rank. This interpretation stands in contrast to textual prescriptions that state that every monk was rigidly ranked, based upon the length of time he had been ordained (Lamotte 1988). While it is possible that those who had been ordained longer would have received privileged positions within the hall (i.e., in rows closer to the central platform), the use of an arena format suggests that these ranks were less central to the typical monastery than stated in either Buddhist monastic texts or the secondary interpretations based upon them. Rather, the monastic hierarchy was more fundamentally two-tiered. The abbot, and perhaps a few important teachers, were distinctly superior to the majority of monks who were, more or less, equal in stature.

Circular Chaitya 1

Chaitya I is a small, round structure with two entrances (see figure 7.1). One faces the interior of the courtyard, while the other leads outside to the west. A similar *chaitya,* in a similar location, is found at Bavikonda as well (see figure 5.8). I suggest that this *chaitya* served as an entrance and exit for the monks into, and out of, the monastery. This indicates that the cloister was sacred ground and that monks engaged in ritual before entering or exiting. That this ritual entrance and exit consisted of a *stupa* with a circumambulatory path further suggests that *stupa* ceremonies and the *stupa* cult were integral to monastic life. This structure also has important possibilities in regard to the rites of passage and liminality as presented by Turner (1966) and van Gennep (1960; see chapter 4).

Both Turner and van Gennep proposed that the beginning and end of rites of passage (separation and reintegration) are often marked architecturally. For example, a special gate was erected at the edge of a village for boys returning from circumcision rites among the Ndembu in Africa (Turner 1966, 253). Passing through this gate served to physically mark the reintegration of these boys into the village in their new social role as men. *Chaitya* I may have served a similar reintegrative function. Its placement as a gateway between the cloister and the outside world, and its religious nature as shown in the presence of a *stupa,* implies that it is more than just a physical passage from the monastery to the outside world. As with the Ndembu gateways, passage through *chaitya* I marked changes in the social positions of those who used it.

Several interpretations of this structure are possible. It may have marked entrances into the cloister, suggesting that the cloister, and the social position of monks, was liminal. Alternatively, monks leaving the monastery to interact with the laity may have passed through this *chaitya,* suggesting that, from the point of view of the monks, time outside of the cloister was liminal. The *chaitya* might have been liminal itself, marking the transition from secular to sacred space. This entrance may have been reserved for more specific ritual functions—as a ceremonial entrance for new novitiates or the path taken to remove monastic dead. Finally, this structure may have been used for all of these different purposes, and more. What is clear is that this structure marked a change in social position between monks within the cloister and the broader outside world. As an architectural marker, this entrance/exit to and from the cloister could have had many meanings, depending upon the social position of the person using it. In different situations, for different people, this *chaitya* could have marked separation, reintegration, or liminality. In any case, this *chaitya* demonstrates that the area within the cloister was different from the outside world—it was a sacred, segregated space. When combined with the evidence of architectural barriers created by the *viharas,* it suggests that the cloister was intended to serve as a retreat where monks could, as Brown (1965, 13) stated, "conduct their observances undisturbed by the distractions of any human environment."

The Refectory

On the eastern side of the cloister, a stone path leads through a break in the *viharas* to the refectory (see figure 7.1). The refectory consisted of four buildings: three storerooms and the refectory building itself. As discussed in chapter 5, a large U-shaped bench in the refectory building would have allowed for the entire monastic population of Thotlakonda to gather for their daily meals. A few times a day the monks would have walked from the cloister, following a path that passed through two buildings before arriving at the refectory. This spatial arrangement, duplicated at Bavikonda (see figure 5.8), would have created a strong architectural separation between the cloister and the refectory. From the point of view of a monk within the cloister, the path to the refectory would have appeared to be little more than another entrance into a monastic cell. The path, therefore, would have preserved the illusion of separation and isolation within the cloister. The question is, why was this separation important? What activities were occurring in the refectory that demanded such a large degree of physical isolation?

Ceramics in the Refectory

In addition to the stone path leading from the cloister into the refectory, several other paths link the refectory with all of the cisterns and the main reservoir. The presence of slicks and mortars at all of these locations attests to food preparation

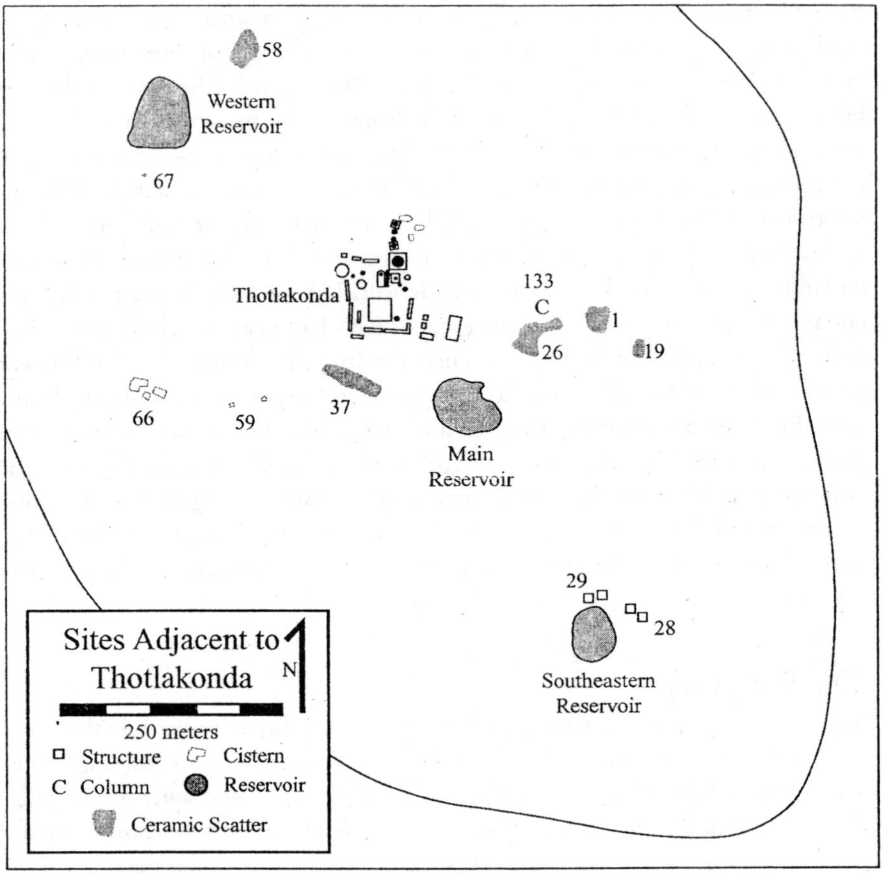

Figure 7.3. Thotlakonda Monastery and adjacent archaeological sites.

and other mundane activities (see figure 7.3). As demonstrated by the APDAM excavations of the refectory (Sastry, Subrahmanyam, and Rao 1992, 49–55) and my investigations of several ceramic scatters east of the refectory, the primary function of this area was food preparation, serving, and storage. As discussed in chapter 6, ceramics from the refectory included a large proportion of jars, most likely used for storage of either liquids or dry goods. Some of these jars, particularly those with "globular lips" and appliqué chain motifs on their shoulders, were very large. Large jars with the same finger-impressed appliqué bands were also found in the ceramic scatters east of the refectory, in the non-monastic settlement below the monastery, and in numerous sites along the eastern coast of India.

Given their size, these jars were almost certainly used for food storage. Their widespread distribution along the east coast, from Arikamedu in Tamil Nadu to

Sisupalgarh in Orissa, suggests that these jars may have been transported great distances. However, their large size and their presence in the non-monastic settlement in the floodplain below Thotlakonda indicate local production of a widespread regional ceramic motif. This latter interpretation is strengthened by the frequencies and types of non-plastic inclusions found within these large jars (see chapter 6). In both type and frequency, the non-plastic inclusions follow the dominant patterns of all the vessels found in the local area. As argued in greater detail in chapter 6, the similarities in non-plastic inclusions among almost all of the ceramics at the monastery and other sites in the area are likely to be the product of the use of a common, local source of clay and similar production techniques. Thus, the large jars with appliqué chain motifs were likely to be locally produced.

The large jars found at the monastery demonstrate that the monks at Thotlakonda did not beg for their food on a daily basis. Rather, the monks engaged in local exchange networks, storing food in sizable quantities. It is likely that these goods were kept in the three storerooms found within the refectory area. What is missing in the refectory is a clear area for food preparation. The ceramic scatters found to the east of the refectory are the most likely location for this activity.

As discussed in chapter 6, several ceramic scatters (NEAMS 1, 19, 26, and 133) and one small structure (NEAMS 133) lie east of the refectory. The frequencies of different ceramic types and wares at these sites are strikingly similar to those found at the non-monastic settlement (see figure 7.4). Assuming that the ceramics from the non-monastic settlement are the product of the activities typical of a village (food preparation, food storage, etc.), people in the areas east of the refectory would have been engaged in a similar range of activities.

In contrast to the refectory, the ceramics from the sites east of the refectory and the non-monastic settlement have significantly higher proportions of bowls (Thotlakonda, 4 percent; settlement, 12 percent; NEAMS 1, 19, 26, and 133, 18 percent). The frequency of bowls from the sites east of the refectory demonstrates that those engaged in preparing food for the monks were also serving themselves. When combined with the evidence for a small structure, as shown by the presence of three columns at NEAMS 133, a picture of the activities in the area east of the refectory and the use of the refectory itself begins to emerge.

The refectory was an interface point between the monks, segregated within the cloister, and the non-monastic labor force centered to the east of the refectory. For the most part, non-monastic laborers worked beyond the monastery walls, using the cisterns and reservoirs for food preparation, cooking, and other activities. Food was stored in the refectory but was taken outside the refectory for preparation. At some point in the day, the prepared food was brought back into the refectory by non-monastic workers and served to the monks at the U-shaped bench. Meanwhile, members of the labor force ate their own meals from ceramic bowls outside the

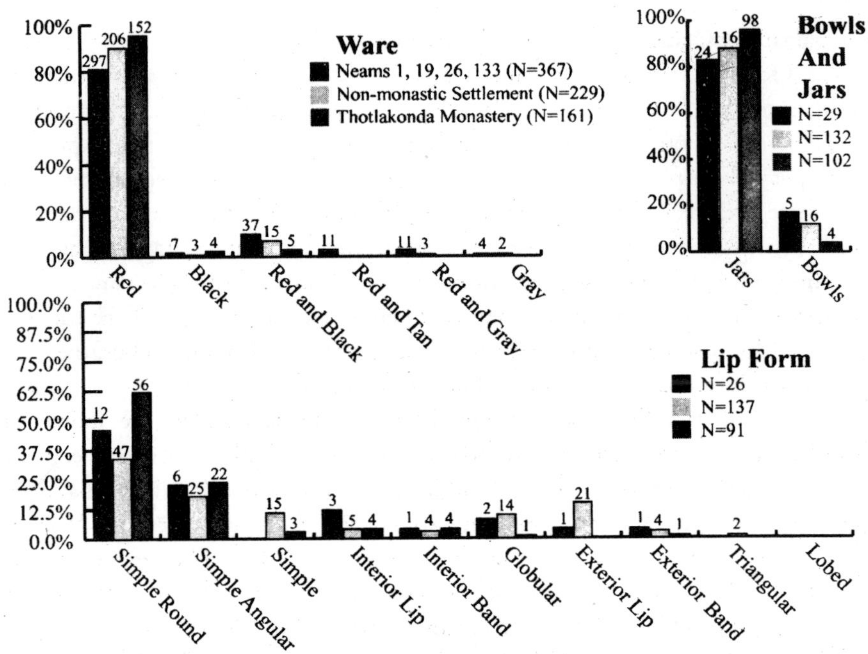

Figure 7.4. A comparison of the ceramics collected from Thotlakonda Monastery, the ceramic scatters east of the monastery, and the non-monastic settlement.

monastery walls. When combined with the architectural evidence for separation of the cloister and refectory, it appears that the monks had an ambivalent perception of the labor force that supported them.

Non-Monastic Labor

As discussed above, the cloister was arranged to isolate the monks from interactions with non-monastic people. The refectory, in contrast, was the location for daily interaction with the non-monastic labor force that supported the monks. A tension existed in these two aspects of monastic life. This tension was reduced through the creation of architectural barriers and the removal, wherever possible, of non-monastic activities beyond the refectory. Thus, only storage (presumably to reduce the potential for theft) and food serving were conducted in the refectory. All other non-monastic activities occurred to the east of the refectory. Following from textual descriptions in the *vinaya* literature, a few monks may have directed the non-monastic labor force. In contrast, the bulk of the monastic population would have interacted with the non-monastic labor force only at meals. In this way, interaction with the labor force was kept to an absolute minimum.

In my discussion of the cloister, I noted the importance of a ritual entrance/exit, defining the sacred space of the cloister versus the mundane world beyond. As with the paths leading behind the *viharas* discussed above, the path to the refectory would have somewhat transgressed these boundaries. For this reason, it is not surprising that a small *stupa* is found adjacent to the path leading to the refectory, near the point where it exits the cloister (see figure 7.1). This *stupa* is neither as large nor elaborate as *chaitya* 1, but its presence suggests that movement to and from the refectory may have required some religious sanction or cleansing.

The refectory was the portion of the monastery that most directly addressed economic interactions beyond the monastery walls. However, despite recent studies that emphasize the role of Buddhist monasteries in long-distance trade (Thapar 1966, 1997, 2002; Ray 1986, 1989; Lahiri 1992), there is no strong evidence for it at Thotlakonda. The large storage jars with appliqué chain motifs are similar to more general east coast ceramic styles, but it is likely that they were produced locally. These jars do suggest that the monastery was acquiring large quantities of food from people in the local area. Why else would storage jars of this size be found at the monastery? Likewise, the presence of non-monastic labor at the monastery suggests that it was employing local people. However, if Thotlakonda was extensively involved in long-distance trade, it should be expected that it would have large storerooms for these goods. The three storerooms in the refectory are relatively small, with only 50 square meters of total floor space. It is likely that they could have stored only the quantities of food necessary to feed a large monastic population.

Within the refectory there is not a single religiously oriented structure. While a few mortuary cairns are found in the areas east of it, in comparison to other portions of the hill, their density is markedly low (see figure 6.5). As discussed in chapter 4, many Marxist approaches argue that religion is used to legitimize the appropriation of wealth and labor. If this was the case in regard to the non-monastic labor force that served Thotlakonda, it should be expected that there would be religious structures, such as votive *stupas* or small shrines, in the areas where this labor was employed, constantly reminding workers of the higher purpose of their efforts. The lack of religious structures in the refectory and the work areas east of it suggest that the relationship between the monks and their staff was not religiously legitimized. Rather, non-monastic labor was more likely supported by tangible payments. While the specific form of payment is difficult to identify, the presence of numerous bowls east of the monastery suggests that food was at least part of the exchange.

As discussed in chapter 3, Schopen (1994) argued that Buddhist monasteries lent money on interest. The proceeds of this activity were used for maintenance and upkeep of the monasteries. With the exception of the accounting records themselves, which are unlikely to have been preserved archaeologically, there is little that can be used to demonstrate the presence or absence of this practice at Thotlakonda. However, the practice of money lending suggests that Buddhist monasteries paid employees and, perhaps, bought goods for use at monasteries. While donation was an important aspect of monastic economies, the focus on money lending demonstrates that monks were also engaged in more traditional economic exchanges. Thus, my suggestion that the non-monastic laborers were paid, in food, money, or other goods, should not be surprising. Given the lack of religious structures within the areas where they worked, tangible payments seem the most likely form of reward.

Public Worship Space

The public worship space is located north of the cloister. Rather than the firm barrier of a *vihara,* only a railing separates the cloister from the ritual structures. Here another exit from the cloister can be found (see figure 7.1). Interestingly, from the point of view of the public area, this entrance is tucked into a corner, preventing outsiders from easily gaining access or views into the cloister. When comparing this layout with Bavikonda, another pattern emerges. The gate between the cloister and public worship area at Thotlakonda leads to the main *chaitya.* At Bavikonda this same passage consists of a side door leading directly into *chaitya* 2 (see figure 5.8). Given this pattern at both monasteries, it appears that the monks were most interested in gaining access to the main *chaitya* while avoiding entanglements with the main *stupa,* votive *stupas,* and other ritual structures in the public worship space.

This pattern of access provides the first evidence that the main *stupa,* the main *chaitya,* and other structures in this area were used by non-monastic populations. Unless other people were using this space, there would be no need to isolate the access route. For that matter, there would be no need for a railing at all. The final line of evidence that this area was public is that there are absolutely no barriers to access—no walls, no railings, nothing to keep onlookers from seeing all of the activities and structures in this area. Given the emphasis on isolation evident in the cloister, it seems unlikely that the monks would have allowed their rituals to be observed, or their own attention to be diverted from their ritual practices, by the stares of curious onlookers. If this area was solely intended for monastic use, it seems likely that it, too, would have had walls or structures enclosing it. The lack of these walls suggests that the use of this area was not limited to the monks alone.

The public worship area was the location for the third monastic role discussed earlier, ritual engagement. Here the resident monks from Thotlakonda interacted with lay worshippers. One question does remain. Did the monks lead worship or only share their ritual structures with the laity? In the first case, as Schopen

(1997) argues, monks would have controlled the *stupa* cult. If the monks were not leading ritual, then it can only be said that the *stupa* cult was monastically centered. In either case, the openness of the public worship space demonstrates that the monastery had to accommodate non-monastic people and rituals in their largest and most important ritual spaces. Ritual engagement is demonstrated; the question remaining is to what degree, and in what manner, did the monks engage with the laity? This question can be partially addressed through analyses of individual structures within the public worship space and investigations of the archaeological remains outside the monastery (to be discussed in chapter 8)

Votive Stupas

In chapter 3, I related the story of the death and memorialization of a prominent monk (see Schopen 1995a). The key elements of this story were that his remains were turned over to a lay disciple who erected a *stupa* in his home. When other lay devotees tried to worship these remains, they found the lay disciple away on business and the house locked. The Buddha then decreed that prominent monks should be memorialized in monasteries to allow for continuous access by lay devotees. This form of memorialization stood in contrast to the funerals of ordinary monks, who were cremated and memorialized beyond the monastery walls. I argued that, if these literary sources were followed in actual practice, it would suggest that those monks interred within monasteries were, conversely, those with the greatest ties beyond it. Also, given that the remains were placed in monasteries to allow access for the laity, it suggests that the laity could gain regular access to the monastery.

This story has several direct material implications for archaeological examination. First, if the memorialization of prominent monks occurred at monasteries, there should be the remains of votive *stupas* within monasteries. This is the case at almost all monasteries, including Thotlakonda. Further, evidence from inscriptions found on votive *stupas* at many sites demonstrates that they memorialized monks and nuns (Schopen 1997, 118–20). A second material expectation more specifically bears upon research at Thotlakonda. If these memorials were intended to be erected and worshipped by lay disciples, they should be located within the portions of a monastery where the laity could gain regular access. As I have already argued, the portion of Thotlakonda Monastery intended for public access is the public worship space. Given this, it should be expected that most, if not all, votive *stupas* would be erected in the public worship space if they memorialized prominent monks as described in the story.

Seventeen votive *stupas* are located within Thotlakonda Monastery. All but three of these are found within the public worship area. The remaining three votive *stupas* are located within the cloister. However, the excavators of Thotlakonda (Sastry,

Subrahmanyam, and Rao 1992) suggest that all three of the votive *stupas* within the cloister date to the earliest phases of the monastery, when the cloister was not yet established. Thus, at the time of their construction, they would have been available for worship by lay devotees. Finally, of the seven readable inscriptions found at Thotlakonda, six were found on *chhatras* (umbrellas) that were likely to have stood on top of votive *stupas*. Three of these six inscriptions—the only three where the status of the donor is decipherable—record a donation from a lay devotee (see chapter 5 for the full text of these inscriptions).

The placement of votive *stupas* within the public worship space and the evidence from inscriptions suggest that, as described in the record of the monastic funeral discussed above, some prominent monks were memorialized at Buddhist monasteries by the laity. This indicates that the monks not only allowed the laity to engage in ritual at the monastery, they promoted it. It also further demonstrates ritual ties between the monks at Thotlakonda and at least some lay devotees. In the following chapter I will examine this issue further, through an analysis of the mortuary landscape surrounding Thotlakonda Monastery.

Main Chaitya

As stated above, the passage from the cloister to the public worship space at both Thotlakonda and Bavikonda leads directly to the main *chaitya* at each monastery. Given this, it is reasonable to argue that, for the monks living at Thotlakonda, the *chaitya* was the most important ritual space within the public worship area. That said, its placement in the public area suggests that it was also intended for use by visiting laity. This point is strengthened by the pattern of architectural development of Thotlakonda discussed earlier. In the earliest phase, Thotlakonda had two *chaityas*. In the middle and late phase, with the creation of the cloister and public worship space, one of these *chaityas* was converted into a *vihara*. Interestingly, the *chaitya* that was demolished would have been located within the cloister, the portion of the monastery reserved for monks. Only the *chaitya* located within what became the public worship space was retained (compare figures 7.1 and 7.2).

The early *chaitya* would have served to architecturally segregate the cloister in the same way as the *vihara* that replaced it. Additional *viharas* could have been constructed elsewhere to accommodate additional monks. With little effort, the monks could have had a *chaitya* for private use within their cloister. The destruction of the *chaitya* cannot be explained as a necessary part of the development of the cloister. The demolition of the early *chaitya* demonstrates that public worship within *chaityas* was not simply desirable but was a necessary function of *chaityas* at Thotlakonda. Conversely, it also shows that the segregation of the cloister was similarly necessary.

In chapter 4, I presented the results of a previous study of Buddhist religious architecture, focusing on the different forms of ritual spaces and their implications for the forms of ritual practiced within them (see also Fogelin 2003a). I argued that halls promoted hierarchical ritual, while arenas promoted a more egalitarian form of worship among ritual participants. In that analysis I also noted that circumambulatory paths, the primary form of individual ritual in early Buddhist religious structures, were deemphasized in monastic *chaityas*. This was shown by the placement of the circumambulatory path on the periphery of *chaityas* rather than immediately adjacent to the *stupa*. In contrast, at those pilgrimage sites favored by the laity, clearly demarcated circumambulatory paths were immediately adjacent to the *stupas*, with an arena format for the ritual spaces beyond. I argued that the emphasis on hierarchical worship by the clergy was an attempt to routinize the charisma of the Buddha for their own benefit. The main *chaitya* at Thotlakonda demonstrates that the resident monks made the same attempt to gain authority.

The *chaityas* at Thotlakonda and Bavikonda do not have circumambulatory paths (see figures 7.1 and 5.8). Within these ritual structures—structures shared with the laity, as shown by their placement in the public worship space—the area for individual worship was omitted. Rather, the *chaityas* consisted of a simple hall, with a *stupa* located at one end. This arrangement would have allowed the abbot or other higher-level monk to position himself between the *stupa* and the audience, monastic or non-monastic, that came to participate in worship. In relation to monastic ritual, this organization demonstrates a two-tiered monastic hierarchy, just as the columned hall in the cloister did. Either the abbot or another individual could position himself as a mediator between the Buddha, symbolized by the *stupa*, and the monastic audience. As discussed earlier, the format of the hall would have reduced the ability for the audience to interact, strengthening the authority of the individual leading worship.

Similarly, the hall form would have allowed monks to assert their authority over the laity when they participated in rituals within the *chaityas*. In sum, the forms of the chaityas at Thotlakonda were designed to facilitate the promotion of a particular form of social solidarity, one with a hierarchical identification with a common leader. Given that this occurred within the public sphere, it demonstrates an attempt by the clergy to promote their authority, derived from their privileged position in regard to the Buddha. This attempt is further demonstrated by the omission of those ritual spaces, circumambulatory paths, that most effectively promoted individual ritual and were favored by the laity. At Thotlakonda, this pattern of omission is further demonstrated by the lack of a clear circumambulatory path at the main *stupa* in the public worship area.

Main Stupa

As discussed in chapter 5, the main *stupa* at Thotlakonda is a somewhat small, simple structure when compared with contemporary *stupas* in Andhra Pradesh and other parts of South Asia. Further, the use of a square drum to support the *stupa* is typically more characteristic of large votive *stupas* than the primary *stupa* within monasteries in Andhra Pradesh (Sastry, Subrahmanyam, and Rao 1992, 25–26). What is most odd about this *stupa* is the lack of a clear circumambulatory path. Circumambulation was possible on the square drum that surrounded the *stupa*. Stairs ascending the drum on the northern and southern sides suggest that it was ascended regularly, and circumambulation was performed. However, no railing defined the circumambulatory path, leaving any worshipper engaging in circumambulation exposed. As stated in chapter 4, the most appropriate space for individual ritual would reduce the potential for distraction and focus attention upon the object of veneration. Without a railing defining the circumambulatory path, it would have been easy for a worshipper's attention to wander from his or her devotions.

By itself, the lack of a circumambulatory path at the main *stupa* at Thotlakonda is suggestive of an attempt by the monks at Thotlakonda to hinder the performance of individual ritual. This could be interpreted as a method of supporting monastic attempts at authority. However, when understood in relation to other *stupas* in the survey area, a more nuanced interpretation is possible.

The main *stupa* at Bavikonda has a clearly demarcated circumambulatory path, with entrances/exits at the cardinal directions. This path, almost two meters wide, had a brick railing covered in plaster. Thus, in comparison to Thotlakonda, the main *stupa* at Bavikonda had ample space for individual ritual. Further, the *stupa* at Bavikonda was larger and more typical of *stupas* found in Andhra Pradesh (see chapter 5). Finally, unlike the *stupa* at Thotlakonda, it contained relics. When compared with Thotlakonda, this *stupa* is clearly the more important and elaborate of the two and was more likely to receive regular worship by the laity. As I suggested above, it appears that Bavikonda was established earlier than Thotlakonda, with the latter developing slowly, perhaps as an offshoot of Bavikonda.

There is no evidence for a large *stupa* at Thotlakonda in the earliest period of occupation. It is possible that the main *stupa* at Thotlakonda may be the memorial of a very prominent monk who lived at Thotlakonda. His memorialization coincided with the expansion of Thotlakonda from a relatively small offshoot of Bavikonda to an independent monastery. The smaller size and limited elaboration of the main *stupa* at Thotlakonda may be the product of the lesser importance of the person memorialized by it. The main *stupa* at Thotlakonda might not have had a clearly demarcated circumambulatory path because it did not warrant one. The main *stupa* at Thotlakonda was more an overgrown votive *stupa* for a locally famous monk than a *stupa* for regular pilgrimage by the laity. That said, evidence from a third *stupa* in the survey area suggests that the lack of a *mahastupa* or any circumambulatory path at Thotlakonda may have been problematic for those laity who hoped to worship there.

The third *stupa* in the survey area (NEAMS 110) is located on the northwestern portion of Thotlakonda Hill adjacent to a quarry, overlooking the non-monastic settlement that I identified in the floodplain. Despite its position on the same hill as Thotlakonda, this *stupa* is not visible from the monastery. I will discuss this *stupa* in more detail in chapter 8. Here, I will only present a few key points. First, this *stupa* has a circumambulatory path. Second, given its position above the settlement in the floodplain, it is likely that this *stupa* was primarily used by the local laity. This, in turn, shows that individual ritual within a circumambulatory path was an aspect of lay ritual in the local area. Thus, the *stupa*'s construction, on the same hill on which Thotlakonda Monastery is found, suggests that the local laity had their own ideas concerning the proper forms for worship. Further, it shows that, despite attempts to establish their own ritual authority in the public worship space, the monks at Thotlakonda were forced to accommodate the ritual interests of the local laity. This *stupa* demonstrates a degree of independence—of resistance—by the local laity to the ritual practices promoted by the monks at Thotlakonda. This issue will be examined in greater detail in the following chapter.

Conclusion

Those who advocate a monastic role in trade could point to the refectory as evidence in support of their model. The large storage jars with appliqué bands and storerooms demonstrate that the monastery was engaging in trade, at least locally, for food. Further, the location of the monastery directly above a protected anchorage suggests that the monastery was ideally placed to participate in coastal trade. Despite this, it is likely that the large storage jars were produced locally, and the storerooms at Thotlakonda were not large enough to hold significant quantities of trade goods (see chapter 5). As demonstrated by the archaeological remains, the economic aspects of the monastery appear to be oriented toward local exchanges of labor and food.

The architectural isolation of the cloister supports the claims of those who see Early Historic Period Buddhist monasteries primarily as places where monks could isolate themselves from the general population for private meditation. Further, through the layout of *chaitya* 1, it appears that the cloister was sacred ground. However, evidence from the public worship area demonstrates that the laity frequented the monastery for ritual activities. This is partially shown in the openness of the architecture in the public worship space. The large number of votive *stupas* also testify to ritual ties with the laity, with some monks at Thotlakonda having lay disciples. Thus, each of the three architectural spaces I have identified at Thotlakonda served a different social function—religious isolation, religious engagement, and economic engagement. Both of the latter roles conflicted with the monastic desire for isolation and detachment from mundane activities.

I believe that the tension between the religious and economic roles of Buddhist monasteries is not simply a debate between historians. It was a tension that existed within the monastic community as well. If the economic activities of the monastery were not viewed as problematic to the conduct of activities in the cloister, there would be no need to go to such architectural lengths to obtain separation. That this same architectural arrangement existed at Bavikonda demonstrates that this was not simply an idiosyncrasy of the layout of one monastery but an element, a tension, in the social role of these monasteries. The architectural separation of these activities served to reduce the tensions created by the performance of the divergent social roles.

In the following chapter I will continue exploring these themes through an analysis of the broader landscape in which Thotlakonda is found. With this movement beyond the monastery, the archaeological remains present information more specifically addressing the lives of the laity. However, evidence from the monastery provides two key insights into the relationship between the clergy and the laity. First, as shown by the layout of the main *chaitya* at Thotlakonda, the monks were attempting to routinize the charisma of the Buddha through the creation of ritual spaces that fostered their authority. This attempt is further demonstrated in the omission of ritual spaces that fostered individual, lay worship of the Buddha. Second, the local laity resisted, to some degree, this attempt at authority through the use of their own ritual space, in a form more appropriate to their ritual desires. This ambivalence between the monks, laborers, and local laity is further demonstrated by the lack of religious structures in those areas of the monastery where the laity performed food preparation and other monastic services. Rather, it appears that monastic labor was based upon an economic relationship of exchange.

In summary, the archaeological evidence from Thotlakonda Monastery suggests that there was a strong degree of ambivalence between the laity and the clergy. While the clergy desired isolation from the laity, they required their labor and attempted to assert ritual authority over them. The laity, though they worshipped at the monastery, preserved their own ritual interests and demanded more tangible rewards for their service. The interests of the different social groups, while related, remained at odds. This same tension is mapped into the broader landscape in which both groups lived, worked, worshipped, and died. One question, however, remains.

Were the laity who worshipped at the main *stupa* and main *chaitya* the same as those who worked in the areas surrounding the refectory? It seems likely that those laity who made pilgrimages to the monastery were drawn from wealthier segments of society. Thus, differences in the treatment of the laity may be the differences in monastic attitudes toward the local laity versus the regional elite. This issue is further investigated in chapters 8 and 9.

Thotlakonda Monastery in Its Local Landscape 8

MANY OF THE ELEMENTS and tensions identified in the architecture of Thotlakonda Monastery are found in the landscape surrounding it. The ambivalence of the monks' relationships with their laborers, and their desire for isolation, is shown in the location of distant work areas, concealed from view of the monastery. The monastic role in public ritual is evident in the creation of a large mortuary landscape combining the memorials of monks and of local laity. Paths were constructed to facilitate the passage of pilgrims to the monastery. Subsidiary cairns and *stupas* were erected along the northern rim of the hill to announce the presence of the monastery to local populations in the floodplain below. Just as in the architecture of the monastery, the surrounding landscape combined divergent monastic roles, employing physical separation to reduce the tensions between them.

A variety of archaeological features, along with their placement in the landscape, can be seen as evidence for independence and resistance by the laity to the attempts by the monks to assert ritual authority over them. This is particularly shown in the placement and form of a large *stupa* on the northern rim of Thotlakonda Hill. This *stupa*, with prominent circumambulatory paths and a location overlooking the floodplain, was a center for lay ritual. Its existence suggests that the monks were obliged to accommodate the ritual desires of the laity and testifies to the subtle negotiation of the social relationships between the monks and the laity in the local area.

In this chapter I discuss the broader landscape of Thotlakonda through examinations of the reservoirs, mortuary landscape of cairns, and other archaeological features. I follow this with a brief analysis of the local and regional settlement patterns.

Reservoirs

As discussed in the previous chapter, three reservoirs are located on Thotlakonda Hill near the monastery (see figure 8.1). All have evidence for slicks and mortars, indicating they were used for food preparation, grinding, and other domestic activities. It is likely that all were used by the non-monastic labor force that worked for the monks on Thotlakonda Hill. Surrounding all of the reservoirs were small terraces, likely used to prevent silt and other debris from filling the reservoirs, reducing yearly maintenance (see Morrison 1995a). While these terraces might have been used for agricultural production, their small size would not have generated significant quantities of food. Rather, as discussed in chapter 6, it is more likely that they were used for herbs, medicinal plants, or other similar crops.

Following from Heitzman's (1984, 1997) studies of agricultural production in Chola period Buddhist monasteries, Ray (1986, 1989) has suggested that monasteries may have had an organizing role in agricultural production. In a similar vein, Shaw and Sutcliffe (2001; Shaw 2000, 2002) have documented a large number of reservoirs at the bases of hills with Buddhist monasteries at and near Sanchi in Madhya Pradesh. They argue that these dams were used for rice cultivation and that cultivation of rice may have accompanied the expansion of "urbanization, monarchical state systems, and Buddhist monasticism" into the region (Shaw and Sutcliffe 2001, 72). While they do not argue that Buddhist monks and nuns were necessarily organizing agricultural production, Buddhism is implicated with techniques of agricultural intensification as new ideas were imported from North India. Given the presence of the large reservoirs on Thotlakonda Hill, it is possible that the same argument could be made for them. However, the evidence from the survey suggests otherwise.

The reservoirs on Thotlakonda Hill are all located in natural depressions, where a small dam could retain a relatively large amount of water. All three are located near the edge of the hill. If these reservoirs had been used for intensive agriculture, they would have required terracing of the hillsides below. During exploration and survey of these hillsides, no evidence for terracing was found. Given this, it seems that the reservoirs on Thotlakonda Hill were intended for use by the residents of the monastery. With no sources of water on the hill, the reservoirs and cisterns collected water in the wet season for use during the dry season.

In the floodplain below Thotlakonda Hill lie several modern reservoirs. All are used to irrigate rice paddies. It is possible that some of these may have been present in the Early Historic Period as well. Despite careful examination, no evidence was found to confirm or deny this proposition. Given the current evidence, the presence of reservoirs on Thotlakonda Hill does not support a monastic role in agricultural production. As for the possibility that reservoirs may have been constructed in the

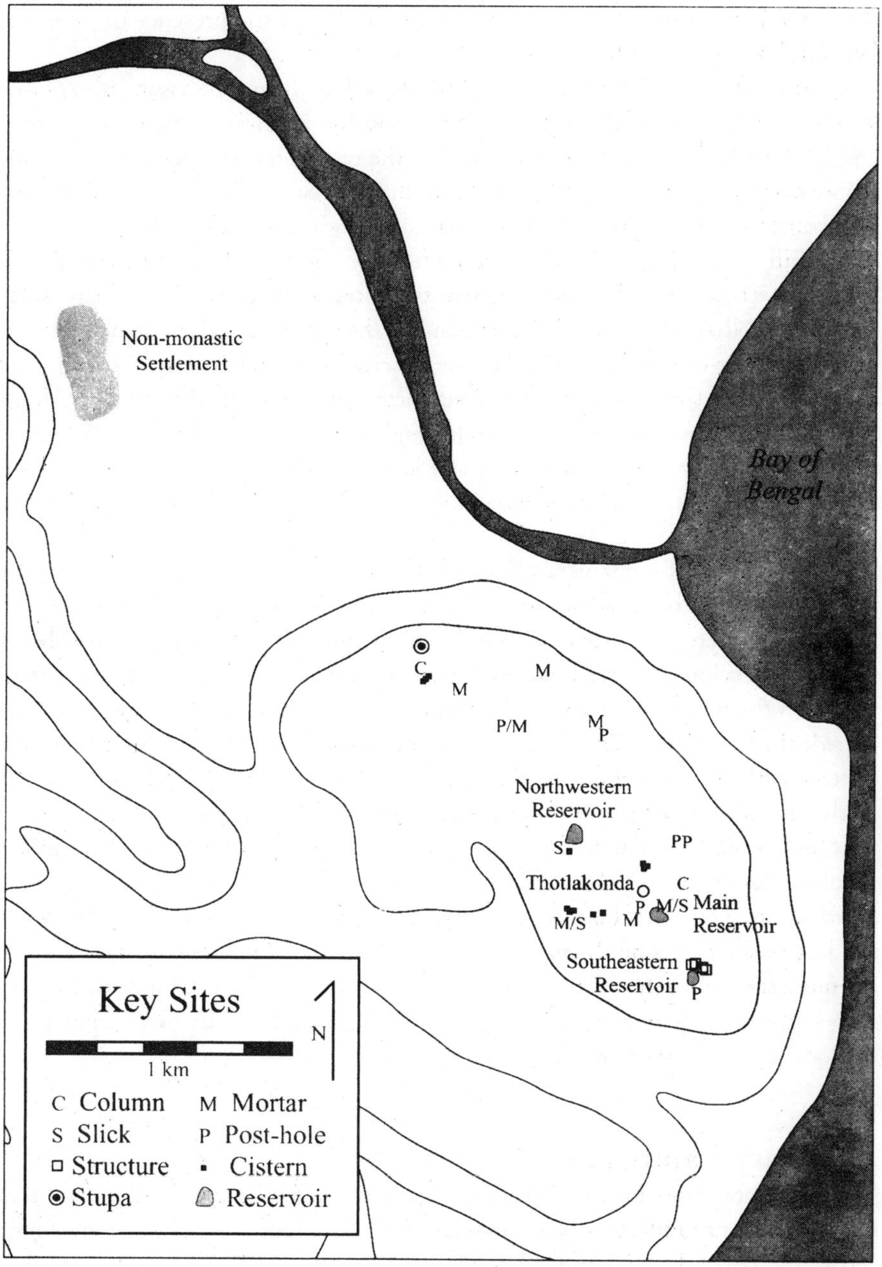

Figure 8.1. Map of key sites.

floodplain, currently there is no evidence for or against the presence of reservoirs beyond Thotlakonda Hill.

The locations of the reservoirs on Thotlakonda Hill and the association of four structures with one of them does inform upon the relations between the monks and laborers who worked for them. Two of the reservoirs (the main reservoir and the western reservoir) were clearly visible to the monastery. The third, and smallest, reservoir (the southeastern reservoir) was located on the other side of a low rise in the hill, concealing it from the monastery (see figure 8.1). On the north and northwestern side of the reservoir were two sites, each consisting of two small structures (NEAMS 28 and 29). Surrounding the reservoir and the structures were a large number of small, memorial cairns (discussed in greater detail below).

All four of the structures were constructed of unmodified boulders. All are poorly preserved. They range between five and eight meters in diameter. As argued in chapter 6, they are similar in size and layout to the thatch huts found in the modern villages below Thotlakonda Hill. Given their size and simplicity, it seems likely that they were used by non-monastic people, though it is possible they were small monastic cells intentionally isolated from the monastery. However, given their placement directly adjacent to a reservoir with ample evidence for use by non-monastic laborers (i.e., slicks and mortars), the former interpretation is more likely.

In the previous chapter I suggested that the monks had an ambivalent relationship with the people who worked for them. For the most part, the laborers worked outside the monastery. The one area where the monks would have come into regular contact with the laborers, the refectory, was architecturally isolated from the rest of the monastery. The southeastern reservoir and the structures located adjacent to it are similarly isolated. This was the only reservoir on Thotlakonda Hill not visible to the monastery. It is also the only reservoir with evidence for simple, non-monastic architecture. Taken as a whole, it appears that non-monastic labor was not just pushed outside the monastery but, when possible, pushed out of sight of the monastery entirely. The ambivalence seen between the monks and the laborers who supported them in the architecture of the monastery is further supported by the location and use of the southeastern reservoir.

Mortuary Landscape

The most common features recorded during the survey were small cairns constructed of unmodified cobbles and boulders. In total, 231 cairns were found across the top of Thotlakonda Hill, two adjacent hills, and in the floodplain below Thotlakonda Hill in areas peripheral to the settlement (see figure 8.3). Given their widespread distribution, almost the entire survey area can be considered a mortuary landscape. As discussed in chapter 7, archaeological and literary sources suggest cairns entombed the ashes of monks, nuns, and lay Buddhists. Just as analyses of the architecture of the monastery suggest a strong degree of ambivalence in the social relations between the monks and local laity, the patterns of distribution of the mortuary landscape demonstrate both interaction and independence in mortuary ritual. Below I examine the mortuary landscape, first at a general level, followed by more specific investigations of particular concentrations of cairns and other associated archaeological features.

Monastic or Lay Memorials?

The first question that must be addressed concerning the cairns is whose ashes are memorialized within them? In chapter 3, I related an account of the funeral of an "ordinary" monk as presented in the *Mulasarvastivada-vinaya* (Schopen 1995a). Upon the monk's death, a gong was sounded. Soon afterward, the monks from his monastery gathered to carry the dead monk out of the monastery. Once outside, the body of the monk was cleaned and cremated. The account does not record what was done with the ashes. Once the cremation was completed, the monks who performed the funeral returned to the monastery, cleaning themselves before re-entering. At this point the possessions of the deceased monk were redistributed among those who participated in the funeral. Throughout the funeral various texts relating to death and rebirth were read, and the merit accrued was transferred to the deceased monk. This story provides the first possible explanation for the cairns found on Thotlakonda Hill. These were the memorials for ordinary monks, those who were not important enough to warrant a burial within the monastery.

A second possibility is that the cairns were memorials for the local laity. As discussed in chapter 3, various *vinaya* texts state that monks were to perform funeral rites for the laity, even in cases where this required them to leave the monastery during the rainy season, a period in which monks were typically sequestered (Schopen 1995b, 105–6). It is important to stress that the monks were obligated to *leave* the monastery, not perform the necessary funeral rites for dead that had been brought to the monastery. In this scenario, the cairns documented during the survey around Thotlakonda were constructed by, and for, lay Buddhists. This interpretation is reinforced by the spatial distribution of the cairns I recorded during the survey. If the cairns were intended to memorialize monks, they should be found on the same hill as the monastery. This is not the case. Numerous cairns were found on the hills next to Thotlakonda Hill, and several others were located in the floodplain below Thotlakonda Hill near the settlement (see figure 6.5). It is unlikely that those monks who lived in relative seclusion within the monastery would be interred next to the non-monastic settlement or on hills distant from the monastery. These more distant cairns are more likely to be memorials for local Buddhist laity.

The mortuary landscape of Thotlakonda seems, therefore, to be a combination of monastic and lay memorials. Given the isolation of monks during their lives, this blending of the mortuary landscape is somewhat surprising. In chapter 7, I argued that the votive *stupas* within Thotlakonda memorialized those monks with the greatest ties with the laity. However, within the large pilgrimage complexes of North India, there is ample evidence for the placement of monastic and lay votive *stupas* side by side (see Schopen 1997, 118–20). At Thotlakonda, the status of those memorialized in votive *stupas* within the monastery is unclear. While several *chhatras* record donations by members of the laity (see chapter 5), it is not clear if the person making the donation was also interred within the votive *stupa* on which the *chhatra* stood. One *chhatra* inscription reads "POYADHI," translated as "one who gained knowledge of the Poya Sutra" (Sastry, Subrahmanyam, and Rao 1992, 84). Thus, one votive *stupa* memorializes a monk, but the others could be either memorials for monks erected by the laity or memorials for the laity themselves.

Social Implications of the Mortuary Landscape

The importance of the cairns is that they are the smallest and least elaborate of a continuum of mortuary memorials ranging from the main *stupa* located at Thotlakonda, through votive *stupas* of a variety of sizes, to the smallest cairns (see figure 8.2). While different in size and elaboration, all of these different mortuary memorials follow the same pattern—a tumulus containing the ashes of a devotee. It is well documented that earlier *stupas* were often constructed of earth and brick (Brown 1965). Over time *stupas* were elaborated and made of superior materials. The cairns I found retain the earlier simplicity but follow the same basic mortuary pattern as even the most elaborate *mahastupa*. In Schopen's terms, all of these smaller cairns served to place the remains of a Buddhist within the perpetual presence of the Buddha, enshrined in the *mahastupa* of the monastery (Schopen 1997, 114–47). Thus, a devotee buried near a *mahastupa* would perpetually perform *puja* (worship), acquiring merit even in death.

Schopen (1997) argued that physical proximity to a *stupa* was the main factor in the placement of votive *stupas*. Within Thotlakonda Monastery this seems to be accurate. The votive *stupas* all seem to be clustered around the main *stupa* (see figure 7.1). However, the cairns outside the monastery follow a different pattern. Seventy-five percent of the cairns were placed in locations with a clear view of the monastery rather than in locations close to the monastery. Thus, visibility was the main factor, not proximity. This pattern is most clearly demonstrated on a hill immediately west of Thotlakonda. During exploration of the hill in January 2002, roughly seventy-five cairns were found on the side of the hill facing Thotlakonda.

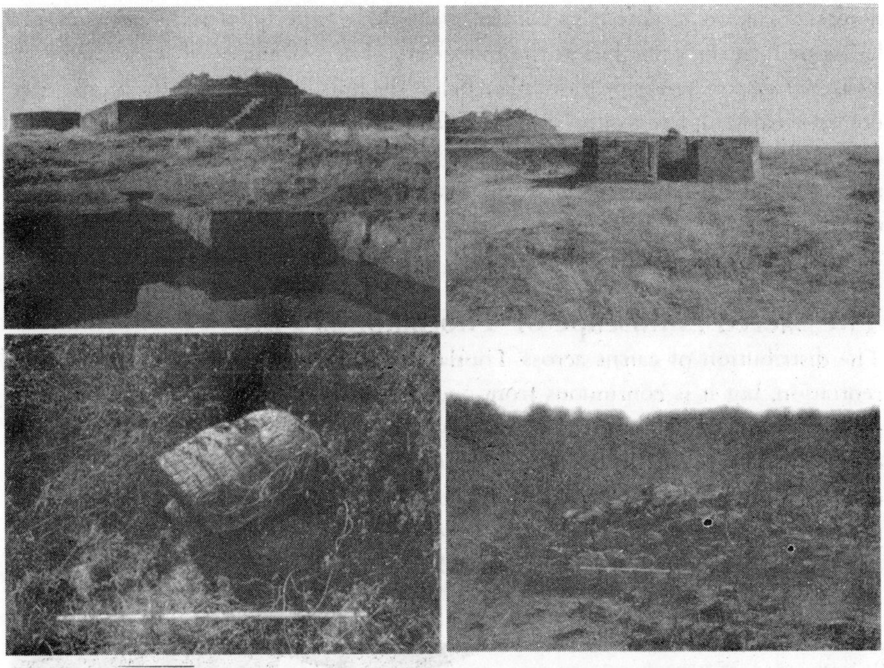

Figure 8.2. The range of mortuary memorials found on Thotlakonda Hill. Clockwise from upper left: the main stupa *at Thotlakonda, a large votive* stupa *at Thotlakonda, a cairn, and a small stone votive* stupa *at Thotlakonda (scale-bar in photographs is 1 meter).*

On the opposite side, where direct view of Thotlakonda is impossible, not a single cairn was found.

The variety of mortuary memorials present may be the result of the memorialization of different classes of Buddhists, all participating in the *stupa* cult. Monks with strong ties with the laity, and perhaps those laity with more wealth or prestige, were buried within the monastery in large, brick votive *stupas*. Less wealthy or prestigious Buddhists employed smaller, carved stone votive *stupas*, either within or close to the monastery. The cairns were the memorials for ordinary monks and laity. Their memorials were located on the hill surrounding the monastery, but more distantly and with less grandeur. In any case, it is clear that the monastery served as the focus of a large mortuary landscape, reinforcing Schopen's (1997, 34) claim that the *stupa* cult was monastically centered. As for his suggestion that the *stupa* cult was monastically controlled, that is less clear.

Control of the *stupa* cult is demonstrated, to some degree, by the simple presence of the main *stupa* at the monastery. However, the haphazard placement of cairns, even on neighboring hills, suggests that monastic control was not complete. If the monks controlled *stupa* ritual and the people who arranged for the entombment of devotees in cairns accepted that control, it should be expected that the cairns should be located on the same hill as the monastery. The placement of these cairns on adjacent hills, or even in the floodplain below the hills, suggests that the monks may not have had complete control over their placement and construction. Whatever the case, the cairns demonstrate at least some degree of ritual engagement between the monks and the local populations who placed their dead in the cairns overlooking the monastery.

The Sacred Landscape of Thotlakonda Hill

The distribution of cairns across Thotlakonda Hill has patches of greater concentration, but it is continuous from one end of the hill to the other. Generally, there are more cairns near the monastery, but a few cairns were found at points distant from the monastery as well. In figure 8.3 I have circled three areas of greater concentration that I investigate in detail below. However, I do not suggest that these patches of greater cairn density are discrete. As figure 8.3 illustrates, the borders of these clusters of cairns are indistinct. My principal reason for examining these

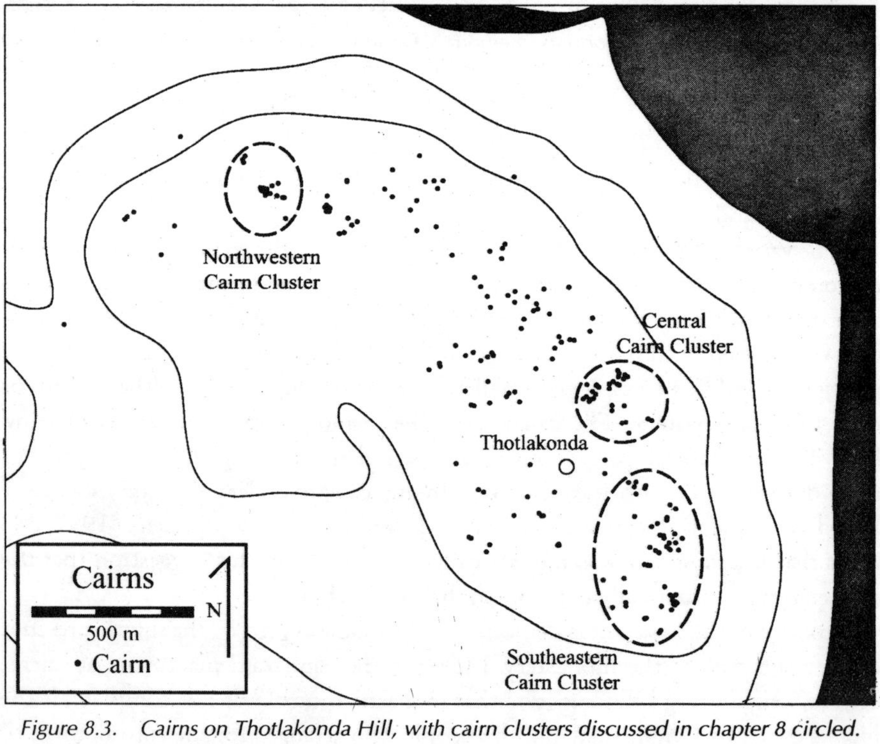

Figure 8.3. Cairns on Thotlakonda Hill, with cairn clusters discussed in chapter 8 circled.

areas in greater detail is the co-occurrence of other archaeological features within these cairn clusters (e.g., reservoirs, structures, and walls).

In my analysis of the distribution of cairns in the survey area, I spent considerable time trying to identify patterns within different cairn clusters. I examined the sizes and positions of different cairns within individual clusters and the layout of clusters in comparison with others. I speculated that if, as argued above, the mortuary landscape consisted of both monastic and lay memorials, there might be differences in the sizes of individual cairns, or the layouts of different cairn clusters. For example, it is possible that even ordinary monks had a few disciples. A large cairn circled by many smaller ones might indicate memorialization of disciples around a moderately prominent monk in the same way that votive *stupas* surround a *mahastupa*. Another possibility is that different cairn clusters might have been used for monks or the laity, maintaining a separation in death that existed in life.

Despite careful analysis, I was unable to identify any significant patterning in the distribution of cairns in relation to their size. Clusters do not appear to be oriented around a large central cairn, nor do the mean sizes of cairns within different clusters appear significantly different. I was not able to identify any common patterns of layout or organization. With the exception of one factor, visibility of the main *stupa* at Thotlakonda, the placement of the cairns appears haphazard.

Southeast Cairn Cluster and Reservoir

As stated earlier, 75 percent (n = 173) of the cairns recorded during the survey are in locations from which Thotlakonda Monastery is visible. Of those that are in positions where the monastery is not visible, the vast majority (n = 38) are located in a cluster surrounding the southeastern reservoir. Otherwise, only a few cairns (n = 10) along the northern rim of Thotlakonda Hill and those located in the floodplain (n = 6) below cannot be seen by the monastery. As discussed above, the southeastern reservoir and the small structures surrounding it were likely used by the labor force that worked for the monastery (see figure 8.4). The ambivalence of their relationship with the monks resulted in the placement of their activities beyond sight of the monastery. Given the proximity of the cairns to the reservoir and structures, and their similar concealment from the monastery, it is likely they memorialize lay Buddhists, perhaps those who worked at the monastery. Their position suggests that in death, as in life, the laborers' interaction with the monastery was kept to a minimum.

The identification of the southeastern cairn cluster as memorials for the labor force that served the monastery remains tentative. Future research, particularly excavations of the cairns, must be conducted to more firmly establish if this interpretation is correct. However, if true, this interpretation provides one mechanism

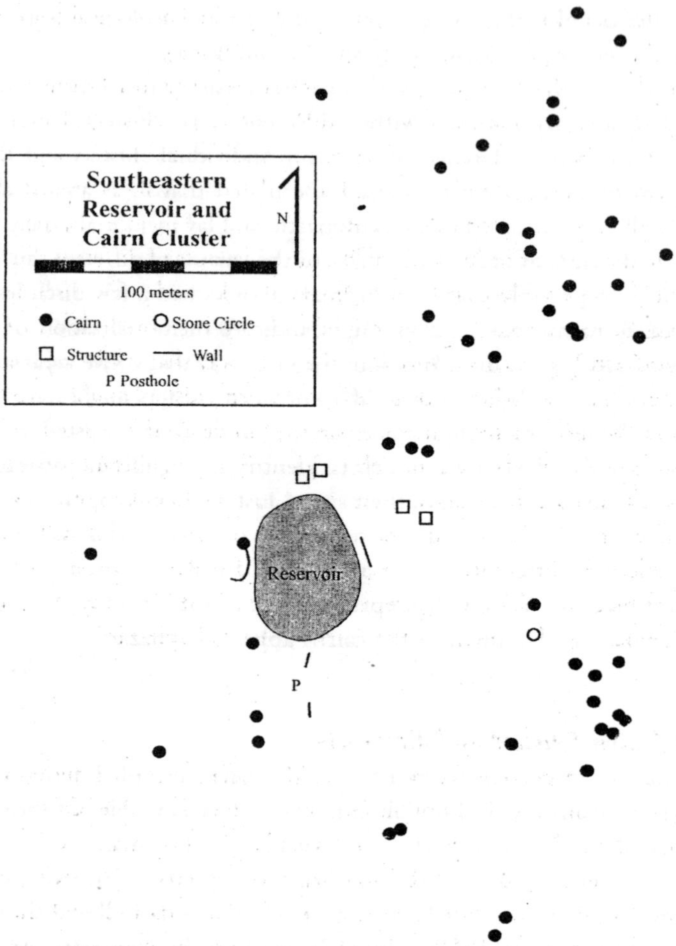

Figure 8.4. Southeastern cairn cluster with associated archaeological features.

for differentiating monastic and lay memorials. On Thotlakonda Hill, locations with views of the monastery may have been reserved for the memorials of ordinary monks. As for the surrounding hills, as suggested earlier, it is likely that these contained memorials constructed by, and for, the laity. Given that all of the cairns found on adjacent hills are located in positions from which the monastery is visible, it seems that monastic authority over the placement of memorial cairns did not extend beyond Thotlakonda Hill. As with so many aspects of the architecture and landscape, the distribution of mortuary cairns seems to demonstrate a degree of ambivalence and resistance in the relations between the monastery and lay Buddhists.

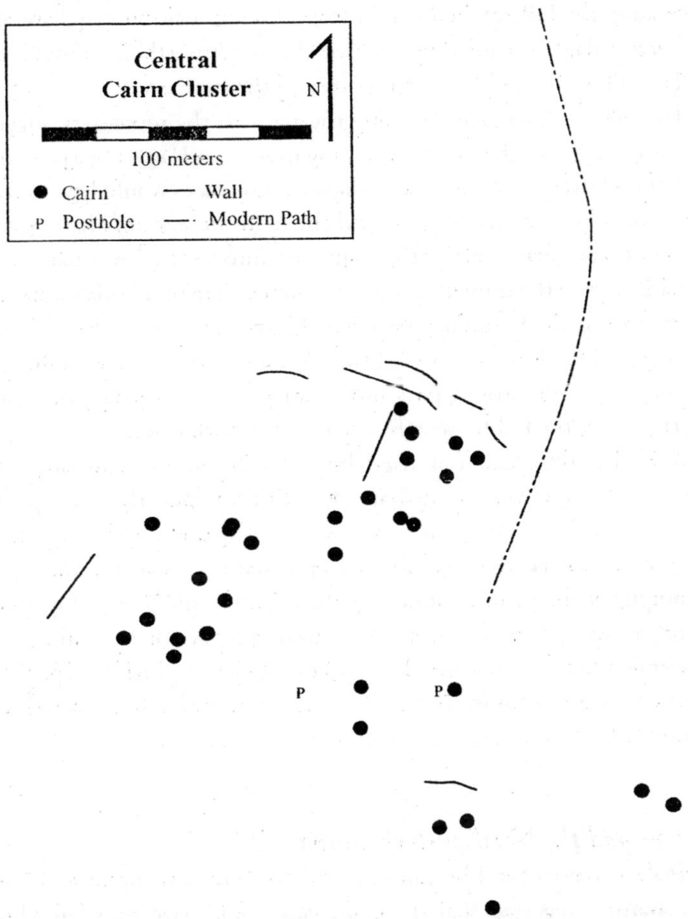

Figure 8.5. Central cairn cluster and associated archaeological features.

Central Cairn Cluster

Unlike the southeastern cairn cluster, the central cairn cluster has a direct view of the main *stupa* at Thotlakonda. Following from the preceding discussion, these cairns likely memorialize monks. The cairns are located on a series of terraces, adjacent to a modern path leading from the floodplain up the hill (see figure 8.5). Two postholes were found on a large patch of sheetrock on the eastern side of the cairn cluster. I believe that this site is best understood in relation with the modern path. This portion of the hill is among the easiest points to ascend. While no archaeological evidence was found to demonstrate that the modern path has greater antiquity, it is likely that ascent to Thotlakonda would have occurred at this location. This cluster of cairns and terraces would have marked the point where a person ascending the hill reached the hilltop. This transition may have also been marked by prayer flags, as shown by the two sheetrock postholes. From here, it is a relatively flat walk to the public worship area of the monastery.

The placement of these cairns along the path to the monastery suggests that cairns had more functions than memorializing monks and laity. For a person ascending the hill, this cluster of cairns, prayer flags, and terraces would have been located at the first point where the monastery, and the main *stupa*, would have been visible. This dense cluster of cairns marked the transition into a sacred, mortuary landscape. Just as *chaitya* I marked the transition into the sacred core of Thotlakonda, this cluster of cairns marked the boundary between the secular world below Thotlakonda Hill and the sacred landscape of the hilltop. As a person continued walking toward the monastery, he or she would pass more cairns before reaching the cisterns on the northern side of the public worship space of Thotlakonda.

It is likely that this path was used by both the monks and laity to ascend Thotlakonda Hill. However, given that the path leads directly to the public worship space, it seems likely that this was the regular route used by pilgrims. Upon arriving at the monastery, they would have cleansed themselves in the cisterns before worshipping at the various ritual structures in the public worship area. Thus, the path, prayer flags, terraces, and cairns were all part of the infrastructure of ritual engagement between the monks and laity. Beyond providing space for nonmonastic ritual within the monastery, routes of access through the sacred landscape of Thotlakonda Hill were created to foster this interaction.

Large Cairns and the Northwestern Stupa

In the original site report for Thotlakonda (Sastry, Subrahmanyam, and Rao 1992, 99), the excavators suggested that the main *stupa* could have served as a beacon or landmark for oceangoing vessels. This is true. However, due to the flat top of the hill on which the monastery is found, the main *stupa* would have been visible only to vessels relatively far out to sea and to other monasteries on neighboring hills. Even the local villages located in the floodplains below Thotlakonda would not have been able to see the central *stupa*.

Shaw (1999) argued that the hilltop locations of the *stupas* at Sanchi and nearby sites created a Buddhist landscape through patterns of intervisibility and prominence. Given their visibility in the local landscapes, the *stupas* at and near Sanchi would have promoted the authority of Buddhism across the region in which they were found. However, because of the topography of Thotlakonda Hill, the main *stupa* at Thotlakonda Monastery was not able to achieve this effect. Rather, one large cairn and one large *stupa* were erected on the northern edge of the hill to mark the presence of the monastery. Both would have been visible over great distances, announcing the presence of the monastery to both passing ships and the local populations of the region.

Four large cairns were found on Thotlakonda Hill during the survey. All but one are located adjacent to the monastery (see figure 8.6). The northernmost large cairn, over twelve meters in diameter, lies directly above the modern anchoring location, in a position prominent to the ocean. As stated in the introduction, I have reserved the term *stupa* for those tumuli with evidence for a circumambulatory path, a *harmika,* or *chhatras.* While this cairn did not have a circumambulatory path, it is possible that it might have had a *harmika* or *chhatras.* Given its location directly on the edge of a steep hillside, both would have rolled down the hill if they eroded from the cairn. The size of this cairn compared with the average size of cairns in the survey area (2.5 m) suggests that it might be best understood as a *stupa.* Whether a large cairn or *stupa,* it would have announced the presence of the monastery to passing ships and people who anchored below the monastery. This latter group could include both local fishermen and coastal traders. However, given the meager amount of trade goods at the monastery, it is likely the former group was targeted.

In contrast to the large cairn discussed above, the *stupa* on the northern edge of Thotlakonda Hill (NEAMS 110) would have announced the presence of the monastery to local populations. The *stupa* is located in a position visible to the interior, particularly the settlement identified in the floodplain, not the ocean or the monastery. As briefly discussed in chapter 7, the inclusion of a circumambulatory path at this *stupa* suggests that it was oriented toward the ritual interests of the laity. This stands in contrast to the main *stupa* at the monastery itself, which does not have a clearly demarcated circumambulatory path. Given the placement of the northwestern *stupa* directly above the settlement in the floodplain, it demonstrates a ritual tie between Thotlakonda Monastery and the local lay Buddhists living in the floodplain below. Further, by employing an architectural form preferred by the laity, the northwestern stupa demonstrates a ritual compromise between the monks and laity. With no circumambulatory paths at the monastery, it is likely that this compromise was the product of resistance to monastic ritual by the local laity.

The northwestern *stupa* is located adjacent to a small concentration of cairns, cisterns, walls, and an unfinished column (see figure 8.7). Previously I argued that the cisterns were created by quarrying stone for construction of the monastery. Thus, like the area surrounding the southeastern reservoir, the area near the northwest *stupa* was used by non-monastic laborers employed by the monastery. It is also likely, then, that the cairns surrounding the northwestern *stupa* were memorials for the laity rather than clergy. Together, the *stupa,* cisterns, and cairns were a subsidiary ritual space intended for use by the laity.

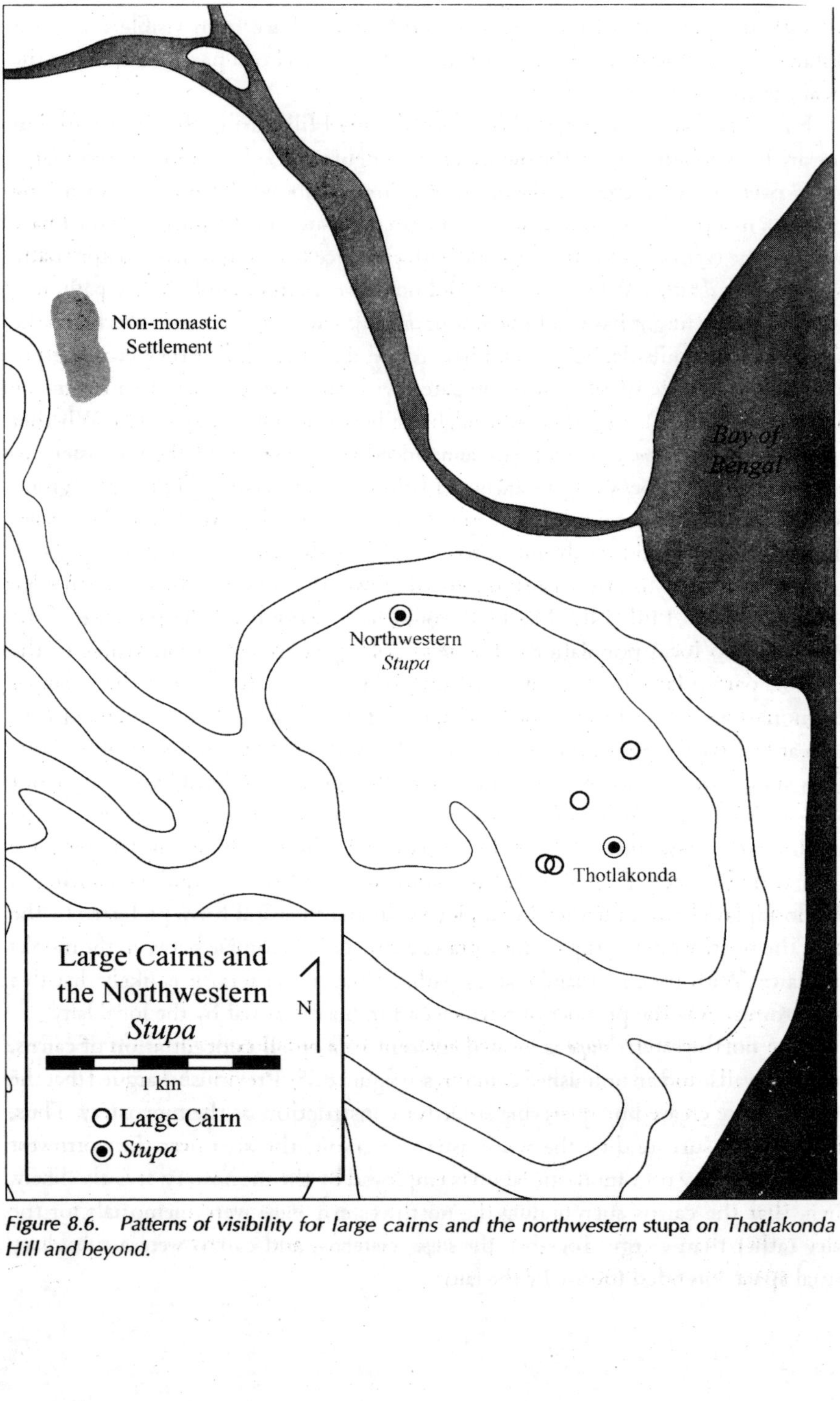

Figure 8.6. Patterns of visibility for large cairns and the northwestern stupa on Thotlakonda Hill and beyond.

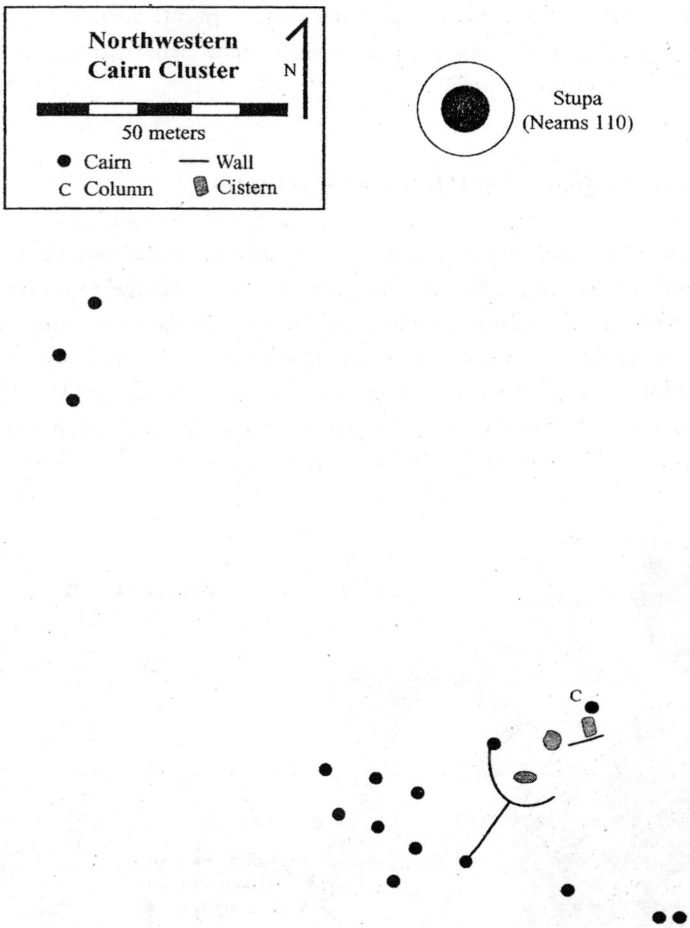

Figure 8.7. Northwestern cairn cluster, cisterns, and nearby stupa.

In chapter 7, I argued that the lack of ritual spaces in the areas east of the monastery indicated that religious legitimization, in a Marxist sense, was not a principal element in the interaction between the monks and their laborers. The northwestern *stupa* and its association with the quarries contradict that argument to some degree. However, given the *stupa*'s distance from the monastery and its lack of visibility from the monastery, it is unclear to what degree the monks at Thotlakonda controlled the northwestern *stupa* or the ritual that occurred around it. The complete lack of similar spaces at, or close to, the monastery, suggests that the monks at Thotlakonda may have accepted this form of worship space grudgingly. The attempts at more direct forms of legitimization at the monastery, as shown by the omission of circumambulatory paths and corporate worship spaces, were not completely successful. Thus, the northwestern *stupa* demonstrates resistance as much as it does legitimization.

Local and Regional Settlement Patterns

With only one non-monastic settlement identified in the survey area, it is difficult to address local settlement patterns. More can be said of the regional settlement patterns, but this is limited by the almost exclusive knowledge of monastic sites. Other than the small settlement I identified below Thotlakonda, only one other non-monastic settlement (Dantapuram; see figure 8.8) has been identified in north coastal Andhra Pradesh (Sarma, Subrahmanyam, and Reddy 2000). This large walled settlement is similar in size and elaboration to Sisupalgarh in Orissa (Lal 1949; Smith 2002). The APDAM began excavations at Dantapuram in 2002,

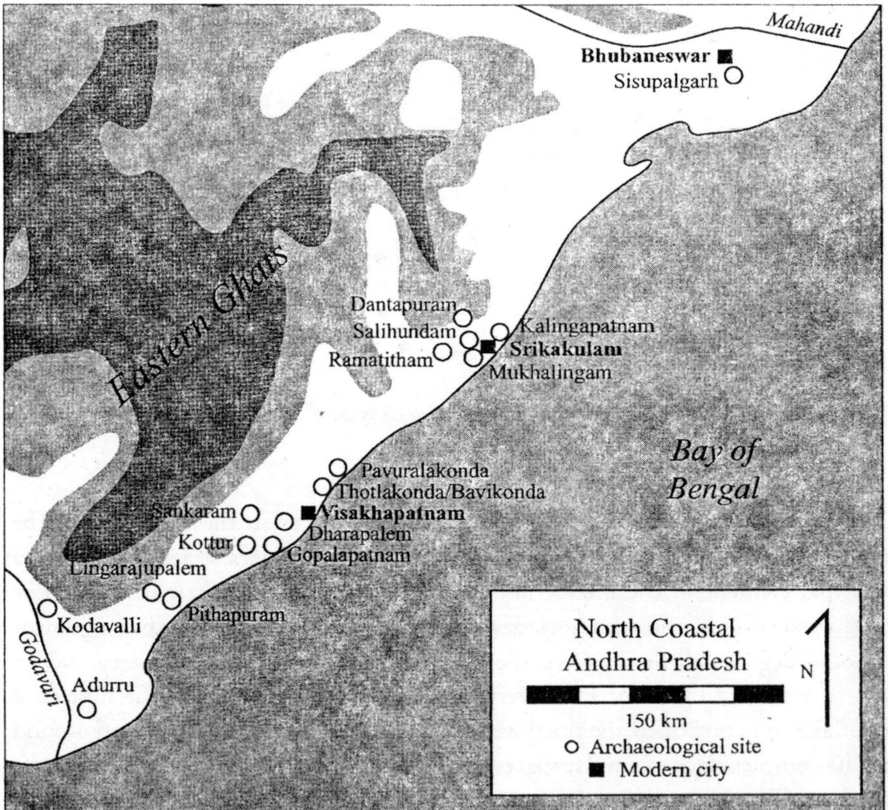

Figure 8.8. Archaeological sites in north coastal Andhra Pradesh.

but it will be several years before reports are available. My discussion of regional settlement patterns, therefore, addresses only the monastic sites.

Local Settlement Patterns

The ceramic scatter indicating the non-monastic settlement in the floodplain below Thotlakonda lies at the base of a large hill. The ceramic scatter ends at the point where the base of the hill meets the floodplain. This may indicate that, like the modern villages in the area today, the floodplain was reserved for agriculture, with villages on the hillsides above. The placement of villages above the floodplain would have also reduced the threat of flooding from cyclones. During survey, only one small ceramic scatter (NEAMS 132) was found in the floodplain. However, it is possible that silt had covered other settlements, making them undetectable by surface survey. Without subsurface prospecting, the possibility of further settlements in the floodplain cannot be ruled out.

Only three square kilometers of the floodplain were surveyed during the course of research (see figure 6.2). Other settlements may lie beyond the survey boundaries. Within seven kilometers of the settlement are three known monasteries: Thotlakonda, Bavikonda, and Pavuralakonda. The combined population of these monasteries, as indicated by the number of monastic cells, would have been approximately 150 people. It is unlikely that a single three-hectare settlement could have provisioned all of these monks. Other settlements almost certainly exist in the region surrounding the monasteries, beyond my survey area.

As has been amply discussed throughout the last few chapters, the ceramics from the settlement are broadly similar in both type and frequency to those found at Thotlakonda. The ceramics are even more similar to those found in the areas used by the laborers who worked for the monastery. It is possible, therefore, that the laborers lived in this village. However, the similarities in the forms of ceramics between the two sites can also be explained by participation in the same trade network and by the similarity of the activities (i.e., food preparation) that occurred at the two sites. Nevertheless, the placement of the northwestern *stupa* in a position overlooking the settlement suggests that the ties between the monastery and this settlement were well established.

It should be remembered that the settlement is equally close to Bavikonda. Likewise, the ceramics at Bavikonda (see Prasad 1994) are similar to those at Thotlakonda and the settlement. It is likely that the settlement had ties with both monasteries. It is also likely that other, unidentified, local villages had similar ritual and exchange relationships with the two monasteries. Given the available information, only the barest outline of the local settlement pattern can be postulated. A more complete appraisal of these patterns requires further survey and perhaps the use of subsurface testing methods in the floodplain.

Regional Settlement Patterns

As discussed briefly in chapter 5, the earliest monasteries in north coastal Andhra Pradesh were established on the coast in the first and second centuries B.C. (e.g., Thotlakonda, Bavikonda, Pavuralakonda, Gopalapatnam, Lingarajupalem; see figure 8.8). Between the second and fourth centuries A.D. the coastal monasteries were abandoned, with new monasteries founded further inland (e.g., Salihundam, Sankaram, and Ramatirtham). The later monasteries are typically found on low hills, adjacent to rivers, amid large parcels of agricultural land (see Sastry 1983). This change in location was accompanied by a change in the typical layout of the monasteries. Where the coastal monasteries had a distinct public worship space, the inland sites had their largest ritual spaces within their cloisters (for maps of Salihundam and Sankaram, see Mitra 1971). A full analysis of these sites would require a separate book and extensive fieldwork. Here I will only suggest that the movement inland may have been related to an increasing role of Buddhist monasteries in agricultural production. While I have argued that there is little evidence for this at Thotlakonda, the establishment of inland monasteries may indicate that Buddhist monasteries in north coastal Andhra Pradesh did, eventually, assume a role in agricultural production.

The earlier placement of monasteries along the coast could be interpreted to suggest that they had a role in coastal trade. However, as I have argued for Thotlakonda, the scant evidence for trade goods and the lack of storage space suggest otherwise. The placement of the monasteries along the coast might have occurred for different reasons. Without a greater understanding of the distribution of non-monastic settlements, these reasons are difficult to identify. Perhaps occupation of the north coast of Andhra Pradesh was centered upon the coast during the early historic period, with monasteries located near the greatest number of villages. Over time, the interior was cleared. As the villages moved inland, the monasteries followed. Perhaps the location of the monasteries is a product of their gradual expansion into a previously inhabited region. Traveling along the coast, the monks would have first established ties with coastal villages, gradually moving inland as their influence increased. An evaluation of these different possibilities must await further research, particularly on the non-monastic archaeological remains of north coastal Andhra Pradesh.

Conclusion 9

MY ANALYSES OF THE ARCHITECTURE and landscape of Thotlakonda have revealed several elements of the broader social role, and social tensions, of the monastery. Each of these relates to the monastic functions proposed by previous researchers (religious isolation, ritual engagement, and economic engagement). This chapter summarizes my analyses, examining the implications of the results for the different understandings of Buddhist monasticism that have been proposed. The emphasis on monastic isolation, as argued by numerous early scholars (Cunningham [1854] 1997; Brown 1965; Basham 1967; Fergusson and Burgess [1880] 1988; Lamotte 1988), is shown in the architectural isolation of the cloister and hilltop placement of the monastery. Ritual interaction with the laity, particularly in regard to the *stupa* cult and mortuary ritual (see Schopen 1997), is evident in the public worship space and mortuary landscape. In contrast, a monastic role in long-distance trade, as proposed by Thapar (1966, 1997, 2002), Ray (1986, 1987), and Lahiri (1992), is not supported by the evidence from Thotlakonda. Rather, economic interactions were locally oriented. All of these monastic roles existed side by side—the tensions between them reduced through separation within the monastery and in the landscape surrounding it.

Monastic Isolation

A focus on isolation is evident in the placement of the monastery on a hilltop, visually and spatially segregated from the non-monastic settlements in the floodplain below. The hilltop was a sacred landscape consisting of the monastery and numerous mortuary features. With the exception of the spaces used by the non-monastic laborers who worked for the monastery, no "secular" structures or sites were found on either Thotlakonda Hill or any of the hills surrounding it. Access to the heart of the monastery, the cloister, passed through a ritual space, defining a transition from secular to sacred ground. The isolation of the monastery is further demonstrated by architectural and spatial barriers to interaction between the monks and the labor force that supported them.

The most conspicuous point of interaction between the monks and the labor force was the refectory. Through architectural isolation, this interaction was kept to a minimum. Most support activities occurred outside the monastery, some visually concealed at the southeastern reservoir. Even the memorial cairns of the laborers seem to have been hidden from direct view. Together, all of this suggests the monks had a strongly ambivalent view of the people who worked for them. While they relied upon them for food preparation and other menial activities, their presence on the hill was concealed to the maximum extent possible. From the inwardly focused cloister to the concealment of the refectory, numerous factors demonstrate that religious isolation was important to the monks at Thotlakonda. However, this interest was tempered by the necessity for economic interactions that allowed the monastery to function and prosper.

Local Economic Interactions

Previous researchers have argued that monasteries acted as facilitators in long-distance trade (see Ray 1986, 1987; Lahiri 1992). My research at Thotlakonda indicates that the monastery was oriented, for the most part, toward local exchange. The evidence for economic interaction consists of donation inscriptions, some limited evidence for long-distance trade, and a variety of indicators demonstrating extensive interest in local exchange systems. The latter includes the employment of the laborers discussed above and the similarities in ceramic types at the monastery and the settlement.

A few artifacts at Thotlakonda are clearly derived from beyond north coastal Andhra Pradesh. The most obvious of these are the Roman and Satavahana coins found by the APDAM. In addition, the two sherds of Rouletted Ware found at the monastery are also likely to have been imported from elsewhere in South Asia. The only other evidence for long-distance trade consists of a large cairn overlooking the modern anchoring location below Thotlakonda Hill. It is possible that this cairn was located to mark the presence of the monastery for traders who stopped there. That said, overall the evidence for long-distance trade at Thotlakonda is limited.

In contrast, the evidence for local economic interaction is extensive. First, the majority of ceramics from the monastery resemble, in both type and frequency of non-plastic inclusions, those found at the settlement. This indicates that ceramics from both sites were locally produced. The two sites also have similar large storage jars with appliqué chain motifs. Given the large size of the storage jars, it is unlikely they were transported great distances. Thus, the monastery likely obtained them through local channels. The large size of these jars demonstrates that the monks stored food in very large quantities. It is unclear if the monastery purchased the food, or if it was directed toward the monastery through donation. In either case, it is likely that it was produced locally.

Another form of economic interaction is shown by the laborers employed by the monastery. If religious conviction underwrote their labor, it should be expected that there would be structures in their work spaces to remind them of the higher purpose of their efforts. Given the paucity of ritual structures within the areas used by the laborers, it seems that their employment was not based upon religious donation. The separation of the non-monastic work spaces and the removal of some activities to the southeastern reservoir further testify to the general level of ambivalence between the monks and those who worked for them. If the monks were dependent on volunteer labor, it seems unlikely that they could have treated the non-monastic workers in this way. Rather, the high frequency of bowls in their work areas may suggest that the laborers received payments of food, if not other tangible benefits as well.

The final evidence for economic interaction consists of donation inscriptions on *chhatras* and other items at the monastery. Unlike the monastic labor discussed above, these are likely to have been motivated by the religious conviction of wealthier laity. However, as suggested by many previous scholars (see Lopez 2001), these were not wholly altruistic donations. Following from Thapar's (2002) arguments, these donations would have conferred prestige upon those who donated them. This partially explains why donation inscriptions are located on *chhatras*. The *chhatras* were located on votive *stupas* in the public worship space. The inscriptions, therefore, would have announced the piety of the donors to a lay audience, enhancing the status of the donor.

These inscriptions would have also served to produce merit for the donors. From an outside perspective, this would seem a less tangible reward, but, for a lay Buddhist, the value of merit was as real as any other benefit. In this way, these donations can be viewed as an exchange. The monks at Thotlakonda balanced their interest in seclusion with engagement in a broadly based *stupa* cult. In this sense, donations were payments for services provided by the monks. That these services were ritual in nature does not diminish their value.

Local Ritual Interactions

While donations have value in understanding the economic interactions of the monastery, they also demonstrate ritual engagement between the monastery and lay Buddhists. The importance of this relationship is further shown in many elements of the architecture and landscape of Thotlakonda. The first is the creation of a public worship space within the monastery. This shows an active interest by the monks in fostering lay ritual, despite their strong desire for seclusion as demonstrated by the cloister. Further, the architectural forms of the ritual spaces in the public worship area illustrate attempts by the clergy to promote more hierarchical ritual, with themselves as leaders. This is shown by the omission of circumambulatory paths and by the construction of the main *chaitya* in the form of a hall.

Another element that demonstrates an attempt by the monks to assert ritual control over the *stupa* cult is the placement of votive *stupas* in the public worship area. These votive *stupas* were memorials for those monks with the strongest ties to lay devotees beyond the monastery. By placing them within the public worship space, the builders forced lay devotees to come to the monastery to pay tribute to, or worship, their former teachers. Paths leading to the monastery were created to assist in fostering these relations. Cairns and flags were strategically placed along the paths to mark the transition to the sacred mortuary landscape of the hilltop. Other large cairns were employed to announce the presence of the monastery to those who lived below the hill. Overall, the architecture and landscape of Thotlakonda demonstrate an active interest in fostering ritual ties with the laity—a relationship through which the monks attempted to assert their own authority. The mortuary landscape of Thotlakonda shows that this attempt was not entirely successful.

The mortuary landscape of Thotlakonda Hill, as well as neighboring hills, combines both monastic and lay memorials. Given the literary evidence, it is likely that monks played a part in the funerals of both. However, the placement of cairns on neighboring hills and in positions below Thotlakonda Hill suggests that the monks had only partial control over their construction. The placement of lay memorials on neighboring hills overlooking the monastery suggests that the mortuary landscape was monastically centered but not necessarily monastically controlled. Overall, the mortuary landscape demonstrates a degree of independence, and perhaps resistance, to the ritual authority of the monks. Lay resistance is more profoundly demonstrated by the layout and placement of the northwestern *stupa*.

The final form of the northwestern *stupa* was a product of negotiation between the monks at Thotlakonda and the lay people who used it. Given its placement adjacent to a quarry, it is likely that those who used it consisted, at least in part, of the laborers who worked for the monastery. The position of this *stupa*, distant from the monastery and prominent to the settlement in the floodplain below, indicates that this *stupa* served to announce the presence of the monastery to the local population. Overall, this *stupa* was oriented toward lay ritual, though its construction and consecration were at least partially dependent upon the monks at Thotlakonda. Thus, it served the interests of both groups. For the laity, the presence of a circumambulatory path allowed for ritual and worship in the form they preferred. For the monks, it established ritual ties with the local laity. On a larger scale, the local laity had their choice of several monasteries at which to worship. The *mahastupa* at Bavikonda followed the ritual preferences of the local laity, with prominent circumambulatory paths. While the chronology of the region is still somewhat difficult to establish, it appears that this was the earliest large *stupa* in the immediate area. The omission of circumambulatory paths at Thotlakonda can therefore be interpreted as a subsequent attempt to manipulate the form of ritual spaces to serve the interests of the local monks. The continued occupation of Bavikonda and the construction of the northwestern *stupa* suggests that the attempt by the monks to establish themselves as ritual leaders over the laity was only partially successful. Monastic control of the *stupa* cult was not absolute. The clergy were forced to take into account the views and desires of the laity who participated in it.

Religion and Ritual: An Archaeological Approach

Throughout this book I have relied upon the perspective of practice theory to investigate the role of ritual in the relationships between the monks at Thotlakonda and the laity who lived below it. It is my hope that this book will serve as one example of how religion and ritual can be studied archaeologically. Given the material focus of archaeology, religion can be productively investigated only if we abandon a view of religion that emphasizes the centrality of abstract religious doctrines and origin myths. It is important to note that I am not suggesting that more abstract aspects of religion are uninteresting or unimportant. Where sources are available (i.e., texts, oral traditions, and artwork), they provide critical insights into the broader social world in which a particular religious tradition existed. These sources, however, typically represent the views of a small, literate minority. It is unclear to what degree they accurately represent the views of the bulk of the population. A complete picture of an early society can best be constructed through a synthesis of literary and archaeological sources.

Ritual, with its regularized and repeated format, leaves material traces of its practice. This in turn allows archaeologists to study it. Once rituals are identified, a wide variety of anthropological approaches toward the social role of ritual can be employed to examine the broader social implications of their practice. Religion, as argued by Durkheim ([1915] 1995), promoted social cohesiveness by reducing and obscuring differences between different segments of society. Common identification with certain religious beliefs, sacred locations, and such promoted a community of followers. At Thotlakonda this sense of community between the monks and laity is shown through the sharing of ritual spaces at the monastery and the construction of a common mortuary landscape. However, the material traces of ritual also demonstrate the limits of the community and the fracture lines that existed within it.

Earlier I argued that the omission of circumambulatory paths at Thotlakonda, along with numerous other archaeological indicators, illustrated attempts by the monks to assert authority over the local laity. This can be interpreted as an attempt at the routinization of charisma by the monks (Weber 1968, 1978). In essence, the monks used their privileged position in regard to the Buddha to promote their power over the laity. Yet again, however, archaeological traces of ritual practice illustrate that this attempt was not entirely successful. The placement of mortuary cairns on adjacent hills and the layout of the northwestern *stupa* suggest that the laity successfully resisted the authority of the monks to some degree, forcing the monks to accommodate their ritual desires. This latter interpretation is founded upon recent discussion of resistance in anthropological discussion of practice.

Different archaeologists and anthropologists might choose one of these issues (social solidarity, the routinization of charisma, and lay resistance) as primary or foundational. I do not. Each has assisted in understanding the conflicting social roles of Thotlakonda Monastery in its local social context. I doubt that a full understanding could have been achieved by relying upon a single anthropological approach. In this way, this research stands in contrast to many archaeological treatments of religion where one view of religion—legitimization—has often dominated. This does not mean that legitimization has no place in an understanding of the social role of Thotlakonda.

Significant quantities of goods were transferred to the monastery through donation. This is shown in several of the inscriptions found at the monastery. The creation of the public worship space and monastic participation in lay rituals further legitimized monastic appropriation. That said, it appears there were limits to what the monks could obtain through religious legitimization alone. The laborers who worked for the monastery do not appear to have been motivated (at least not entirely) by charity. This is shown by the lack of ritual structures in the areas where they worked and the overall ambivalence of their relationship with the monks. Evidence of lay resistance demonstrates that the monks were not given free rein. The support they received was based upon their fulfillment of ritual and social obligations. This, in turn, limited their ability to isolate themselves, a desire expressed in monastic literature and demonstrated in the architecture of the cloister. While valuable, legitimization cannot account for the full diversity of social ties in which the monastery was engaged.

Despite its focus on ritual, this research was able to identify aspects of Thotlakonda that were not religiously oriented. In order to accomplish the religious and ritual functions of the monastery, the monks engaged in local exchange networks and employed local labor. By focusing on ritual interaction, this analysis has also identified those mundane aspects of monastic life that lie outside the depictions of Buddhist monasteries in religious texts. In this way my archaeological research serves to complement traditional, textually based, scholarship.

Unresolved Questions

It is my hope that this book will serve as an example of the value of archaeological survey in South Asia. To date, most archaeological research on the Early Historic Period has focused on the excavation of Buddhist monasteries and a few larger urban centers. In a sense, this has created islands of understanding, but the broader social relations remain somewhat vague. That said, several of the implications of this research demand excavations to address them.

Throughout my analyses, the laity have been treated, for the most part, as a single, homogenous community. Yet, it is clear that there were significant social, economic, and religious divisions in the lay community that my analysis has failed to take into account. For example, those laity who donated *chhatras* to Thotlakonda Monastery were likely to have been comparatively wealthy, while the laborers employed to support and build the monastery were undoubtedly less so. The order of monks and nuns was primarily drawn from the wealthier families in the Early Historic Period. Thus, the differences in treatment between pilgrims and laborers could be heavily informed by differences in wealth and status of the lay communities from which they came. Different segments of the lay community likely had different attitudes toward Buddhist worship and support.

Given the paucity of literary information concerning the day-to-day activities of the laity during the Early Historic Period, an examination of the different attitudes toward ritual among the laity requires the archaeological study of their communities. As part of these studies, several issues could be investigated. First, it is likely that the laity engaged in domestic rituals. As stated earlier, numerous Buddhist literary sources state that monks were to perform "life cycle" rituals for the laity, outside the monastery. Archaeological investigations of Early Historic Period domestic architecture could serve to identify domestic ritual and examine the differences between it and the rituals performed in and around monasteries. This, in turn, would allow for religious differences between Buddhist monks and laity to be further elucidated. Through comparisons between the rituals practiced in wealthy and less wealthy homes, the variation in attitudes toward religion and ritual could also be examined between different segments of laity.

A second issue that should be examined is religious heterodoxy. During the Early Historic Period, several different monastic orders (e.g., Jainism and Brahmanism) existed side by side with Buddhism in many areas of South Asia. It is likely that adherents of many religious traditions lived within single communities. It is also possible that individuals may have engaged in rituals of multiple religious sects. A complete understanding of Early Historic Period religious interaction must take these into account. Careful archaeological examination of the variety of domestic rituals that occur within a community and within individual households could lead to understandings of this variability.

Another issue that must be addressed concerns chronology. As discussed earlier, particularly in regard to ceramics, the archaeological materials used to identify chronological periods in South Asia tend to cover broad periods and large geographic areas. Given that many sites may have been occupied for less than a century, the existing chronological periods do not allow for the precise identification of contemporary sites. In order to minimize this problem, greater attention must be paid to the construction of regional chronologies with tighter temporal resolution. These more robust local chronologies will, in time, allow for the relationships between different archaeological sites to be investigated with far greater clarity than is currently possible.

Finally, the architectural analyses I performed in this book were, for the most part, based upon the APDAM excavations of Thotlakonda. While the information I gained from survey was critical to the construction of my interpretation, it should be possible to apply these techniques to other Buddhist monasteries and other architectural structures. Existing archaeological site reports from South Asia provide ample documentation of the architectural layout from numerous locations and contexts. Reanalysis of these sites, focusing upon the experiential aspects of their architecture and layout, could be extremely productive. Research of this sort could examine not only regional differences in the social roles of Early Historic Period Buddhist monasteries, but also issues concerning other religious sects and the long-term development of individual sects.

Conclusion

In the end, the picture of the broader social relations I have developed for Thotlakonda Monastery is messier than typical depictions of early Buddhist monasticism. The interpretation here resembles more the practice of modern Buddhist monasteries, with all of their conflicting roles, idiosyncrasies, and practical demands of feeding and maintaining a large monastic community. In part, this is the result of the methods I used to investigate Thotlakonda. Previous interpretations of Early Buddhist monasticism rested upon readings of Buddhist monastic texts and archaeological excavations of monasteries in isolation from their surroundings. In essence, archaeologists and historians have relied upon a single perspective to develop their interpretations—the perspective of the monks themselves. It is not surprising that this view would be more coherent than one that incorporates the conflicting interests of multiple social groups. By moving my investigations beyond the monastery walls, my analyses emphasize the tensions, conflicts, and complex ritual relationships between the monks at Thotlakonda and the lay Buddhists who engaged, both economically and spiritually, with them. Rather than the idealized monastery of Buddhist literature, my analyses focus on the practice of Buddhist monasticism, with all of its discordant aspects intact.

References

Adams, Robert McC. 1965. *Land behind Baghdad: A history of settlements on the Diyala Plain.* Chicago: University of Chicago Press.

———. 1981. *Heartlands of Cities: Surveys of ancient settlements and land use on the central floodplain of the Euphrates.* Chicago: Chicago University Press.

Alcock, Susan E. 1993. *Graecia Capta: The landscapes of Roman Greece.* Cambridge: Cambridge University Press.

Allchin, Bridget, and Raymond Allchin. 1982. *The Rise of Civilization in India and Pakistan.* Cambridge: Cambridge University Press.

Allchin, Raymond, ed. 1995. *The Archaeology of Early Historic South Asia: The emergence of cities and states.* Cambridge: Cambridge University Press.

———. 1995. Early cities and states beyond the Ganges Valley. In *The Archaeology of Early Historic South Asia: The emergence of cities and states,* edited by R. Allchin. Cambridge: Cambridge University Press.

———. 1995. The Mauryan state and empire. In *The Archaeology of Early Historic South Asia: The emergence of cities and states,* edited by R. Allchin. Cambridge: Cambridge University Press.

Ammerman, Albert V. 1981. Surveys and archaeological research. *Annual Review of Anthropology* 10:63–88.

Arnold, D. E. 1985. *Ceramic Theory and Cultural Process.* Cambridge: Cambridge University Press.

Ashmore, Wendy, and A. Bernard Knapp, eds. 1999. *Archaeologies of Landscape.* Malden: Blackwell.

Bareau, André. 1974. La Parinirvana du Bouddha et la naissance de la religion bouddique. *Bulletin de L'Ecole Française d'Extrême-Orient* 64:275–99.

———. 1985. Etude du Bouddhisme: I. Aspects du Bouddhisme Indien décrits par les pèlerins chinois. *Annuaire du Collège de France 1984–1985.*

Barnes, Gina L. 1995. An introduction to Buddhist archaeology. *World Archaeology* 27(2): 165–82.

———. 1999. Buddhist Landscapes of East Asia. In *Archaeologies of Landscape,* edited by W. Ashmore and A. B. Knapp. Malden: Blackwell.

Barrett, John C. 2001. Agency, the duality of structure, and the problem of the archaeological record. In *Archaeological Theory Today,* edited by I. Hodder. London: Polity.

Barua, Benimadhab. 1979. *Barhut: Parts 1, 2, and 3.* Varanasi: Indological Book House.

Basa, Kishor K., and Pradeep Mohanty, eds. 2000. *Archaeology of Orissa.* Delhi: Pratibha Prakashan.

Basham, A. L. 1967. *The Wonder That Was India.* Calcutta: Rupa and Co.

Beal, Samuel. 1908. *Si-yu-ki. Buddhist Records of the Western World.* 2 vols. New York: Paragon Book Reprint Corp.

Bechert, Heinz. 1978. The beginnings of Buddhist historiography: *Mahavamsa* and political thinking. In *Religion and Legitimation of Power in Sri Lanka,* edited by B. L. Smith. Chambersburg, Pa.: ANIMA Books.

———, ed. 1995. *When Did the Buddha Live? The Controversy on the Dating of the Historical Buddha.* Delhi: Sri Satguru Publications.

Begley, Vimala. 1983. Arikamedu reconsidered. *American Journal of Archaeology* 87:461–81.

———. 1986. Rouletting and chattering: Decoration on ancient and present-day pottery in India. *Expedition* 28(1):47–54.

———. 1988. Rouletted ware at Arikamedu: A new approach. *American Journal of Archaeology* 92:427–40.

———. 1992. Ceramic evidence for pre-*Periplus* trade on the Indian coasts. In *Rome and India: The ancient sea trade,* edited by V. Begley and R. D. DePuma. New Delhi: Oxford University Press.

———. 1993. New investigations at the port of Arikamedu. *Journal of Roman Archaeology* 6:93–108.

———, ed. 1996. *The Ancient Port of Arikamedu: New excavations and researches, 1989–1992.* Vol. I. Pondichery: Ecole Française d'Extrême-Orient.

Begley, Vimala, and R. D. De Puma, eds. 1992. *Rome and India: The ancient sea trade.* New Delhi: Oxford University Press.

Bell, Catherine. 1997. *Ritual: Perspectives and dimensions.* Oxford: Oxford University Press.

Binford, Lewis. 1962. Archaeology as anthropology. *American Antiquity* 28:217–25.

Bintliff, J. L. 1991. The Roman countryside in central Greece: Observations and theories from the Boeotia Survey (1978–1987). In *Roman Landscapes: Archaeological Survey in the Mediterranean Region,* edited by G. Barker and J. Lloyd. London: Archaeological Monographs of the British School at Rome.

Blanton, R. E. 1982. *Monte Alban's Hinterland, Part 1.* Vol. 23, *Memoirs of the Museum of Anthropology, University of Michigan.* Ann Arbor: Museum of Anthropology, University of Michigan.

Bloch, Maurice. 1977. The past in the present. *Man* 12:278–92.

———. 1989. *Ritual, History, and Power: Selected papers in anthropology.* London: Athlon Press.

Bourdieu, Pierre. 1973. The Berber house. In *Rules and Meanings,* edited by M. Douglas. Middlesex: Penguin Books.

———. 1977. *An Outline of a Theory of Practice.* Translated by R. Nice. Cambridge: Cambridge University Press.

Bradley, Richard. 1991. Ritual, time, and history. *World Archaeology* 23:209–19.

———. 1998. *The Significance of Monuments: On the shaping of human experience in Neolithic and Bronze Age Europe.* London: Routledge.

———. 2000. *An Archaeology of Natural Places.* London: Routledge.

Bradley, Richard, ed. 1990. Monuments and the monumental. *World Archaeology* 22.

Braudel, F. 1969. *Ecrits sur l'Histoire.* Paris: Flammarion.

Breckenridge, Carol A., and Peter van der Veer, eds. 1993. *Orientalism and the Postcolonial Predicament: Perspectives on South Asia.* Philadelphia: University of Pennsylvania Press.

Briant, Pierre. 2002. *From Cyrus to Alexander: A history of the Persian Empire.* Translated by P. T. Daniels. Winona Lake: Eisenbrauns.

Brown, Percy. 1965. *Indian Architecture: The Buddhist and Hindu periods.* Bombay: D. B. Taraporevala Sons and Co.

Brubaker, Robert. 2000–2001. Aspects of mortuary variability in the South Asian Iron Age. *The Bulletin of the Deccan College Post-Graduate and Research Institute* 60–61:253–302.

Brumfiel, Elizabeth. 1992. Breaking and entering the ecosystem: Gender, class, and faction steal the show. *American Anthropologist* 94:551–67.

———. 1995. Heterarchy and the analysis of complex society: Comments. In *Heterarchy and the Analysis of Complex Society,* edited by R. Ehrenreich, C. Crumley, and J. Levy. Washington, D.C.: American Anthropological Association.

Brumfiel, Elizabeth, and John W. Fox, eds. 1994. *Factional Competition and Political Development in the New World.* Cambridge: Cambridge University Press.

Caldwell, Robert. 1856. *A Comparative Grammar of the Dravidian or South-Indian Family of Languages.* London: Harrison.

Campbell, Alexander D. 1816. *A Grammar of the Teloogoo Language, Commonly Termed the Gentoo, Peculiar to the Hindoos Inhabiting the North Eastern Provinces of the Indian Peninsula.* Madras: College Press of Fort St. George.

Cane, H. 2002. Hurricane Alley. www.hurricanealley.net/bob.htm.

Carmichael, David L., Jane Hubert, Brian Reeves, and Audhild Schanche, eds. 1994. *Sacred Sites, Sacred Spaces.* London: Routledge.

Carrithers, Michael. 1983. *The Forest Monks of Sri Lanka: An anthropological and historical study.* Delhi: Oxford University Press.

Casson, Lionel. 1989. *The Periplus Maris Erythraei.* Princeton, N.J.: Princeton University Press.

Chakrabarti, D. K. 1995. Post-Mauryan states of Mainland South Asia (c. BC 185–AD 320). In *The Archaeology of Early Historic South Asia: The emergence of cities and states,* edited by R. Allchin. Cambridge: Cambridge University Press.

Chakrabarti, Dilip K. 1995a. *The Archaeology of Ancient Indian Cities.* Delhi: Oxford University Press.

———. 1995b. Buddhist sites across South Asia as influenced by political and economic forces. *World Archaeology* 27(2):185–202.

———. 1997. *Colonial Indology: Sociopolitics of the ancient Indian past.* Delhi: Munshiram Manoharlal.

———. 2001a. *Archaeological Geography of the Ganga Plain: The lower and the middle Ganga.* Delhi: Permanent Black.

———. 2001b. *A History of Archaeology: From the beginning to 1947.* Delhi: Munshiram Manoharlal.

Chakravarti, Ranabir, ed. 2001. *Trade in Early India.* New Delhi: Oxford University Press.

Chauley, G. C. 2000. Excavated remains at Lalitagiri, a Buddhist site in Orissa. In *Archaeology of Orissa,* edited by K. K. Basa and P. Mohanty. Delhi: Pratibha Prakashan.

Cherry, John F. 1982. A preliminary definition of site distribution on Melos. In *An Island Polity*, edited by C. Renfrew and M. Wagstaff. Cambridge: Cambridge University Press.

Cherry, John. F., J. L. Davis, and E. Mantzourani. 1991. *Landscape Archaeology as Long-Term History: Northern Keos in the Cycladic Islands*. Los Angeles.

Collins, Steven. 1990. On the very idea of the Pali Canon. *Journal of the Pali Text Society* XV:89–126.

Comfort, H. 1991. Terra Sigillata at Arikamedu. In *Rome and India: The ancient sea trade*, edited by V. Begley and R. D. DePuma. Madison: University of Wisconsin Press.

Coningham, Robin. 1995. Monks, caves, and kings: A reassessment of the nature of Early Buddhism in Sri Lanka. *World Archaeology* 27:266–81.

———. 1997. The spatial distribution of craft activities in early historic cities and their social implication. In *South Asian Archaeology 1995: Proceedings of the 13th International Conference of the European Association of South Asian Archaeologists*, edited by R. Allchin and B. Allchin. Cambridge: The Ancient India and Iran Trust.

———. 1998. Buddhism "rematerialized" and the archaeology of Gautama Buddha. *Cambridge Archaeological Journal* 8:121–26.

———. 2001. The archaeology of Buddhism. In *Archaeology and World Religion*, edited by T. Insoll. London: Routledge.

Coomaraswamy, Ananda K. 1927. *History of Indian and Indonesian Art*. New York: E. Weyhe.

Cosgrove, D. E. 1984. *Social Formations and Symbolic Landscape*. London.

Cosgrove, D. E., and S. Daniels, eds. 1988. *The Iconography of Landscape: Essays on the symbolic representation, design, and use of past environments*. Cambridge: Cambridge University Press.

Cowgill, George. L. 1972. Models, methods, and techniques for seriation. In *Models in Archaeology*, edited by D. L. Clarke. London: Methuen.

———. 1990. Toward refining concepts of full-coverage survey. In *The Archaeology of Regions: A case for full-coverage survey*, edited by S. K. Fish and S. A. Kowalewski. Washington: Smithsonian Institution Press.

Crumley, Carole. 1987. A dialectical critique of hierarchy. In *Power Relations in State Formation*, edited by T. Patterson and C. Gailey. Washington, D.C.: American Anthropological Association.

———. 1995. Heterarchy and the analysis of complex society. In *Heterarchy and the Analysis of Complex Society*, edited by R. Ehrenreich, C. Crumley and J. Levy. Washington, D.C.: American Anthropological Association.

Cunningham, Alexander. [1854] 1997. *The Bhilsa Topes or Buddhist Monuments of Central India*. New Delhi: Munshiram Manoharlal.

———. [1876] 1962. *The Stupa of Bharhut: A Buddhist monument ornamented with numerous sculptures*. Varanasi: Indological Book House.

———. [1892] 1998. *Mahabodhi or the Great Buddhist Temple under the Bodhi Tree at Buddha-Gaya*. New Delhi: Munshiram Manoharlal.

Das, Dharmanarayan. 1977. *The Early History of the Kalinga: A socio-economic and cultural history of coastal Orissa*. Calcutta: Punthi Pustak.

Davids, T. W. Rhys. 1900. Buddhism. *North American Review* 171:517–27.

———. 1910. *Buddhism: Being a sketch of the life and teachings of Gautama, the Buddha.* London: Society for Promoting Christian Knowledge.

Dehejia, Vidya. 1972. *Early Buddhist Rock Temples.* Ithaca, N.Y.: Cornell University Press.

Dharmanarayanadas, Das. 1977. *The Early History of the Kalingas: A socio-economic and cultural history of coastal Orissa.* Calcutta: Punthi Pustak.

Dirks, Nicholas B. 1993. *The Hollow Crown: Ethnohistory of an Indian kingdom.* Ann Arbor: University of Michigan Press.

———. 2001. *Castes of Mind: Colonialism and the making of modern India.* Princeton: Princeton University Press.

Dobres, Marcia-Ann, and John E. Robb, eds. 2000. *Agency in Archaeology.* London: Routledge.

Douglas, Mary. 1966. *Purity and Danger: An analysis of the concepts of pollution and taboo.* New York: Routledge.

Dundas, Paul. 1992. *The Jains.* New York: Routledge.

Dunnell, Robert C., and William S. Dancey. 1983. The Siteless Survey: A regional scale data collection strategy. In *Advances in Archaeological Method and Theory*, vol. 6, edited by M. Schiffer. New York: Academic Press.

Durkheim, Emile. [1893] 1984. *The Division of Labor in Society.* Translated by W. D. Halls. New York: Free Press.

———. [1897] 1951. *Suicide: A study in sociology.* Translated by J. A. Spaulding and G. Simpson. Glencoe, Ill.: Free Press.

———. [1915] 1995. *The Elementary Forms of Religious Life.* Translated by K. E. Fields. New York: Free Press.

Dutta, Mala. 1990. *A Study of Satavahana Coinage.* New Delhi: Harman Publishing House.

Ehrenreich, Robert, Carole Crumley, and Janet Levy, eds. 1995. *Heterarchy and the Analysis of Complex Societies.* Washington, D.C.: Archaeological Papers of the American Anthropological Association.

Eliot, John, ed. 1906. *Climatological Atlas of India*: Indian Meteorological Department.

Ellis, Francis Whyte. 1816. Note to the Introduction. In *A Grammar of the Teloogoo Language*, edited by A. D. Campbell. Madras: College Press of Fort St. George.

Elster, Jon. 1985. *Making Sense of Marx.* Paris: Cambridge University Press.

———, ed. 1986. *Karl Marx: A Reader.* Cambridge: Cambridge University Press.

Erdosy, George. 1985. Settlement archaeology of the Kausambi region. *Man and Environment* 9:66–79.

———. 1988. *Urbanization in Early Historic India, British Archaeological Reports: International Series.* Oxford: British Archaeological Reports.

———. 1993. The Archaeology of Early Buddhism. In *Studies in Buddhism in Honour of A. K. Warder*, edited by N. K. Wagle and F. Watanabe. Toronto: University of Toronto, Center for South Asian Studies.

———. 1995. City states of North India and Pakistan at the time of the Buddha. In *The Archaeology of Early Historic South Asia: The emergence of cities and states*, edited by R. Allchin. Cambridge: Cambridge University Press.

Fergusson, James, and James Burgess. [1880] 1988. *The Cave Temples of India.* New Delhi: Munshiram Manoharlal Publishers Pvt. Ltd.

Fish, Suzanne K., and Stephan A. Kowalewski, eds. 1990. *The Archaeology of Regions: A case for full–coverage survey*. Washington, D.C.: Smithsonian Institution Press.

Fogelin, Lars. 2003a. Ritual and presentation in Early Buddhist religious architecture. *Asian Perspectives* 42(1).

———. 2003b. Beyond the monastery walls: Buddhism in Early Historic Period society in Northeast Andhra Pradesh. In *Buddhism in Andhra: Papers in Commemoration of Dr. Hanumantha Rao*, edited by A. Parsher-Sen. New Delhi: Bharatiya Kala Prakashan.

———. 2003c. Beyond the monastery walls: The archaeology of Early Buddhism in north coastal Andhra Pradesh, India. Ph.D. dissertation, Anthropology, University of Michigan, Ann Arbor.

———. 2004. Sacred architecture, sacred landscape: Early Buddhism in coastal Andhra Pradesh. In *Archaeology as History: South Asia*, edited by H. P. Ray and C. M. Sinopoli. New Delhi: ICHR.

———. in press a. Recent research at the Buddhist monastery of Thotlakonda. In *South Asian Archaeology, 2001*, edited by C. Jarrige. Paris: Editions Recherche sur les Civilisations–ADPF.

———. in press b. History, ethnography, and essentialism: The archaeology of religion and ritual in South Asia. In *The Archaeology of Ritual*, edited by E. Kyriakidis. Los Angeles: Cotsen Institute of Archaeology.

Foley, Robert. 1981. Off–site archaeology: An alternative approach for the short-sited. In *Patterns of the Past*, edited by I. Hodder. Cambridge: Cambridge University Press.

Foucault, Michel. 1977. *Discipline and Punish*. Translated by A. Sheridan. New York: Vintage Books.

Frauwallner, Erich. 1956. *The Earliest Vinaya and the Beginnings of Buddhist Literature*. Vol. 8, *Serie Orientale Roma*. Rome: Is. M. E. O.

Fritz, John. 1978. Paleopsychology Today: Ideational systems and human adaption in prehistory. In *Social Archaeology: Beyond subsistence and dating*, edited by C. Redman. New York: Academic Press.

Fussman, Gerard. 1988. Central and Provincial Administration in Ancient India: The problem of the Mauryan Empire. *The Indian Historical Review* 14:43–72.

———. 1999. La Place des Sukhavati-Vyuha dans les Bouddhisme Indien. *Journal Asiatique*:523–86.

Garwood, Paul, David Jennings, Robin Skeates, and Judith Toms, eds. 1991. *The Sacred and Profane: Proceedings of a conference on archaeology, ritual, and religion*. Oxford: Oxford University Committee for Archaeology.

Giddens, Anthony. 1984. *The Constitution of Society: Outline of a theory of structuration*. London: Polity.

Giles, Herbert Allen. 1923. *Gems of Chinese Literature*. London: B. Quaritch.

Godelier, Maurice. 1978. Infrastructures, societies, and history. *Current Anthropology* 19(4): 763–68.

Gomez, Luis O. 1996. *The Land of Bliss: The Paradise of the Buddha of Measureless Light*. Honolulu: University of Hawai'i Press.

Goyala, Srirama. 1995. *The Dynastic Coins of Ancient India*. Jodhpur: Kusumanjali Prakashan.

Guha, Ranajit, and Gayatri Chakravorty Spivak, eds. 1988. *Selected Subaltern Studies*. New York: Oxford University Press.

Gurumurthy, S. 1981. *Ceramic Traditions in South Inda (Down to 300 A.D.)*. Madras: University of Madras.

Habib, I., and F. Habib. 1990. Mapping the Mauryan Empire. *Proceedings of the Indian History Congress 1989–90*:57–79.

Hanumantha Rao, B. S. L. 1976. *The Age of the Satavahanas*. Hyderabad: Andhra Pradesh Sahitya Akademi.

Hanumantha Rao, B. S. L., N. S. Ramachandra Murthy, B. Subrahmanyam, and E. Sivanagi Reddy. 1998. *Buddhist Inscriptions of Andhradesa*. Secunderabad: Ananda Buddha Vihara Trust.

Hawkes, Christopher. 1954. Archaeological method and theory: Some suggestions from the Old World. *American Anthropologist* 56(2):155–68.

Heitzman, James. 1984. Early Buddhism: Trade and empire. In *Studies in the Archaeology and Paleoanthropology of South Asia*, edited by K. A. R. Kennedy and G. Possehl. New Delhi: Oxford University Press.

———. 1997. *Gifts of Power: Lordship in an early Indian state*. Delhi: Oxford University Press.

Hillier, B., and J. Hanson. 1984. *The Social Logic of Space*. Cambridge: Cambridge University Press.

Holt, John. 1981. Assisting the dead by venerating the living: Merit transfer in the early Buddhist tradition. *Numen* 28:1–28.

Horner, I. B. 1957. *The Book of Discipline (Vinaya-Pitaka)*. 6 vols. Oxford: Pali Text Society.

Inden, Ronald B. 1990. *Imagining India*. Cambridge, Mass.: Basil Blackwell.

Indian Archaeology: A Review (IAR). New Delhi: Archaeological Survey of India.

Indian Meteorological Department. 2002. Historical records of severe cyclones which formed in the Bay of Bengal and made landfall at the eastern coast of India during the period from 1970–1999. www.imd.ernet.in/section/nhac/static/cyclone–history–bb.htm.

———. 2002. Tropical Cyclones. www.imd.ernet.in/services/cyclone/tropical–cyclone .htm.

Insoll, Timothy. 2001. Introduction. In *Archaeology and World Religion*, edited by T. Insoll. London: Routledge.

———. 2004. *Archaeology, Ritual, Religion*. London: Routledge.

Irwin, John. 1980. The axial symbolism of the early stupa: An exegesis. In *The Stupa: Its religious, historical, and architectural significance*, edited by A. L. Dollapiccola and S. V. Lallemant. Wiesbaden: Franze Steiner Verlag.

Jameson, M. H., C. N. Runnels, and T. N. Van Andel. 1994. *A Greek Countryside: The southern Argolid from prehistory to the present day*. Stanford, Calif.: Stanford University Press.

Jaswal, I. J. S. 1990. Skin colour in India. Paper read at Human Variations in India, July 1977.

Johnson, Gregory A. 1980. Rank–size convexity and system integration: A view from archaeology. *Economic Geography* 56(3):234–47.

———. 1981. Monitoring complex system integration and boundary phenomena with settlement size data. In *Archaeological Approaches to the Study of Complexity*, edited by S. E. van der Leeuw. Amsterdam: University of Amsterdam.

Jones, William. 1786. Asiatic researches. Paper read at 3rd Anniversary Discourse, at Royal Asiatic Society.

———. 1824. *Discourses delivered before the Asiatic Society: And miscellaneous papers on the religion, poetry, literature, etc. of the nations of India.* London: C. S. Arnold.

Kenoyer, Jonathan Mark. 1997. Early City-States in South Asia: Comparing the Harappan Phase and Early Historic Period. In *The Archaeology of City-States: Cross-cultural approaches*, edited by D. L. Nichols and T. H. Charlton. Washington, D.C.: Smithsonian Institution Press.

———. 1998. *Ancient Cities of the Indus Valley Civilization*. Islamabad: Oxford University Press.

Kent, Susan, ed. 1990. *Domestic Architecture and the use of Space: An interdisciplinary cross-cultural study*. Cambridge: Cambridge University Press.

Khan, F., J. R. Knox, and K. D. Thomas. 2000. The Bannu Archaeological Project: Archaeological explorations and excavations in Bannu Division, North-West Frontier Province, Pakistan, 1985–2000. *Journal of Asian Civilisations* 23(2):1–6.

Kintigh, Kieth W. 1990. Comments of the case for full-coverage survey. In *The Archaeology of Regions: A case for full–coverage survey*, edited by S. K. Fish and S. A. Kowalewski. Washington: Smithsonian Institution Press.

Kosambi, D. D. 1965. *Ancient India: A history of its culture and* civilization. New York: Pantheon Books.

———. 2002. *Combined Methods in Indology and Other Writings*. New Delhi: Oxford University Press.

Kowalski, Jeff Karl, ed. 1999. *Mesoamerican Architecture as a Cultural Symbol.* Oxford: Oxford University Press.

Kramer, Carol. 1997. *Pottery in Rajasthan: Ethnoarchaeology in two Indian cities.* Washington: Smithsonian Institution Press.

Krishnaswami, V. D. 1949. Megalithic types of South India. *Ancient India* 5:35–45.

Lahiri, Nayanjot. 1992. *The Archaeology of Indian Trade Routes* (*Up to c. 200 B.C.*). Delhi: Oxford University Press.

Lal, B. B. 1949. Sisupalgarh 1948: An Early Historical fort in Eastern India. *Ancient India* 5:62–105.

———. 1955. Excavations at Hastinapura and other explorations in the Upper Ganga and Sutlej Basins. *Ancient India* 2:5–151.

Lal, M. 1984. *Settlement History and the Rise of Civilisations in the Ganga-Yamuna Doab (from 1500 BC–AD 300)*. Delhi: B. R. Publishing Corporation.

Lamotte, Etienne. 1988. *History of Indian Buddhism from the Origins to the Saka Era.* Translated by Sara Webb-Boin under the supervision of J. Dantinne. Louvain-la-Neuve, Belgium: Institute Orientaliste, Université de Louvain.

Lewarch, Dennis E., and Michael J. O'Brian. 1981. The expanding role of surface assemblages in archaeological research. In *Advances in Archaeological Method and Theory*, edited by M. B. Schiffer. New York: Academic Press.

Liu, Xinru. 1988. *Ancient India and Ancient China: Trade and Religious Exchanges, AD 1–600.* Delhi: Oxford University Press.

Lopez, Donald S. 1995. Introduction. In *Buddhism in Practice,* edited by D. S. Lopez. Princeton: Princeton University Press.

———. 2001. *The Story of Buddhism: A concise guide to its history and teachings.* San Francisco: HarperSan Francisco.

Luders, H. 1912. A list of Brahmi inscriptions. *Epigraphia Indica* 10.

Lukacs, John R., ed. 1984. *The People of South Asia: The biological anthropology of India, Pakistan, and Nepal.* New York: Plenum.

Marcus, Joyce. 1998. *Women's Ritual in Formative Oaxaca: Figurine-making, divination and the ancestors.* Vol. 11, *Prehistory and Human Ecology of the Valley of Oaxaca,* edited by K. V. Flannery and J. Marcus. Ann Arbor: University of Michigan Museum of Anthropology.

Margabandhu, C. 1985. *The Archaeology of the Satavahana-Kshatrapa Times.* Delhi: Sundeep Prakashan.

Markus, T. A. 1993. *Buildings and Power.* New York: Routledge.

Marriot, McKim, ed. [1955] 1969. *Village India: Studies in the Little Community.* Chicago: University of Chicago Press.

Marshall, John. [1951] 1975. *Taxila: An illustrated account of archaeological excavations carried out at Taxila under the orders of the Government of India between the years 1913 and 1934.* 3 vols. Delhi: Motilal Banarsidass.

Marshall, John, and Alfred Foucher. 1983. *The Monuments of Sanchi.* 3 vols. Delhi: Swati Publications.

Marx, Karl. [1844] 1970. *A Critique of Hegel's Philosophy of Law.* Translated by A. Jolin and J. O'Malley. Cambridge: Cambridge University Press.

———. [1845–1846] 1998. *The German Ideology.* Amherst: Prometheus Books.

———. [1852] 1964. *The 18th Brumaire of Louis Bonaparte.* New York: International Publishers.

———. [1859] 1970. *A Contribution to the Critique of Political Economy.* Translated by S. W. Rayazanskaya. New York: International Publishers.

McCrindle, John W. [1901] 1979. *Ancient India as Described in Classical Literature.* Delhi: Munshiram Manoharlal.

———. [1926] 2000. *Ancient India as Described by Megasthenes and Arrian.* Delhi: Munshiram Manoharlal.

———. [1927] 2000. *Ancient India as Described by Ptolemy.* Delhi: Munshiram Manoharlal.

Miller, Daniel, Michael Rowlands, and Christopher Tilley, eds. 1989. *Domination and Resistance.* London: Unwin Hyman.

Mirashi, Vasudev Vishnu. 1981. *The History of Inscriptions of the Satavahanas and the Western Kshatrapas.* Bombay: Maharastra State Board for Literature and Culture.

Mishra, Jitu. 2000. Radhanagar: Early Historic Buddhism, urban structure and trade. In *Archaeology of Orissa,* edited by K. K. Basa and P. Mohanty. Delhi: Pratibha Prakashan.

Mitra, Debala. 1965. *Sanchi.* New Delhi: Archaeological Survey of India.

———. 1971. *Buddhist Monuments.* Calcutta: Sahitya Samsad.

———. 1975. *Udayagiri and Khandagiri.* New Delhi: A.S.I.

Moore, Jerry D. 1996. *Architecture and Power in the Ancient Andes.* Cambridge: Cambridge University Press.

Moorti, Udayaravi S. 1994. *Megalithic Culture of South India: Socio-economic perspectives.* Varanasi: Ganga Kaveri Publishing House.

Moran, D. 2000. *Introduction to Phenomenology.* London: Routledge.

Morley, Sylvanus G. 1946. *The Ancient Maya.* Stanford: Stanford University Press.

Moron, Eleanor. 1977. Configuration of time and space at Angkor Wat. *Studies in Indo-Asian Art and Culture* 5:217–67.

Morrison, Kathleen. 1995a. *Fields of Victory: Vijayanagara and the course of Intensification.* Berkeley: University of California, Archaeological Research Facility.

———. 1995b. Trade, urbanism, and agricultural expansion: Buddhist monastic institutions and the state in Early Historic Western Deccan. *World Archaeology.*

———. in press. Brahmagiri revisited: A re-analysis of the South Indian sequence. In *South Asian Archaeology, 2001,* edited by C. Jarrige and V. Lefevre. Paris: Recherche sur les Civilisations–ADPF.

Mueller, James W., ed. 1975. *Sampling in Archaeology.* Tucson: University of Arizona Press.

Mughal, M. R. 1982. Recent archaeological research in the Cholistan Desert. In *Harappan Civilization: A contemporary perspective,* edited by G. L. Possehl. New Delhi: Oxford and IBH Publishing Co.

Muni, Bharata. 1986. *Natyasastra: English Translation with Critical Notes.* Translated by A. Rangacharya. Bangalor: IBH Prakashana.

Munsell. 2000. *Munsell Soil Color Charts.* New Windsor, N.Y.: Munsell Color.

Mus, Paul. 1978. *Barabudur.* New York: Arno Press.

Nagaraja Rao, M. S. 1971. *Protohistoric Cultures of the Tunghabadra Valley (A Report on the Hallur Excavations).* Dharwar: Nagaraja Rao.

Nagaraju, Seshabhatta. 1981. *Buddhist Architecture of Western India.* Delhi: Agam Kala Prakashan.

Nance, Jack G. 1983. Regional sampling in archaeological survey: The statistical perspective. In *Advances in Archaeological Method and Theory,* vol. 6, edited by M. Schiffer. New York: Acadmic Press.

Narain, A. K., and T. N. Roy. 1976. *Excavations at Rajghat, 1957–58, 1960–65.* Varanasi: Banaras Hindu University.

Narain, A. K., and P. Singh. 1977. *Excavations at Rajghat.* Varanasi: Banares Hindu University.

Obeyesekere, Gananath. 1978. Gajabahu and the Gajabahu Synchronism: An inquiry into the relationship between myth and history. In *Religion and Legitimation of Power in Sri Lanka,* edited by B. L. Smith. Chambersburg, Pa.: ANIMA Books.

Oldenberg, Herman. 1882. *Buddha: His life, his doctrine, his order.* Translated by W. Hoey. London: Williams and Norgate.

Ortner, Sherry B. 1989. *High Religion: A cultural and political history of Sherpa Buddhism.* Princeton, N.J.: Princeton University Press.

Parasher-Sen, Aloka. 1993. Introduction: Problems and interpretations. In *Social and Economic History of the Early Deccan: Some Interpretations,* edited by A. Parasher-Sen. Delhi: Manohar.

———. 1996. Small localities and the writing of regional history. Paper read at Andhra Pradesh History Congress, January 5–7, 1996, at Jagarlamudi Kuppuswamy Choudary College, Guntor.

Parker, Grant. 2001. Porous connections: The Mediterranean and the Red Sea. *Thesis* 11(67):59–80.

Patnaik, J. 2000. Ceramics of Lalitagiri. In *Archaeology of Orissa*, edited by K. K. Basa and P. Mohanty. Delhi: Pratibha Prakashan.

Payne, Darwin Reid. 1993. *Scenographic Imagination*. Carbondale: Southern Illinois University Press.

Pearson, Michael Parker, and Colin Richards, eds. 1994. *Architecture and Order*. London: Routledge.

Plog, Fred. 1974. *The Study of Prehistoric Change*. New York: Academic Press.

Plog, Stephen, Fred Plog, and Walter Wait. 1978. Decision making in surveys. In *Advances in Archaeological Method and Theory*, vol. 1, edited by M. Schiffer. New York: Academic Press.

Possehl, Gregory L. 1980. *Indus Civilisation in Saurashtra*. Delhi: B.R. Publishing Corporation.

Powell, Shirley. 1983. *Mobility and Adaptation: The Anasazi of Black Mesa, Arizona*. Carbondale: Southern Illinois University Press.

Pradhan, Debaraj, Pradeep Mohanty, and Jitu Misra. 2000. Manikapatana: An ancient and medieval port on the coast of Orissa. In *Archaeology of Orissa*, edited by K. K. Basa and P. Mohanty. Delhi: Pratibha Prakashan.

Prasad, N. R. V. 1993. *Recent Buddhist Discoveries in Visakhapatnam District Andhra Pradesh: Relic caskets at Bavikonda*. Hyderabad: Department of Archaeology and Museums, Government of Andhra Pradesh.

———. 1994. *Bavikonda: A Buddhist site in North Coastal Andhra Pradesh*. Hyderabad: Department of Archaeology and Museums, Government of Andhra Pradesh.

Prebish, Charles S. 1996. *Buddhist Monastic Discipline: The Sanskrit Pratimoksa Sutras of the Mahasamghikas and Mulasarvastivadins*. New Delhi: Motlilal Banarsidass.

Rajan, K. 1991. Stratigraphical position of Russet Coated Painted Ware. In *Indian Archaeological Heritage*, edited by C. Margabhandu, K. S. Ramachandran, A. P. Sagar and D. K. Sinha. Delhi.

———. 1994. *Archaeology of Tamilnadu (Kongu Country)*. Delhi: Book India Publishing.

Ramachandran, T. N. 1953. *Nagarjunakonda 1938*. Memoirs of the Archaeological Survey of India. Delhi: Manager of Publications.

Rapoport, A. 1982. *The Meaning of the Built Environment*. Beverly Hills, Calif.: Sage Publications.

Ray, Himanshu P. 1986. *Monastery and Guild: Commerce under the Satavahanas*. Delhi: Oxford University Press.

———. 1989. Early Historical trade: An overview. *The Indian Economic and Social History Review* 26:437–57.

———. 1994a. Kanheri: The archaeology of an early Buddhist pilgrimage center in western India. *World Archaeology* 26:35–46.

———. 1994b. *The Winds of Change*. New Delhi: Oxford University Press.

———, ed. 1999. *Archaeology of Seafaring*. Delhi: Pragati Publications.

———. 2004. The Archaeology of sacred space: Introduction. In *Archaeology as History in Early South Asia*, edited by H. P. Ray and C. M. Sinopoli. New Delhi: Indian Council of Historical Research.

Ray, Himanshu P., and Carla M. Sinopoli, eds. 2004. *Archaeology as History in Early South Asia*. New Delhi: Indian Council of Historical Research.

Rea, A. 1907–1908. *A Buddhist Monastery on the Sankaram Hills*. Calcutta: M.A.S.T.

Read, Dwight W. 1986. Sampling procedures for regional surveys: A problem of representativeness and effectiveness. *Journal of Field Archaeology* 13:479–91.

Reddy, R. S., C. R. Shiva Prasad, and C. S. Harindranath. 1996. *Soils in Andhra Pradesh*. Nagpur: National Bureau of Soil Survey and Land Use Planning.

Renfrew, Colin. 1985. *The Archaeology of Cult*. London: Thames and Hudson.

———. 1994. The archaeology of religion. In *The Ancient Mind*, edited by C. Renfrew and E. Zubrow. Cambridge: Cambridge University Press.

Renfrew, Colin, and J. M. Wagstaff, eds. 1982. *An Island Polity*. Cambridge: Cambridge University Press.

Renfrew, Colin, and E. Zubrow, eds. 1994. *The Ancient Mind*. Cambridge: Cambridge University Press.

Rice, Prudence M. 1987. *Pottery Analysis: A sourcebook*. Chicago: University of Chicago Press.

Richards, Colin. 1990. The Late Neolithic house in Orkney. In *The Social Archaeology of Houses*, edited by R. Samson. Edinburgh: Edinburgh University Press.

Robb, John E., ed. 1999. *Material Symbols: Culture and economy in prehistory*. Carbondale, Ill.: Center for Archaeological Investigations.

Rocher, Ludo. 1986. *The Puranas*. Wiesbaden: O. Harrassowitz.

Rowlands, Michael. 1993. The role of memory in the transmission of culture. *World Archaeology* 25:141–51.

Rye, O. S. 1981. *Pottery Technology: Principles and reconstruction*. Washington, D.C.: Taraxacum.

Sahu, Bhairabi Prasad. 2000. Authority and patronage in early Orissa. In *Archaeology of Orissa*, edited by K. K. Basa and P. Mohanty. Delhi: Pratibha Prakashan.

Said, Edward W. 1978. *Orientalism*. New York: Vintage Books.

Sanders, W., J. Parsons, and R. Santley. 1979. *The Basin of Mexico: Ecological processes in the evolution of a civilization*. New York: Academic Press.

Sarkar, H. 1966. *Studies in Early Buddhist Architecture of India*. New Delhi: Munshiram Manoharlal.

Sarkar, H., and B. N. Mishra. 1966. *Nagarjunakonda*. New Delhi: Archaeological Survey of India.

Sarma, Inguva Karthikeya. 1980. *Coinage of the Satavahana Empire*. Delhi: Agam.

Sarma, M. Radhakrishna, B. Subrahmanyam, and E. Sivanagi Reddy. 2000. *Lotus Petals*. Hyderabad: Dept. of Tourism.

Sastri, Nilikanta. 1966. The Satavahanas and their successors. In *A History of South India*. Oxford: Oxford University Press.

Sastri, T. V. G., M. Kasturi Bai, and J. Vara Prasada Rao. 1984. *Veerapuram: A Type Site for Cultural Study in the Krishna Valley*. Hyderabad: Birla Archaeological and Cultural Research Institute.

Sastry, V. V. Krishna. 1983. *The Proto and Early Historical Cultures of Andhra Pradesh*. Hyderabad: The Government of Andhra Pradesh.

Sastry, V. V. Krishna, B. Subrahmanyam, and N. Rama Krishna Rao. 1992. *Thotlakonda: A Buddhist site in Andhra Pradesh*. Hyderabad: Department of Archaeology and Museums, Government of Andhra Pradesh.

Schiffer, Michael B. 1983. Toward the identification of formation processes. *American Antiquity* 48(4):675–706.

Schoff, W. H. 1974. *The Periplus of the Erythrean Sea.* Translated by W. H. Schoff. New Delhi: Munshiram Manoharlal.

Schopen, Gregory. 1994. Doing business for the lord: Lending on interest and written loan contracts in the Mulasarvastivada-vinaya. *Journal of the American Oriental Society* 114(4).

———. 1995a. Deaths, funerals, and the division of property in a monastic code. In *Buddhism in Practice,* edited by J. Donald, S. Lopez. Princeton, N.J.: Princeton University Press.

———. 1995b. Monastic law meets the real world: A monk's continuing right to inherit family property in classical India. *History of Religions* 35(2):101–23.

———. 1997. *Bones, Stones, and Buddhist Monks: Collected papers on the archaeology, epigraphy, and texts of monastic Buddhism in India.* Honolulu: University of Hawai'i Press.

———. 2000. The Mahayana and the Middle Period in Indian Buddhism: Through a Chinese looking glass. *Eastern Buddhist* 32(2):1–25.

Seneviratne, S. 1981. Kalinga and Andhra: The process of secondary state formation in early India. In *The Study of the State,* edited by H. J. M. Claessen and P. Skalnik. The Hague: Mouton.

Shaffer, Jim G. 1984. The Indo-Aryan invasions: Cultural myth and archaeological reality. In *The People of South Asia: The biological anthropology of India, Pakistan, and Nepal,* edited by J. R. Lukas. New York: Plenum Press.

Sharma, G. R. 1960. *The Excavations at Kausambi (1957–59).* Allahabad: Department of Ancient History, Culture and Archaeology, University of Allahabad.

———. 1969. *The Excavations at Kausambi (1949–50).* Memoirs of the Archaeological Survey of India. Delhi: Manager of Publications.

Sharma, H. V. 1987. *The Theatres of the Buddhists.* Delhi: Rajalakshmi Publisher.

Shastri, Ajay Mitra. 1987. *Early History of the Deccan: Problems and perspectives.* Delhi: Sundeep Prakashan.

Shaw, Julia. 1999. Buddhist landscapes and monastic planning: The elements of intervisiibility, surveillance and the protection of relics. In *Case Studies in Archaeology and World Religion,* edited by T. Insoll. Oxford: Archaeopress.

———. 2000. Sanchi and its archaeological landscape: Buddhist monasteries, settlements and irrigation works in Central India. *Antiquity* 74:775–76.

———. 2002. Methodological and theoretical frameworks for the archaeological survey of Central India. *Archaeological Review From Cambridge* (June).

Shaw, Julia, and John Sutcliffe. 2001. Ancient irrigation works in the Sanchi area: An archaeological and hydrological investigation. *South Asian Studies* 17:55–75.

Sinopoli, Carla M. 1991. *Approaches to Archaeological Ceramics.* New York: Plenum Press.

———. 1993. *Pots and Palaces: The earthenware ceramics of the nobleman's quarter of Vijayanagara.* Delhi: American Institute of Indian Studies and Manohar Press.

———. 2001. On the edge of empire: Form and substance in the Satavahana Dynasty. In *Empires: Perrspectives from archaeology and history,* edited by S. E. Alcock, T. N. Daltroy, K. D. Morrison, and C. M. Sinopoli. Cambridge: Cambridge University Press.

Sinopoli, Carla M., and Kathleen Morrison. 1992. Archaeological survey at Vijayanagara. *Research and Exploration* 8(2):237–39.

———. in prep. *The Vijayanagara Metropolitan Survey*. Ann Arbor: University of Michigan, Museum of Anthropology.

Smith, Alexander, and Alison Brookes, eds. 2001. *Holy Ground: Theoretical issues relating to landscape and material culture of ritual space objects*. Oxford: Archaeopress.

Smith, Bardwell L. 1978. Kingship, the Sangha, and the process of legitimization in Anuradhapura Ceylon: An interpretive essay. In *Religion and Legitimation of Power in Sri Lanka*, edited by B. L. Smith. Chambersburg, Pa.: ANIMA Books.

———, ed. 1978. *Religion and Legitimation of Power in Sri Lanka*. Chambersburg, Pa.: ANIMA Books.

Smith, Monica L. 1997. Strong economies, weak polities: The archaeology of Central India in the early centuries A.D. Ph.D. dissertation, Anthropology, University of Michigan, Ann Arbor.

———. 2002. Systematic survey at the Early Historic urban site of Sisupalgarh, Orissa. In *Archaeology of Eastern India: New perspectives*, edited by G. Sentupta and S. Panja. Kolkata: Center for Archaeological Studies and Training, Eastern India.

Snodgrass, Adrian. 1992. *The Symbolism of the Stupa*. Delhi: Motilal Banarsidass.

Srinivas, M. N. 1966. *Social Change in Modern India*. Berkeley: University of California Press.

———. [1955] 1969. The Social System of a Mysore Village. In *Village India*, edited by M. Marriot. Chicago: University of Chicago Press.

———. 1976. *The Remembered Village*. Delhi: Oxford University Press.

———. 1989. The cohesive role of Sanskritization. In *The Cohesive Role of Sanskritization*. Delhi: Oxford University Press.

Srinivasan, K. R., and N. R. Banerjee. 1953. Survey of South Indian megaliths. *Ancient India* 9:102–15.

Strong, John S. 1983. *The Legend of King Asoka*. Princeton: Princeton University Press.

———. 1994. Images of Asoka: Some Indian and Sri Lankan legends and their development. In *King Asoka and Buddhism: Historical and literary studies*, edited by A. Seneviratne. Kandy: Buddhist Publication Society.

Subrahmanyam, B. 1993. Administrative Report 1992–93. Hyderabad: Andhra Pradesh Dept. of Archaeology and Museums.

———. 1998. *Buddhist Inscriptions of Andhradesa*. Secunderabad: Ananda Buddha Vihara Trust.

———. 1999. *Buddhist Relic Caskets in Andhradesa*. Secunderabad: Ananda Buddha Vihara Trust.

Subrahmanyam, R. 1964. *Salihundam—A Buddhist Site in Andhra Prades*. Andhra Pradesh Government Archaeological Series, no. 17. Hyderabad: Government of Andhra Pradesh.

Sullivan, Alan, ed. 1998. *Surface Archaeology*. Albuquerque: University of New Mexico Press.

Tambiah, Stanley J. 1969. Animals are good to think and good to prohibit. *Ethnology* 8:424–59.

———. 1976. *World Conqueror and World Renouncer: A study of Buddhism and polity in Thailand against a historical background*. Vol 15, *Cambridge Studies in Social Anthropology*, edited by J. Goody. Cambridge: Cambridge University Press.

———. 1984. *The Buddhist Saints of the Forest and the Cult of Amulets: A study in charisma, hagiography, sectarianism, and millenial Buddhism.* Vol. 49, *Cambridge Studies in Social Anthropology*, edited by J. Goody. Cambridge: Cambridge University Press.

Thapar, Romila. 1966. *A History of India.* Vol. 1. London: Penguin Books.

———. 1984. *From Lineage to State: Social formations in the mid-first millennium B.C. in the Ganga Valley.* Delhi: Oxford University Press.

———. 1997. *Asoka and the Decline of the Mauryas: With a new afterword, bibliography, and index.* Delhi: Oxford University Press.

———. 2000. *Cultural Pasts: Essays in early Indian history.* Delhi: Oxford University Press.

———. 2002. *Early India: From the origins to AD 1300.* Berkeley: University of California Press.

Thomas, David Hurst. 1975. Nonsite sampling in archaeology: Up the creek without a site? In *Sampling in Archaeology*, edited by J. W. Mueller. Tucson: University of Arizona Press.

Thomas, Julian. 1996. *Time, Culture and Identity.* London: Routledge.

———. 2001. Archaeologies of place and landscape. In *Archaeological Theory Today*, edited by I. Hodder. Oxford: Polity.

Thompson, Edward P. 1963. *The Making of the English Working Class.* New York: Vintage Books.

Thompson, J. Eric S. 1950. *Maya Hieroglyphic Writing.* Washington, D.C.: Carnegie Institution.

Tilley, Christopher. 1994. *A Phenomenology of Landscape.* Oxford: Berg.

Tilley, Christopher, Sue Hamilton, Stephen Harrison, and Ed Anderson. 2000. Nature, Clutter, Clitter: Distinguishing between cultural and geomorphological landscapes; the case of hilltop tors in South-West England. *Journal of Material Culture* 5(2):197–224.

Townsend, R. F. 1982. Pyramid and sacred mountain. In *Ethnoastronomy and Archaeoastronomy in the American Tropics*, edited by A. F. Aveni and G. Urton. New York: Annals of the New York Academy of Sciences.

Trainor, Kevin. 1997. *Relics, Ritual, and Representation: Rematerializing the Sri Lankan Theravada tradition.* Cambridge: Cambridge University Press.

Trautmann, Thomas R. 1971. *Kautilya and the Arthasastra: A statistical investigation of the authorship and evolution of the text.* Leiden, Netherlands: Brill.

———. 1981. *Dravidian Kinship.* Cambridge: Cambridge University Press.

———. 1997. *Aryans and British India.* Berkeley: University of California Press.

Trautmann, Thomas, and Carla M. Sinopoli. 2002. In the beginning was the word: Excavating the relations between history and archaeology in South Asia. *Journal of the Economic and Social History of the Orient* 45(4):492–523.

Turner, Victor. 1966. *The Forest of Symbols: Aspects of Ndembu ritual.* Ithaca: Cornell University Press.

van der Leeuw, S. E. 1977. Toward a study of the economics of pottery making. In *Ex Horreo*, edited by B. L. Van Beek, R. W. Brandt and W. Goeman-van Waateringe. Amsterdam: University of Amsterdam.

Van Dyke, Ruth M., and Susan E. Alcock, eds. 2003. *Archaeologies of Memory.* Malden: Blackwell.

van Gennep, Arnold. 1960. *The Rites of Passage.* London: Routledge & Kegan Paul.

Wallace, Anthony F. C. 1966. *Culture and Personality*. New York: Random House.

Weber, Max. 1968. *On Charisma and Institution Building*. Chicago: University of Chicago Press.

———. 1978. The routinization of charisma. In *Economy and Society*, edited by G. Roth and C. Wittich. Berkely: University of California Press.

Wheeler, R. E. M. 1948. Brahmagiri and Chandravalli 1947: Megalithic and other cultures in Chitaldurg District, Mysore State. *Ancient India* 4:180–310.

———. 1954. *Rome Beyond the Imperial Frontiers*. London: George Bell and Sons.

Wheeler, R. E. M., A. Ghosh, and Krishna Deva. 1946. Arikamedu: An Indo-Roman trading station on the East Coast of India. *Ancient India* 2:17–125.

Willey, Gordon R. 1953. *Prehistoric Settlement Patterns in the Viru Valley*. Bureau of American Ethnology Bulletin No. 155. Washington: Smithsonian Institution.

Wright, Henry, and G. Johnson. 1975. Population, exchange, and early state formation in Southwest Iran. *American Anthropologist* 77:267–89.

Zukin, S. 1991. *Landscapes of Power: From Detroit to Disney World*. Berkeley: University of California Press.

Glossary

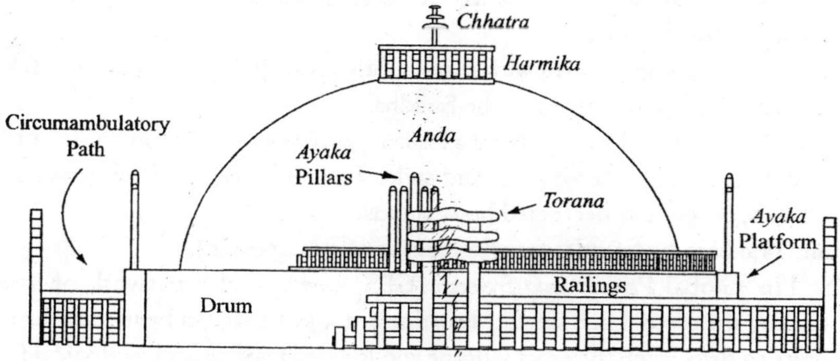

Figure gloss.1. A schematic diagram of a stupa.

Anda: The central earth, brick, or stone tumulus of a *stupa* (see figure gloss.1).

APDAM: The Andhra Pradesh Department of Archaeology and Museums.

Artifact scatter: Any concentration of usually small artifacts found on the modern ground surface. Artifact scatters often indicate the presence of subsurface archaeological features.

Ayaka pillars: Lines of five columns, erected at the cardinal points of some *stupas*. *Ayaka* pillars are common at many *stupa* complexes in Andhra Pradesh (see figure gloss.1).

Ayaka platforms: Platforms on the cardinal points of a *stupa* that supported *ayaka* pillars.

Burnish: A technique in pottery manufacturing where the surface of a vessel is polished to a high degree using a smooth stone, bead, or similar smooth material.

Cairn: A small pile of stones (typically only a few meters in diameter) that served as a memorial for a Buddhist monk or layperson. A cairn is distinguished from a *stupa* by the lack of a *harmika*, *chhatra*, or circumambulatory path. Cairns are the simplest form of mortuary feature identified in the Northeast Andhra Monastic Survey.

Chaitya: A building containing a *stupa*. Typically *chaityas* are either round or apsidal (see figure 4.1).

Chakravartin: A Buddhist ruler with religious sanction. A ruler who promotes Buddhism through both mundane and, at times, supernatural means.

Chhatra: A stylized umbrella made of wood or stone, erected on top of *stupas* (see figure gloss.1).

Circumambulatory path: Also known as a *pradakshina*, the circumambulatory path encircles larger *stupas*. This path was used to ritually walk around a *stupa* (see figure gloss.1)

Collection Unit: A clearly demarcated area in which artifacts are collected. Collection units allow for the density of different parts of a ceramic scatter to be accurately determined.

Dharma: A very complex term with many subtle meanings. As used here it refers to the teachings or doctrines of the Buddha.

Diagnostic ceramics: Those parts of a broken pottery vessel that are most indicative of its larger form, decoration, and style. Typically diagnostic ceramics consist of rims, bases, and decorated body sherds.

Drum: The base or foundation of a *stupa* (see figure gloss.1).

GPS: The Global Positioning System (GPS) consists of a network of satellites circling the earth. Each satellite broadcasts a signal that can be used by handheld units to determine the exact latitude and longitude of an archaeological feature. The accuracy of these units varies, but the average unit will typically have an error of less than +/− 10 meters. GPS units have become common tools for archaeologists in the field.

Harmika: The topmost portion of a *stupa*, often resembling a small railing (see figure gloss.1).

Mahastupa: A *stupa* containing the relics of the Buddha or one of his more prominent disciples. This term is often used to label the largest stupa of a Buddhist site, whether it memorialized the Buddha or not.

Mandapa: A columned hall.

Midden: The remains of an ancient garbage dump. Middens are often found in abandoned rooms or on the peripheries of ancient settlements.

Monastic cell: A small room used as the private quarters of a monk.

Moonstone: A semicircular stone threshold at the base of staircases.

Mortar: Small circular depressions created by grinding foods, pigments, or other substances into powder (see figure 6.11).

NEAMS: The Northeast Andhra Monastic Survey.

Non-plastic inclusions: The material within pottery that is not clay (e.g., sand and/or shell).

Paste: The material that forms a piece of pottery. The paste consists of clay, non-plastic inclusions, and temper. The paste is best viewed in cross-section on a broken piece of pottery.

Railing: An architectural element used to separate the circumambulatory path from other portions of a *stupa* complex (see figure gloss.1). Railings were made of wood, stone, and brick. The surfaces of railings were often used for carvings and inscriptions.

Sangha: The order of Buddhist monks and nuns. In some discussions it is also used as a label for the monks and nuns who make up a particular Buddhist sect, or as a term for those who inhabit a monastery. Given its multiple meanings, the term is avoided here.

Sheetrock: Large exposed portions of bedrock.

Slick: Slicks are smoothed areas of sheetrock used for grinding foods, pigments, and other materials (see figure 6.11).

Slip: A thin application of colored clay to the surface of a ceramic vessel. This results in a finer finish than is usually achieved on an unslipped vessel.

Stupa: A memorial tumulus of earth, brick, or stone (see figure gloss.1). Although predating the Buddha, over time *stupas* became a focus of Buddhist ritual. The most important *stupas* (*mahastupas*) contained relics of the Buddha. Smaller *stupas* housed the remains of other individuals, or lacked relics completely. *Stupas* are surrounded by circumambulatory paths and/or capped by a *harmika* and *chhatra*.

Temper: Material intentionally added to clay to alter the physical properties of a piece of pottery. For example, seeds or other organic materials added to clay result in ceramic vessels more resistant to cracking when placed in a fire.

Torana: A gateway leading into a circumambulatory path (see figure gloss.1). *Toranas* were often located at the cardinal points of a *stupa*.

Vihara: A row of monastic cells sharing a common verandah (see figure 5.3). The term is often used as a synonym for "monastery," though not here.

Vinaya: Buddhist texts focusing on codes of conduct for monks and nuns.

Votive stupa: Small *stupas* of brick or stone erected around a larger *stupa*. Unlike cairns, votive *stupas* often have a *harmika* or *chhatra*, but typically do not have circumambulatory paths (see figure 8.2).

Index

About the Author

Lars Fogelin is assistant professor of anthropology at Albion College, Michigan. He received a BA in anthropology from Ithaca College, New York, an MA from the University of Hawai'i at Manoa, and a PhD in anthropology from the University of Michigan in 2003. His research and publications center on South Asian archaeology, religion, architecture, and landscape. For the last five years he has led archaeological investigations of a 2000-year-old Buddhist monastery near the modern city of Visakhapatnam, India. He is also coeditor, with Carla M. Sinopoli, of *Imperial Imaginings: The Dean C. Worcester Photographic Collection of the Philippines, 1890–1913*, a CD-ROM addressing American colonialism in the Philippines. Prior to his first trip to India in 1994, he participated in archaeological research in Israel, the Mediterranean, Peru, and the Dutch West Indies.